21/9/13

F

D0715698

WITHDRAWN

Please return or renew this item by its due date to
avoid fines. You can renew items on loan
by phone or internet:

023 9281 9311
www.portsmouth.gov.uk

Portsmouth
CITY COUNCIL
Library Service

TIM MOORE

You Are Awful
(But I Like You)

Travels Through Unloved Britain

VINTAGE BOOKS
London

Published by Vintage 2013

2 4 6 8 10 9 7 5 3 1

First published in Great Britain in 2012 by
Jonathan Cape

Vintage
Random House, 20 Vauxhall Bridge Road,
London SW1V 2SA

www.vintage-books.co.uk

Addresses for companies within The Random House Group Limited
can be found at: www.randomhouse.co.uk/offices.htm

The Random House Group Limited Reg. No. 954009

A CIP catalogue record for this book
is available from the British Library

ISBN 9780099546931

The Random House Group Limited supports The Forest Stewardship
Council (FSC®), the leading international forest certification
organisation. Our books carrying the FSC label are printed on FSC®
certified paper. FSC is the only forest certification scheme endorsed
by the leading environmental organisations, including Greenpeace.
Our paper procurement policy can be found at:
www.randomhouse.co.uk/environment

Printed and bound by CPI Group (UK) Ltd, Croydon, CR0 4YY

To Valdis

Prologue

RIGHT WAY WRONG WAY

On a footloose impulse one fair Saturday morning, in that
faraway time before all such weekend whimsy was dashed
away by parenthood and giving a shit about the garden, my
wife and I set out for a motoring mystery tour. After enjoying
breakfast, a leisurely and expansive affair of the type then
popular in building society TV adverts, we popped sunglasses
on the top of our heads and strolled out to my old Rover. It
seems like we ought to have worn jumpers over our shoulders
with the arms knotted, and possibly even thrown back our
heads and laughed.

As we burbled out of west London, my wife leafed rumina-
tively through the road atlas. 'Let's go to Leeds Castle,' she
said, once we were nosing into the green belt. 'We've never
been there, and it's supposed to be lovely.'

Except we didn't go to Leeds Castle. Somehow – perhaps we
were too busy congratulating ourselves for knowing it wasn't
in Yorkshire – this substantial moated edifice completely evaded
us. One minute we were homing in on it through the smooth
and sunny Kentish hills, counting down the miles on those
brown tourist information signs, and the next we were out in
some lonely, unkempt coastal plain. The brown signs were no
more, replaced by tilted finger-posts pointing the way to
Whither Island and Fuck-Knows-by-Sea. At length we arrived
at a roundabout whose accompanying navigational information

unequivocally demonstrated that we had overshot our intended destination by some distance. After a brief and amicable inquest – like I say, it was a long time ago – we agreed to head on rather than turn back.

'Let's go to Whitstable,' I said. 'We've never been there, and it's supposed to be lovely.'

Except we didn't go to Whitstable. The next wrong turn took us down a spectacularly unappealing peninsula that probed deep into the Thames Estuary's brownest waters, and identified itself as the Isle of Grain. I've just established that this area is named after the Old English word for gravel, and that in 1918 it hosted Britain's last recorded outbreak of malaria. Throw in a sprawl of refineries, a vast commercial port and an oil-fired power station crowned by the UK's second-highest chimney, and you have a full appreciation of its merits as a day-trip destination.

Looking at the map now, our subsequent directional mishap seems no more than a continuation of the extravagant U-turn that put the Isle of Grain in our mirrors. Almost straight away our chosen escape route veered up a broad and sinuous concrete bridge, which carried us across a wide estuarine creek and offered an overview of Grain's belching awfulness. Then it was down into a thick band of coastal fog that had rolled in from nowhere.

'Must be the Isle of Sheppey,' said my wife, nose to the atlas. A convoy of enormous container lorries roared towards us out of the mist and were swallowed up by it behind. Then emptiness and silence. It wasn't a fair summer's day any more: we'd gone from July to November, from the heart of the Garden of England to its bleak and steaming compost heap. When at last something else loomed out of the fog, it was the entrance sign to a prison. As a small, flat island engulfed by estuary mud and huge-scale industrial filth, Sheppey certainly seemed a good place for one. So good, indeed, that within moments we'd driven past the entrances to a further two. Just after the third a rather less obvious adaptation suggested itself: a family in beachwear lugging buckets, spades and a large inflatable shark out through the gates of a compound, home to the shadowy silhouettes of several hundred static caravans. Improbably, impossibly, this barren, befogged offshore correction facility managed to lead a double life as a place that people came to voluntarily, in search of fun.

'Only way out is back over that bridge,' my wife murmured. But curiosity, in its brow-crevassing, jaw-slackening, morbid essence, drove us on. Presently the roadside family groups swelled, and the murky gaps between caravan parks were filled with chip shops and purveyors of lurid plastic beach accessories. A sign welcomed us to Leysdown-on-Sea. We turned down this settlement's main drag, a densely peopled thoroughfare lined with amusement arcades that bleeped and winked at us through the fog. The road terminated at what must have been the sea wall, though in these conditions it was hard to be sure. A flip-flopped stream of holidaymakers slapped away towards a gloomy space in the concrete, and in silence we watched the vapour claim them, one by one.

It was extraordinary to think that we had lived our lives – short and beautiful as they then were – entirely ignorant of the existence of this evidently popular resort, despite it lying just a 30-mile drive from our front door, had we gone there directly and on purpose, and lived in Bexleyheath. More extraordinary still to wonder how a fog-smothered mudbank in the Thames Estuary had ever become a holiday resort in the first instance, and little short of truly, madly, cow-hurlingly preposterous to discover that it still was one. As we drove back to the mainland these thoughts coalesced into loud and rather hysterical words, which is no doubt why we missed the turning for Whitstable, and ended up in Margate.

This whole curious misadventure recurred to me as I drove home from Gatwick Airport one morning twenty summers later, having dropped my family off for the annual visit to their Icelandic motherland. I'd stayed behind to meet several professional deadlines and fulfil a long-standing commitment relating to the refreshment of our exterior woodwork, which may explain why at a crucial juncture I found myself turning right instead of left. Of course I was going to compose many thousand words on manorexia, celebrity druids and the Battle of the Somme, and of course I was going to sit on a window ledge for a week listening to Eurosport's coverage of the Tour de France while holding a wire brush. But first, just one sunny afternoon of Kentish prevarication, the righting of a twenty-year wrong. I'd had an idea: I was going to Leeds Castle. Forty minutes later I exited the M20 at the requisite turn-off, spotted another name on the big blue sign at the roundabout above it, and had a better idea, or at least a different one.

That long-ago evening my wife and I hit Margate in a state of exhausted delirium, one that led seamlessly into a night of dimpled pint pots and period disco stylings at an establishment called the Ace of Clubs. We stumbled into a seafront b. & b., and stumbled out some hours later in blinding sun and bleary befuddlement. The beach was already filling up with bucket-and-spaders; that bracing seaside whiff of brine and vinegar hung in the air. As a place that people came to on holiday, Margate made sense in a way that Leysdown-on-Sea hadn't. Indeed, as we ran through the previous day's events in the cold light of a terrible hangover, the whole Leysdown experience already seemed anomalous and unreal, a fogged-up, fucked-up fantasy. The stuff, indeed, that legends are made of. So it was that Leysdown-on-Sea had matured over the years into our yardstick for seaside misery, a metaphor for any truly terrible place – a hyphenated triplet to be muttered over a plastic cup of weak tea in a draughty promenade cafeteria, or bawled in gleeful disgust across a rural yard full of doorless fridges flat on their backs in oily mud.

But had it really been so mad and bad? Was there any truth in the myth? Leeds Castle be damned – I was going back to the Temple of Doom. On sea.

Chapter One

Iapproached Sheppey under a big blue sky streaked lightly with cirrus, the sort of sky that Michael Caine's burning Spitfire spiralled out of in *The Battle of Britain*, in fact the actual sky in which the actual battle was fought. No Hammer Horror mists that day: the bridge across the Swale channel delivered me from one bright and treeless flatland to another. The signpost at the Isle of Sheppey's first roundabout was dominated by destinations beginning with HMP, but with the sea a-twinkle, my window down and the scent of warm meadow gusting in through it, I could sense that Leysdown would struggle to live up to its legend.

I parked up at the top of the road that led down to the seafront. Static caravans and garden-shed holiday chalets were still tightly crammed into surrounding fields. The chip shops were all present and correct, hawking jellied eels and pie and mash, so too the beach-crap vendors (FOLDING SUNBEDS – £12 – MAX WEIGHT 16 STONE). The pavement down to the promenade was still packed on both sides with amusement arcades, some of industrial enormity. It was all very much as I remembered, in every respect but one: here we were on a sun-kissed, fog-free afternoon two weeks into the school holidays, and the whole place was deserted. No one in the chip shops or on the streets. No one in the expansive promenade conveniences to defy the stern edict on the washing of feet in hand basins. No one on the promenade to gaze out at the view: two distant clusters of old sea forts, like Nissen huts on stilts, the revolving Mercedes stars of an offshore wind farm, a container vessel as massive and graceless as a Gorbals tower block pushed on to its side. And right round to the east, looking yachty and clean and fresh, visibly thriving even from this distance, Whitstable. I've still never been there.

I peered over the dour sea wall: high tide, with the calm, moss-mud sea drawn right up to a sliver of beach more gravel than sand. At last I discovered I wasn't alone, not quite. A man in goggles was performing slow and methodical breaststroke a few yards offshore. Right up by the concrete squatted a skinhead aged about ten, manically excavating deep into the gritty shingle. Some way off to the west, a clutch of distant figures was either playing a very slow-paced game of hockey or detecting metal.

What had happened? I'd seen this place packed in a pea-souper. Concern was tempered with slight irritation: it felt as if I'd come a long way to visit a distant relative in some rather rundown care home, and found them unrousably asleep.

One possible explanation suggested itself in the 'Bathing Water Quality' chart I now found prominently displayed on the seafront 'information point'. By means of a simple coding system – a smiley green face, a straight-mouthed amber one and a grumpy red – this recorded levels of 'faecal coliform' and 'faecal streptococci' present in samples drawn from Leysdown beach, going back many years. The faces, like faeces, were a blend of green and yellow, but as the footnotes explained, even the smiles merely denoted that untreated human waste was present in quantities someone had deemed acceptable. A tip for Swale Borough Council tourist officials: there are certain things that you should never boast about finding only some of on your beaches. Landmines and paedophiles would be two of these; faeces a third.

I walked north-west along the blowy seafront, where someone had etched 'I HATE THIS FUCKING PLACE' into the top of a mossy groyne. At length the coastal backdrop rose into a steep hill and the sea wall petered out. Beyond it the waves had gone to work, bringing down the landscape in great clods that blocked the path. And not just the landscape: the lumps of mud were studded with hunks of masonry and tiling, even a few shattered urinals, presumably the remains of some clifftop holiday complex.

I turned back and soon chanced upon a caravan village, dug down into the tussocked dunes. With its tight-packed rows of statics hemmed in around a bow-fronted retaining wall, from above it resembled one of those awful diagrams of an eighteenth-century slave ship. In lumpy open grass at its centre, a quorum of holidaymakers finally presented themselves: a couple of pottering grandfathers in cardigans and sharp-creased trousers, four fat dads hoofing a St George beachball about. But well over half the caravans were shuttered up and flagrantly unoccupied, and most of those that weren't had stripy windbreaks staked out by their doors. It's always seemed to me that any holiday requiring such equipment is fatally flawed from the outset. Would you send your kids to a school that handed out Geiger counters at the gate? There is literally no difference.

It was a further half an hour before I found everyone, or at least the balance of the three dozen people who apparently sustained the town. As a risk-averse econophile I'm not a natural gambler, but walking up past the first arcade I saw a sign yelling 10P BINGO – IT'S BACK! That sounded like my kind of low-rolling joint; I walked into the garish cacophony and found myself amongst friends.

In fact no one was playing bingo, 10p or otherwise. Nor had the patrons been enticed by the complimentary shrink-wrapped sarnies and packets of cheese-and-onion on offer in the roped-off 'Over 18s VIP area', with its £500-jackpot fruit machines. A couple of youths were engaged in a desultory round of air hockey. Absolutely everyone else, from seven to seventy, was pressed up against the glazed façade of one of the ranks and ranks of that fairground gaming staple of my youth, Crompton's Penny Falls. For those unfamiliar with this hallowed arcade institution, here's the procedure: players release a coin (in this instance an inflation-adjusted 2p) into a lofty slot, and watch it drop down to a stack of other such coins on the highest of two moving, mirrored shelves. The aim is to dislodge coins from this shelf to the one beneath, and in turn – with a glorious clatter of ill-gotten gain – into a winnings slot somewhere down at knee level.

I palmed a pound's worth of twos from a dead-eyed young woman in the sentry-box change booth, and after a quick recce installed myself before a teetering shelf of coppers. As any tight-arse of a certain age will confirm, it is possible to harvest a steady profit from such machines with no more than a grasp of the basic laws of gravity, an unusually high boredom threshold and at least one functioning eye. But without wishing to do my fellow gamblers down, they seemed deficient in one of these departments, and it certainly wasn't either of the last two. My regular tuppenny landslides were going unechoed; nobody else was winning. Faces old and young were set in that joyless death-mask of recidivist slot-feeders the world over – it's funny how little amusement you ever see at these eponymous places – but practice had not made perfect. Low-stakes arcade gambling appeared to be the only thing that anyone ever did in Leysdown, and they were all still really bad at it. Indeed the muffled metallic crashes and occasional yelps of pain suggested many regulars had yet to master the entry-level skill: inserting coins into a slot without spilling them all over the carpet or really hurting themselves.

When, after perhaps forty-five minutes, I noisily piled my winnings on to the change-girl's counter, she looked down at the heap as if it was some sort of dying seabird.

'Wossat?'

I acquainted her with what was clearly an unencountered situation, that of a customer who had played the shelves and come out on top, and now wished to exchange many coins of low denomination for a smaller number with higher individual value. Eventually, and with impressive truculence, she counted up my profits aloud, at a rate that pegged pennies to elapsing seconds. One hundred and twenty-eight, to be exact. I really am the daddy.

It wasn't yet seven, but the chip shop at the top of the road was already putting chairs upside-down on its tables. I hurried in, and emerged a moment later with a tray of chips recklessly doused in that watery brown sauce made from Bovril and Sunny Delight. I ate what I could – the whole sickly lot, as it turned out – and roamed Leysdown's main thoroughfare in the dying sun, hunting for ways to string out these last moments of workshy freedom. There were only two, and both were pubs. The first was a slab-sided edifice down by the seafront. *The Talk of the Town – A Fun Pub!* read a legend that ran the full length of the building. I peered in and found it entirely empty but for a barman and a denim-suited DJ, leaning arms-folded against his PA speakers. The second, a stoutly traditional affair called the Rose & Crown, was home to half a dozen drinkers, and the most appalling stench.

'Fuckinell, wossat stink?'

I faltered inside the dim threshold, wavering between a diplomatic half-pint and brusque flight.

'Is it you, mate? You done summing in your trousers?'

Amidst unvarnished cackles I looked over and met a trio of weathered and extremely happy male faces. 'Don't mind them,' said the old barmaid when I presented her with my craven features. 'It's the farmer up the road, muck-spreading. Terrible business. Want to sign our petition?' I did so, and rather than sit alone beside my tormentors, then stayed at the bar to sip my half in the barmaid's company. Thus did I come to learn of Leysdown-on-Sea's astounding past, challenging present and utterly hopeless future.

My own subsequent research has captured the Isle of Sheppey's significance to such historical big-hitters as the Vikings (being the place they spent their first British winter), Henry VIII (who honeymooned with Anne Boleyn at Shurland Hall, just outside Leysdown), and the Dutch navy (which occupied the island for a week in 1667, securing Sheppey's infamy as the only part of the British mainland to have endured a foreign invasion since 1066). But the barmaid's history focused on Leysdown-on-Sea's more recent and most extraordinary contribution to the annals. 'Cradle of aviation,' she said with an arch smile, explaining how in the summer of 1909, the Aero Club's flying ground at Leysdown had witnessed the first flight by a British pilot in Britain. 'Couple of weeks later, same feller went up with a pig in a basket,' she said. 'He was just having a laugh about flying pigs, but it went down as the world's first cargo flight!' Indeed, the centenary of John Moore-Brabazon's pioneering achievements had just been marked by a carnival parade through Leysdown. She tilted her head at a poster beneath the pub's telly: I'd missed it by two days.

Our conversation charted Leysdown's descent from these high-flying glory days. As a Cockney Club Med it had been in steady decline since the Fifties, when the railway closed, every summer quieter than its predecessor. The hotels and guest houses had all gone, and occupancy at the caravan and chalet parks was now falling steeply away. It didn't help that annual rates and ground rents apparently ran to £2,500 per pitch: 'I mean, come on: you could have a proper olerdy for that, somewhere nice!' These days, scratching a living in Leysdown meant feverish seasonal multi-tasking: cab driving, bar work, cleaning and maintenance in the holiday villages. When I mentioned how bustling the town had seemed one unpromising afternoon twenty years before, she barked a mirthless laugh. Since then the bus station and even the church had been demolished, she said. 'Come back in another twenty and there'll be nothing left.'

One of the burnished regulars had overheard all this, standing at the bar as he waited for his half-poured Guinness to settle. 'If you think this place is buggered,' he said, a little more amiably than the words imply, 'you should go to Great bloody Yarmouth.' All right, I thought as I walked out into the smelly night and made towards my car, maybe I will.

* * *

The revelations of Leysdown's noble history and its ongoing, drawn-out demise nagged at me, stirring a melancholy that flourished deep into those family-free summer nights. In the small hours of one I found myself clicking through some online photos of Leysdown's heyday, and gathered from a linked discussion forum that The Talk of the Town had abruptly closed down. Leysdown was on its deathbed, but those gathered around it hadn't come to pay their respects. Declaring it the second-worst seaside resort in Britain, a travel blog encapsulated Leysdown as 'an abandoned wilderness at the end of a 10-mile-long cul-de-sac'. A man who had spent a lot of time there while visiting his son in a Sheppey prison told the internet: 'Come to Leysdown if you're excessively fat and ugly, you will blend in . . . It's the end of the world, nobody finds it by accident and only the demented go there more than once.' (A twin failure on my part.)

Yet countless thousands clearly *had* gone there more than once, had in fact gone there year after year. There they were in the archived photos, packing the beach and having the Brylcreemed, black-and-white time of their lives, and there they were in my memory, filing happily away into the late-Eighties summer fog. I wasn't just mourning Leysdown, I realised, but the passing of a heroic breed of hardy, stiff-upper-lip Britons. The Windbreak Generation: our austere forefathers who didn't mind a bit of fog and faecal coliform in their holiday mix. Now that spirit had died, and Leysdown-on-Sea was slipping into oblivion just as surely as the holiday complex I'd found in chunks at the foot of that crumbling cliff.

My portentous nostalgia soon outgrew the Isle of Sheppey. One night I found myself reminiscing on the iconic hangouts from a childhood spent in Ealing: the Wimpy and the Berni Inn on the Broadway, the Grace Brothers department-store double act of Bentalls and John Sanders, the ABC cinema in West Ealing. All cheerfully inept or tatty, or both, and all now long gone, replaced with sleek, competent and studiously unendearing commercial successors, or one of those dreary new-build residential blocks with kettle barbecues set out on a thousand never-used balconies. This same blandification would be ongoing right across the country, and in settlements far more significant, and far more awful, than the self-styled Queen of the Suburbs had ever been. There were so many fascinatingly terrible, terribly fascinating places all around Britain that I had never visited, never even been near, and as the fate of Leysdown made plain, time was running out.

Hunched at the computer on that final pizza-stubbled night of bachelor dishevelment, I tried to make sense of the beery melodrama sloshing around in my brain. At its core was a native weakness for the underdog, that very British affection for the neglected, the down-at-heel, the uselessly crap. A bass note of awed admiration for those who had no choice but to put up with it. And topping it all off a sudden, earnest conviction that this was my last chance to see these places before they were all knocked down and claimed by the ghostly Leysdown sea-fog, taking their stories with them.

By rights I should have calmed down after the family came home, but I'm afraid I absolutely didn't. The nocturnal histrionics of summer begat a properly bonkers autumn, and when it ended there I was, juddering along behind a queue of brake lights as 'There's No One Quite Like Grandma' gave way to Des O'Connor's 'Dick-A-Dum-Dum'. With Hanger Lane Gyratory System behind me I had successfully negotiated Britain's worst road junction, and endured two of the most unpopular songs in the history of British popular music. A wisp of steam coiled forth from the bonnet of Britain's least esteemed car, and a man endowed with Britain's ugliest regional accent ordered me to turn right at the fucking roundabout, third exit. It was an early Saturday afternoon at the fag-end of November, four months since I'd come home from the Kentish seaside with my fingers stinking of chips and change. And half an hour since I'd set off on a Leysdown-inspired tour of the unloved, the rundown, the half-arsed and the hideous. All the brilliantly miserable crap, in short, that makes our country so bloody great.

As a basic understanding of animal behaviour tells us, it's hard for any rational entity to commit a deliberate foreseeable wrong. I don't mean moral transgressions or other such complexities, just any action with an obvious and instant negative impact upon one's own well-being. 'I am glad to have this fire; it was cold, and now I am warm. But oh! I have removed my trousers and sat down upon it.' Or: 'This porridge is both filling and delicious, yet I am pouring sand into it. Now it is less enjoyable to eat. Perhaps some more sand?'

Planning my trip meant unlearning several million years of such painfully accrued human knowledge. It meant asking friends and family for places they particularly wouldn't recommend, clicking on the website tabs that sorted reviews from lowest to highest, conducting internet searches beside a thesaurus folded open on 'bad'. This was the road-trip from hell, and to it.

I have to say I proved a fast unlearner, and swiftly rose to the challenge of making the worst of a bad job. Quite soon, indeed, I found myself looking for more and more wrong boxes to tick. If I was to visit the worst British towns, then it seemed only appropriate to stay in their worst hotels. To go to the worst restaurants and eat the worst food. Drink in the worst pubs, see the worst sights, drive the worst car while listening to the worst music. I confess I had begun to find the whole prospect rather exhilarating, in an oddly masochistic fashion: this was to be my down-and-dirty homage to the Windbreak Generation.

The basic framework for my tour was provided by a survey of the worst places to live in Britain, compiled in 2007 for property-based TV show *Location, Location, Location*. I approached this with extreme caution, suspecting that as a Channel 4 venture it would have been collated by Gok Wan, and based solely on the average household's total of matching scatter cushions. In fact, the conclusions were derived from reams of sober and incontestable statistics related to things like air quality, crime, hours of sunshine, life expectancy, leisure facilities, employment rates, educational achievement. I might get sick of the programme's stupid name (and did, immediately), but I couldn't argue with their survey's methodology or conclusions: any town that made the bottom twenty was an indubitably horrid place. (I might as well explain right now that although some of these places lay within the confines of greater London, I shall not be covering any of them. Partly as I've spent my entire life living in the capital, and was keen only to visit places I'd never been to, and partly as I've already written an entire – and wholly wonderful – book about London. I am consequently fated to come across in this one as the worst sort of sneering, hypocritical metropolitan ponce. Huzzah!)

I also drew upon a number of more opinionated but statistically credible polls organised by various magazines, radio and television shows and websites to find the nation's most dreadful albums, buildings, high streets, beaches, foodstuffs, sea zoos, and so on. Beyond these came sundry harvested sources of diminishing credibility, on a scale that ran from the ropily agenda-driven to the frankly laughable. In descending order:

1) TripAdvisor and the many internet-based rivals offering user reviews of hotels, restaurants, visitor attractions and so forth. Beyond filtering out sparsely reviewed establishments whose dire ratings might be down to no more than some rogue individual grudge, my main challenge here was to root out any sore-thumb thumbs-ups: contributions supplied by a proprietor or lackey, in order to counter the welter of damning criticism and bump up a lowly average score. Happily, most seemed incapable of mustering even the tiniest degree of subtlety, singing their own five-star praises with a magnificent disregard for the language of genuine opinion. There was transparent bitterness: 'All I can say is some people wouldn't be satisfied if the Queen's butler served them.' There was

hyperbole bred of rank desperation: 'Please ignore all the negative reviews. Everything about this hotel is completely fantastic, and my wife cried when we left.' Best of all, there was praise lavished where no sane visitor would ever lavish it: 'The sign-posting was excellent'; 'Refreshments were reasonably priced and there was ample parking'. How I loved that. 'Is this parking amplc, or what? I say we go straight home and positively review the hell out of it!'

2) Places and stuff that other people, drawing on personal experience, had assured me were disastrously run, ugly, daft, unpalatable or in some other way very badly wrong.

3) Places and stuff I'd always thought might be a bit rubbish.

4) Sky 3's *Britain's Toughest . . .* series of television programmes, an empirical nationwide investigation covering villages, pubs and twenty-four-hour dry-cleaners, would you believe (though you absolutely shouldn't)?

5) Surveys compiled by market-research companies for corporate clients in the interests of garnering publicity. That which pronounced the Hanger Lane Gyratory System to be Britain's worst road junction ranked amongst the more coherent of these, having been commissioned on behalf of some insurance company and thus bearing at least vague relevance to the client's core business. More typically I encountered a cheerfully brazen disconnect. You know the sort of thing: 'Two out of three Welshmen would eat a bar of soap for £800, reveals a poll carried out on behalf of Jack Russell's, Guildford's leading twenty-four-hour pet-supplies warehouse.' Only an idiot would place any faith in the legitimacy of such asinine investigations. I must have used at least a dozen.

I was putting a lot of pins in my map, but still had to decide on the vehicle in which I'd be joining them all up. The runaway winner of most 'worst ever British car' polls was the Austin Allegro, that definitive 1970s British Leyland disaster: a wallowing, bulbous oaf swiftly nicknamed the 'flying pig', launched with a rectangular steering wheel and so ineptly designed that a wind-tunnel test found it was more aerodynamic going backwards. But even the newest Allegros were already twenty-seven years old, and it didn't seem quite fair to put a geriatric through what I had in mind. Plus, the Allegro was already heading around the horn of post-modern irony, now so bad it was good, an object of ugly-duckling retro affection. I didn't want any of that rubbish. In its dotage as the Austin Rover Group, our nationalised motor manufacturer had knocked out a bewildering array of truly abysmal cars; it was just a question of deciding upon the most awful, the least loved, the still unforgiven.

My epiphany was delivered one evening by a BBC4 re-run of a mid-Nineties BBC programme about people and their cars, entitled *From A to B: Tales of Modern Motoring*. In the course of this, I watched a sales representative being interviewed while driving the car he'd been given to replace his Vauxhall Cavalier. 'Obviously my wife knew I was getting a new company car,' he said, knuckles whitening on the wheel. 'When I told her it was an Austin Maestro, we both literally sat down and cried – we physically cried.'

I literally stood up and cheered – I physically cheered.

Since that happy moment I have acquired a great store of knowledge about the Austin Maestro, and I'm afraid I'm going to share a little of it with you now. No matter what my wife keeps telling me, I like to think that as a very British tale of delusion, sloth, incompetence and on-the-cheap botch-jobbery, it is the enthralling embodiment of everything my trip was about.

One day in the early 1980s, Austin Rover's top brass sat down to do something they were good at: mulling over recent embarrassments. What had their globally successful Mini and Morris Minor possessed that the Allegro so patently lacked? Innovative design, reliability, circular steering wheels – these were the obvious answers. But there was another, and it came cheap: a name beginning with M. In great excitement the management drew up an appropriate shortlist of such names with which to endow the Allegro's hatchbacked successor. To placate the perpetually troublesome trade unions, they even allowed their factory-floor workforce to vote on this short list. (I'm assuming the other options were things like Mudblood and Manbag, as Maestro seems very much like the best of a bad bunch. Sounds awful and looks worse: even members of the Maestro Owners' Club still have trouble getting those vowels in the right order.)

No one knew then that the Austin Maestro would turn out to be the final ever British-designed, British-built mass-produced family car (its booted sister model, the Montego, was snarkily dubbed BL's 'last-chance saloon'). No one except perhaps Roy Axe, newly installed as Austin Rover's head of design just before the car was launched in 1983. Some years later he recalled his first encounter with a pre-production example: 'I was ushered into a room and stood in front of this object and asked, "What do you think of that?" It was the Maestro. I couldn't believe my eyes. The car's whole stance and proportion were wrong. Design was moving into more rounded forms and this car was back in the old folded-paper era. Its proportions were peculiar, too. In short, it was a complete shambles. I thought so and said so.'

Poor old Roy was surveying a design that had left the drawing board way back in 1976, and worse was to come when he lifted the bonnet and beheld an engine that had powered its first Austin over thirty years previously. 'It was engineering of the Fifties not of the Eighties . . . The interior was even worse. The fascia panel was like a wet codfish, all floppy. The whole car was decades old in its thinking. When I said, "We have got to start again", it was made clear to me that production was only four months off, so there was nothing anybody could do.' One motoring magazine's launch review drolly encapsulated the Maestro thus: 'Truly a car for the 80s – or any 90-year-olds still up to driving.'

Then there were the build-quality issues that came to dominate – in fact, comprise – the Maestro-owning experience.

The plastic bumpers shattered in the cold, and the dashboard swelled up and split in the sun. Wheels would randomly detach themselves, and when the car was jacked up to replace them, the windscreen popped out. Leaks sprang out everywhere – passengers sat in the back rather than endure the ever-water-logged front seat, and for drivers, even the standard under-arse plastic bag sometimes wasn't enough: 'In bad weather,' recalled one owner, 'I had to wear a raincoat.' Living with the Maestro meant a permanent oil stain on your driveway, and a mechanical soundtrack that has been memorably compared to 'a skeleton wanking in a biscuit tin'. 'It wasn't that unpleasant to drive,' said Roy Axe, trying to find something nice to say about the car, 'but things fell off it all the time.'

You might be starting to see where that tearful sales rep was coming from. But in doing so, you underestimate the more typically undiscerning, because-we're-not-worth-it British motorist of the era. The Allegro was a terrible disappointment because in 1973, when it appeared, Britain still expected great things from its national motor manufacturer. Ten years later we expected nothing, and in the Maestro we got it. Wet pants, oil stains, a canned skelly knocking one out under the bonnet: small beer for the long-suffering, make-do, Leysdown-bound Windbreak Generation. In eleven years, 600,000 Maestros dribbled and creaked out of British showrooms.

Most weren't around for long. The enthusiasm with which the car welcomed and retained water rolled out the browny-red carpet for Sir Rampant Corrosion, and early Maestros were being scrapped almost as fast as new ones rolled off the lines. Without any fond farewells, production quietly ceased in 1994. You may therefore imagine my surprise when I chanced upon a 1998 Maestro for sale – and in Slough, which seemed like the kind of place I ought to be going to anyway.

The realm of David Brent and the butt of John Betjeman's come-friendly-bombs jibe, Slough is a trailblazing bad joke of a town – and just 15 miles down the road from me, the proverbial shit on my doorstep. I'd arranged to view this curious Maestro on a Saturday morning, and as the sun was out I went there on my bike. In fact, Slough proved disappointingly acceptable beneath blue skies, and via a route that bypassed the witheringly drab centrepiece structures featured in *The Office* title sequence. The last street I turned into was an inoffensive suburban cul-de-sac of recent construction, fronted by a petrol station with an en suite Tesco Express, and lined with compact pale-brick houses. A gawky, angular presence on one drive meant I didn't need to check the door numbers.

It was a very long time since I'd seen an Austin Maestro in the flesh. The design had a flimsy, creased and somehow unconvincing air, too tall, too thin. And what an awful lot of glass: there'd be no hiding place in that Popemobile. But what really struck me about the car had nothing to do with all Maestros, just this particular one. From bumper to bumper it was almost eerily pristine, and gleamingly, sombrely black. I knew straight away that I would never find a more appropriate conveyance for my valedictory tour of rubbish Britain.

The vendor was a van driver called Craig, mild of manners and smooth of pate. Craig was a sensible, straightforward bachelor whose single eccentricity was a passion for the kind of anti-charismatic vehicles that Jeremy Clarkson likes to drop anvils on. (In addition to his Maestros – there was another parked across the road – he was bringing a dumpy 1980s single-decker bus back to whatever passed for its original glory.) He told me he'd bought the car I'd come to see from an elderly gent in the Midlands, who'd owned it from new; in twelve years' combined ownership, the pair had clocked up just 14,546 evidently gentle miles. And why only twelve years, when the newest Maestro should just have turned sixteen? Craig smiled a little ruefully. 'You'd better come inside,' he said.

A cup of tea later I had the whole story. After the Maestro went out of UK production, Rover's management team sought to offload the obsolete manufacturing machinery to East Europeans, echoing the deal that FIAT had struck with Soviet Russia to spawn the Lada. An arrangement was soon made with the Bulgarian government: in 1995, a production facility opened on the Black Sea coast, manufacturing Maestros tailored for the domestic market. To cope with Bulgaria's challenging roads they were endowed with more rugged suspension and gearboxes, and to satisfy the nation's evident Windbreak Extreme sense of hair-shirted unworthiness, there would be only one dourly spartan model. The intention was to sell ten thousand of these cars a year. When production ceased after seven months, the new company had managed to persuade just two hundred Bulgarians to buy a Maestro. Two hundred! Bulgarians!

It's hard to imagine a more pathetic finale for the British motor industry, though the hapless Maestro managed to contrive one anyway. Around six hundred of the unsold Bulgarian cars were shipped to Britain by a West Country entrepreneur, who converted them to right-hand drive in a big shed round the back of a petrol station in Ledbury, Herefordshire. At £4,995 on the road they were the cheapest new cars you could buy in 1997, but it still took him four years to shift them all. And here I was being offered one for £500. A shiny, pampered motor vehicle with almost nothing on the clock and a full year's MOT – that had to be worth £500 of anyone's money. But at the end of the day, this was a Maestro. I offered Craig £450 and we shook on it.

In any other low-value second-hand-car transaction, that would have been that. Instead, like a father quizzing a prospective son-in-law, Craig began to probe my intentions. What was I planning to do with his pride and joy? Without lying, though not without feeling like a bit of a tosser, I said that I just fancied a tour around the country. For the first and only time his features hardened. 'And what about when you're done doing that?' So it was that a while later, sat at Craig's kitchen table over the registration documents and a pile of twenties, I heard myself pledging that when the moment came to part with my new acquisition, I would offer it exclusively to the membership of the Maestro Owners' Club. 'I'm very happy to hear you say that,' Craig said quietly, as we walked out to the car. 'It's been bothering me all night.' Then I bullied my bike into the boot, slammed it shut at the fifth violent attempt, and under Craig's sombre gaze drove away.

Chapter Two

'F-f-fookin left turn ahead!'

In 2008, a team of British linguistic researchers asked volunteers to estimate the intelligence of people recorded speaking in a range of regional accents. One emerged as the runaway loser, ajudged even less astute than the section of total silence included as a statistical control. Five years earlier, a sociological study found that the same accent 'consistently fares as the most disfavoured variety of British English'. Or put another way in an online forum discussion: 'Brummie is so droning and depressing, it makes people sound stupid and lazy, like moaning six-year-olds.'

So it was that via a downloaded package of celebrity voices, I had placed my satellite-guided navigation in the hands – or rather the filthy, stuttering mouth – of John Michael 'Ozzy' Osbourne, Birmingham-reared lead vocalist of Black Sabbath and fuck-happy, semi-coherent paterfamilias in MTV's long-running reality series *The Osbournes*. With the M25 still to be broached, Ozzy's relentless nasal profanity was already causing my jaw to clench, and my brain to run through the less awful guiding voices that were just a few screen-clicks away: Sean Connery, Darth Vader, George and Zippy from *Rainbow* (in fairness, a few months later I gave that last pair a go and almost put my fist through the LCD at the first roundabout). But Ozzy had to be and would be endured. The unwritten ground rules of my trip allowed for no backsliding, no weakness. It was the same with the soundtrack: no fast-forwarding, no next-tracking, just a dour vigil through a Bermuda Triangle of bombastic guitar wails and plinking novelty gibberish, the very worst of British music as voted for by us, the public, or them, the critics, or you, the time-rich, poll-happy internet curmudgeon.

Once again, digital technology had made all my nightmares come true. A little memory-card-cum-transmitter wedged in the Maestro's fag lighter had transformed the humble neighbouring radio into a jukebox packing 3.8 gigabytes of terrible sounds, and with no display screen I never knew what was coming next. Great artistes at their addled, deluded or indulgent worst; total idiots yammering their way through awful one-hit rubbish. The tuneless, the endless, the cloying, the Wurzels: 358 native musical offerings that wouldn't have me tapping my fingers on the wheel so much as repeatedly dashing my forehead against it.

The compilation process was a grim ordeal with two fleeting moments of joy: the first when I found out that Crazy Frog was Swedish, and therefore ineligible, and the second when I gave up trying to trace a copy of *Urban Renewal: the Songs of Phil Collins*. (I was initially mystified as to how this collation of hip-hop-inspired covers should have disappeared off the face of the earth, but the explanation turned out to be quite simple: spontaneous combustion and a vengeful god.)

In the pick-and-mix iPod age, we are no longer exposed to the character-building effects of terrible music. We don't have to tolerate duff album tracks or cheesy chart-toppers, and have therefore lost that shade which lets the light shine through, those dismal troughs that put the majestic peaks in their full and glorious perspective. Thus did I attempt to convince myself that this sonic suffering was for my own good, before giving up somewhere near Stansted Airport, when Mr Lennon and Ms Ono began to address each other thus:

'Yoko?'

'John?'

'Yoko?'

'John?'

So they went on for twenty-three minutes, unaccompanied by any other sound, except a loop recording of their heartbeats and the steady drip of my puréed cerebellum en route from nostrils to lap. In that time I travelled two and a half miles, and forgot many important online passwords. When the pub-piano intro to 'Grandad' struck up, I began to whoop with joy. Then I remembered that Clive Dunn was only five years older than I was when he recorded it, and stopped.

Into Essex, into darkness. The Saturday traffic was thinning now, and for the first time I was able to find out what Craig was really made of. Answer: corrugated iron and chewing gum. I'm not sure exactly when I started to think of the Maestro as Craig. At some point during my obsessive classification of all things rubbish, I'd done a little research into out-of-favour first names and found it near the top of a list of those that had fallen most dramatically from grace. From a peak in the late Seventies, its popularity with British parents had dropped away so steeply that even in the Craigish heartlands of Scotland, fewer than eighty male bairns were given the name in 2009. The original inspiration wasn't my Craig, Craig's previous owner Craig, but him out of *The Royle Family*. It somehow seemed a perfect name for the Maestro – unpretentious and well-meaning, but at the same time pudgy, unfashionable, clueless, shabby and just generally a bit crap.

Craig's CV – fewer than 15,000 miles patiently accrued over twelve years – pointed to light suburban pottering with the odd leisurely weekend run, no doubt heading a long queue of apoplectic horn-jabbing Clarksons through the byways of the West Midlands. Sustained high speed was a novel experience, and one he reacted to with a touching blend of exuberance and fear. The little engine – a very modestly updated variant, let's remember, of a 1952 design – seemed eager, in fact over-eager, to prove it was still up to the job.

'Well, look at me go! We must be doing, what, fifty? Sixty, you say! Gosh – how . . . how exciting!'

After twenty minutes or so the engine began to race, sounding desperate and overwhelmed; I kept thinking I'd put Craig in third gear instead of fifth.

'Listen, there's absolutely no problem here, and I'm definitely coping with this, but I just wanted to check – you do realise those big numbers are *miles* per hour? That we're doing sixty *miles* per hour?' The under-bonnet skeleton was pleasuring himself with reckless gusto, and I pulled over before he could blow his bony load all over the hard shoulder.

To a man in search of the inadequate and disheartening, few British catering options exert a more magnetic pull than our native garage chiller cabinets. I strode towards this example expecting to be spoilt for pallid, strip-lit choice, but happily there was one stand-out winner. Grabits Original Chicken on a Stick – 75g of impaled poultry, reduced to clear at 90p. As demonstrated by the success of the microwaveable burger, Britain's forecourt diners do not lightly reject a snack product. I unsheathed my neglected Grabit in ignorance of a recent product recall related to 'raw chicken meat', and took a nibble as the trees closed in. A dash of camphylobacter might at least have added a little zing: this was the most tasteless substance I have ever willingly put into my mouth, and that included the many strips of *Guardian* I chose to ingest during childhood. As drab and watery as the prostrate landscape hiding out there in the gloom, as Craig and I were Ozzied off the f-f-fookin motorway, up the f-f-fookin A11 and into the middle of f-f-fookin nowhere.

The road was dead straight, dead flat and – beyond a blurt of excitement at the oppressively floodlit, stop-who-goes-there entrance to USAF Mildenhall – dead dull. After bypassing the orange glow that was Norwich, we pretty much had the tarmac and its dim hinterland all to ourselves. There was a pitch-black, small-hours feel to proceedings, but a glance at the frail butter-scotch digits on Craig's LED clock told me that the 3 p.m. kick-offs weren't yet into added time.

The final stretch towards Britain's eastern extremity empha-sised that no one goes where I was going by mistake. In a protracted silence that I later traced to another long moment of Lennon/Ono pretentiousness, we made an unwavering dash across reclaimed land, atop a narrow raised road flanked by old drainage windmills and red warning triangles. The net effect was of driving down a long, narrow pier to the end of the world. Or Great Yarmouth, as it's known to online connoisseurs of English seaside decay.

'No! No, I won't have that!' cries the Major, in retort to a fellow guest who has just damned Fawlty Towers as the worst hotel in western Europe. 'There's a place in Eastbourne.' I'd recalled these words when that Leysdown Guinness drinker had nominated the Norfolk resort as one whose depths out-plumbed his own. I recalled them again now, as Ozzy swore me away from the signs marked 'seafront' – and the evocative promise of clean and cosy beachside b. & b.s – and off down a gloomy, silent road that arced past shadows of corrugated warehouse sheds and the occasional cargo vessel.

These were the ghostly docksides where Yarmouth had once made its stinky mint as the world's busiest herring port, home in the mid-Victorian, pre-seaside age to ten thousand fishermen working one thousand boats. My Scout troop used to belt out a dedicated shanty: 'It was on a fair and a pleasant day, out of Yarmouth harbour I was faring, as a cabin boy on a sailing lugger, for to hunt the bonny shoals of herring.' Ah, what bitter-sweet emotion those lines stirred within me: both a celebration of the red-cheeked spirit of adventure I'd hoped would define Scouting and a poignant requiem for a hope that died on the Flora Gardens housing estate, when a young Scout realised that hurling huge bin-liners full of collected jumble off a fourth-floor balcony thrilled him in a way that clapping out jokes in Morse code never would.

'You have raiched your f-f-fookin dustinoition.'

I pulled over and looked up: ahead reared the stately clock-towered bulk of what looked like, and proved to be, Great Yarmouth town hall. To my left, gazing out at the long and empty quayside across a matching taxi rank, stood the half-timbered, monochrome-gabled frontage of the Star Hotel. It was a disarmingly grand face for an establishment that had attracted my attention as the most poorly reviewed hotel in town, indeed in all of East Anglia. TripAdvisor's contributors laboured to trump previous criticisms: 'The worst I have ever stayed in'; 'I can safely say that I will never stay in this hotel again'; 'Although most hotels in Great Yarmouth are in need of a lot of TLC, this one exceeds them all'; 'Falling apart'; 'I felt uneasy about sleeping in the beds, using bathroom, etc.' The only consistent positives were praise for the staff's Dunkirk spirit.

I bullied open Craig's increasingly reluctant boot catch, pulled my bag out and made towards the Star's entrance. Shortcomings now asserted themselves: the window frames were flaky and crevassed, as if they'd been knocked up from driftwood, and the columns supporting the first-floor veranda were set at a jaunty tilt. A certain sort of guest would already have been making unkind mental notes, but as I pushed through the mahogany revolving door and walked into a panelled, low-beamed lobby dominated by a big old fireplace, I felt a prickle of excitement, a sort of nostalgic anticipation. I had entered a building of character, marinaded in salty marine history, a place with tales to tell, where adventures had begun and ended. It wasn't built for your kiss-me-quickers or your stag-weekenders, or the self-loathing, churlish carpet-tile sales representative who I'd already begun to think of as TripAdvisor's archetypal hotel reviewer. The Star dated from the days when Yarmouth was indubitably Great, when the people who checked in here were shipping merchants and fishery administrators, when the civic ambience was more *Onedin Line* than *Quadrophenia*. I saw it all encapsulated in a sepia photograph on the wall opposite the little reception desk: a throng of smart and happy Edwardians promenading across the quayside on an early summer's evening, with a line of horse-drawn carriages in front of the Swan and the town hall clock at ten to six. And a one-night slice of this heritage could be mine, as the quiet old chap at reception now gently informed me, for £33 including a full breakfast. Stick that up your Travelodge, carpet-boy.

There had been a suggestion of it in the receptionist's strained smile, the smile of a good man making the best of a bad job. There was another when the lift revealed itself as one of those manually operated, double-shuttered, concertina-door-grate affairs, which meant my ascent was preceded by an entire *Porridge* title sequence of clanking and creaking, then accompanied by the terrible conviction that an errant trouser hem or coat sleeve would billow out through the open grating and snag in some protuberance in the lift shaft, ensuring I'd arrive at the second floor one limb down. But full realisation that the TripAdvisor misanthropes might in fact have had a point only took hold when I yank-clunk, clunk-yanked my way out of the lift. The corridor was a study in mothballed neglect, panelled with the flanks of a derelict caravan and carpeted in mismatched strips of rusty doormat. It was so cold I could see my breath, a phenomenon I hadn't experienced indoors since a week spent re-enacting 1474 at a castle in the Alsace with a party of living-history fundamentalists. Two dungeon-weight fire-doors later, I heaved my way into a post-war annexe and a thick wave of old heat, heavy with the fetid legacy of waste-water mismanagement. The silence was deafening. I opened my door with something close to morbid curiosity.

Compact would be the first word that sprang to mind, with regard to everything but the beefy old telly that teetered on an occasional table at the foot of the bed: I could have changed channels with my big toe – and later did so. Everything else seemed to have been designed for the very little. The bed itself was a thinly padded church pew: in the morning I didn't so much roll out of it as off it, winding up flat on the floor. Of such modest plumpness was the pillow that I initially took it for a folded towel; the folded towel I initially took for a flannel. I stooped to open the wardrobe, expecting to find Peter Rabbit's waistcoat hung up inside. Instead there was a blanket the size of a dishcloth.

The bathroom ventilation fan paid thunderous aural homage

to the last moments of a stricken Lancaster bomber, yet did nothing to disperse the stench that had annexed the corridor and was in here, too, seeping from every orifice in the sanitary ware. Though the hot water was hot, so too was the cold. I ran the blue tap at full blast and felt its output warm ominously from hour-old coffee to freshly drawn blood. Any connection with the smell didn't bear thinking about, so for some time I thought about nothing else.

Still, the fixtures gleamed, and beside the kettle lay a brimming basket of beverage sachets. The presence of a Corby trouser press expressed the spirit of a nobler, more genteel executive era, and I established that the olfactory badness could be effectively contained by wedging the bedspread under the bathroom door. While doing so I noted and admired the refreshing honesty of the mirror-mounted notice regarding towel reuse, which simply asked guests to place towels they wanted laundered in the bath. No recourse to the gut-pumping hypocritical blackmail that's become de rigueur in the hotel industry.

'Have you ever stopped to think of the ecological damage caused by unnecessarily washing towels? Please help us to save the bunnies hopping about an Alpine brook in the drawing beneath these words by using your towel again and again and again.' Heavens, that gets my goat, then punches it hard in the stomach. Why can't they just be upfront and admit their only concern is saving themselves a few quid on Daz? For that matter, why don't they go the extra mile and roll out the initiative across every area of guest-related budgetary management? 'Have you ever stopped to think about the pigs that died to bring you this breakfast buffet? Just have toast, you bastard. Oi, Fatty – one slice.' Anyway, I saluted the Star's management for not setting off down this road, and a minute later pushed through the Victorian airlock of its revolving doors with a modest spring in my step.

Great Yarmouth, I came to learn, is effectively two towns. The old one, home to the Star, lay clustered around the docks. I stuck my gloved hands in my armpits and walked stiffly across to the empty quayside, that spring in my step swiftly rusted by the elements and a haunted silence. This part of Yarmouth has certainly endured more than its share of tragedy, most of it improbable. On 2 May 1845, the townspeople crowded on to their new suspension bridge to watch a clown in a barrel being pulled down the River Yare by harnessed geese; as this memorable convoy passed beneath, the audience rushed from one side of the bridge to the other, triggering a collapse in which seventy-nine people drowned. In the First World War, Old Yarmouth beat off more obvious targets as the first English town to suffer a Zeppelin raid, and in the Second, its unfortunate proximity to the Luftwaffe's cross-Channel airfields established it as the most-bombed town in Britain per capita.

More drawn out but far more damaging was the death of the maritime trade that once kept these docks and the Star so busy. Over-fishing seems a strange concept. You can't imagine an agricultural labourer lying in bed at night worried that he might have been over-farming, or tradesmen being ticked off for over-plumbing. Over-curating is not the scourge of the museum world. But then few of us contemplate the bigger picture when considering the consequences of what we do for a living: if we did, every hedge-fund manager in the land would come home from work and immediately plunge a fork deep into his own thigh. The mundane truth is that as a natural resource, fish stocks are rather tricky to monitor. You can see a forest disappearing tree by tree, or a lake drying up, or a herd of wild animals being hunted to extinction. But in Great Yarmouth's pre-ultrasound golden age, by the time the sailing luggers noted a certain shortfall in shoal-bonniness, it was already too late. A tipping point had been passed, and from the 1920s the decimated herring population just shrank away into oblivion. No mean achievement when you consider that a single shoal of North Atlantic herring could contain four billion fish – enough to give everyone on earth a hearty kipper breakfast. Certainly everyone who actually wanted one. By the 1980s the Yarmouth fleet was down to twenty boats, and a fortnight after my visit, Great Yarmouth's last remaining fishermen, a pair of brothers in their thirties whose family had been in the business for four generations, gave it up as a bad lot.

As tourism took over from fishing, so the civic centre of gravity tilted towards the seafront, which I now discovered to be rather a long way off, into the sharp teeth of a vicious wind. The bulk of this journey was down Regent Road, a long, broad thoroughfare rendered claustrophobically festive by a low-slung net of wind-whipped blue fairy lights. A pedestrian zone, at least nominally, because at 7.30 p.m. on a Saturday, there were no pedestrians.

In planning my itinerary, I had made a conscious decision to see bad things in the worst possible light: for a seaside resort, late November was surely as bad as it got. The days of sunburn and candyfloss already seemed woefully distant, yet in grim reality the off-season was barely into its stride. Trembling above the cold and silent street, the Christmas illuminations seemed a bitter parody of the garish neon winks and flashes that would have jollied the crowds along on a balmy, boisterous summer evening. Every chilled gust seemed to carry before it the whisper of a harsh and vindicated Leysdown laugh.

All retail premises were comprehensively shuttered up: some for the night, some for the off-season, some for ever. A moth-balled gypsy clairvoyant. A discount store trading under the poorly conceived slogan: *£1 and much much more!* A tattoo parlour advertising daily specials to a customer base that had clearly come to consider permanent skin-stains as an impulse purchase: *Thursday: spend £30 or over on a tattoo and get a free name in any script font!* And a lone, dark, haunted-looking Victorian villa, set back from the shopfronts, shooing away the curious with a stark signposted legend: WAX MUSEUM – NOW CLOSED. I gazed at its dim frontage for some time, expecting Scooby Doo and Shaggy to pelt out through the front door, wailing.

Regent Road terminated before the radiant façade of the Britannia Pier. Huge billboards advertised the seasonal attractions at its end-of-pier theatre, one of the very few to survive. From these I learnt that the Chuckle Brothers would shortly be in town for their Christmas Chuckle, after which there was nothing on until 28 July, when the Chuckle Brothers would be in town. It's difficult to despise the Chuckle Brothers, though over-exposure to their breezy inanity on CBBC did once cause me to refer to them in a rhyming appellation ill-suited to the family environment. On the other hand, it's much, much easier to despise the performer who was booked to take to the Britannia Pier stage on 1 August. If I'm honest, Great Yarmouth's close association with Jim Davidson was a dominant reason – all right, the only reason – why I'd happily accepted all negative pronouncements on the town. What hope was there for a place that not only welcomed Britain's Horridest Man year after year, but charged people £20 to see him? That allowed this man to buy up a number of their most iconic seafront leisure facilities, including the town's second pier? That commiserated when his local investments backfired and the pier was demolished? That smiled indulgently when he chose to blame the resort itself, in these endearing terms: 'Great Yarmouth is full of overweight people in flip-flops, and fat children of all colours and no class'?

But it was too cold to sustain fury for long, and after shuddering along the pier's boardwalk, and around its trim but very closed entertainment booths and deep-fried, sugarcrusted snack stalls, I trotted down a side staircase and jogged back to the promenade across the soft sand. The beach was vast: you couldn't even hear the distant sea, let alone make out any silvery breakers. Marine Parade, the beachfront esplanade, was laid out on a sympathetically grand scale. On the seaward side, a broad pavement lined with hibernating food stalls (ROD'S SEAFOOD SHACK – SHRIMPLY THE BEST). On the other, across a generous sweep of under-trafficked tarmac, a parade of well-kept three- and four-storey Victorian residences – ex-boarding houses by the looks of them, now converted into apartments. Every other ground floor was home to a doggedly traditional restaurant, or more precisely a 'steak house', the kind that advertises 'English and Continental dishes'.

Like *Emmerdale* or a pint of Baileys, Marine Parade went on for ever and steadily leached appeal as it did so. The stolid old buildings gave way to garish and flimsy-looking Vegas-lite contemporary amusement arcades, embellished with pseudo-classical façades and slogans like: *The Atlantis – Open Every Day Throughout The Winter!* Why had they bothered? The mirrored walls, intended to amplify the flashing and colourful excitement, served instead to emphasise the total absence of humanity within. Every so often an old couple would shuffle past, triggering open the automatic doors and letting out a waft of heat and bleeping jingles. It was as if the owners had based their business model on the works of Edward Hopper. Somebody was losing an awful lot of money here, and I was struck with a sudden tragic thought: it might not have been Jim Davidson.

The viability of redevelopment declined as the promenade continued. Grubby, long-dark windows advertised OAP menus or the availability of a commercial lease. Pubs had died, been renamed and reborn, and died again. I later read that half of the town's public houses had closed over the previous five years, a decline one local councillor explained through a forthright demographic analysis that cast an unflattering light across Yarmouth's social scene: 'Pubs in Yarmouth are largely populated by older people who are prepared to stand out in the wind and rain to smoke. Younger drinkers prefer to get a case of cheap lager from supermarkets and stay at home.'

The civic pulse grew weaker, then flat-lined in a long parade of moribund retail premises (NEW INTERIORS – CLOSING-DOWN SALE). The wind was getting colder, compressing my features into a clenched grimace. It occurred to me that I'd eaten nothing since that reduced-to-clear handheld meat snack. I squinted into the dead distance, then turned back towards the gaily lit realm of English and Continental dishes.

It had always seemed likely that any day's final meal was going to provide my stiffest challenge. The traditional reward for enduring grim travails on the road is a really nice dinner, a reward entirely incompatible with my mission statement. Before setting off I'd decided that if the absence of sufficient related reviews and opinions prevented me from selecting a restaurant of certified ill-repute in advance – as was the case in Great Yarmouth – I'd do a quick tour of the local options on arrival, and select the least appealing. But even as I made that vow, I feared fulfilling it would demand mental reserves of self-denial and self-discipline that, deep into pampered middle-age, I wasn't sure I still possessed. I imagined myself striding into cosy little candle-lit bistros, and having to trudge out with a thwarted sigh. Gazing at mouth-watering, belt-loosening menus clustered with dishes I loved or knew I would, swallowing hard, and moving on. And keep moving until at last I came upon a catering establishment that no one in their right mind would voluntarily wish to enter, serving food that no one in their right mind would voluntarily wish to eat. Happily, for my mental reserves at least, Great Yarmouth seemed to offer nothing but.

I could probably have selected any of the seafront steak-houses, but plumped for the one that displayed the doughtiest disregard for developing fashions in catering ambience, and as a bonus served spam fritters.

As I took the first of the four tiled steps to the entrance, a plump old couple squeezed out through the door. 'See you tomorrow, then,' called the husband over his shoulder, in a flat tone disguised by the unlit fag already wedged in his lips, but which certainly originated far to the north-west of Norfolk. I walked inside and found myself alone in a dim red room with a matronly grey-haired waitress. It was looking as if the town's entire off-season economy was shored up by an inevitably dwindling population of retired gentlefolk, come to smoke away their twilight years by the sea. How would Great Yarmouth cope when they were all sparking up outside that big pub in the sky?

From the swirly carpet to the Festival of Britain typefaces, the dining experience that lay in wait could have been styled by Martin Parr, deadpan photographic chronicler of decaying seaside kitsch. Not seedy or surly, in other words, just deeply traditional and curling up slightly at the edges. Well-meant but careworn: an old-fashioned place for old-fashioned people. The waitress handed me a menu heavy on gammon steak and fried liver, served with every possible permutation of chips, beans and peas. Heart FM jangled out from the kitchen. A little display case by the till housed a pair of Barbie-sized plastic dancers in Greek national costume, which along with the waitress's rolling, guttural greeting suggested a family-run business dating back to an early wave of post-war economic migration. Only in the atlas index would you find Great Yarmouth anywhere near Greece. It was terribly sad to think that the search for a better life had led her from the glittery, sun-dappled Eastern Mediterranean to the muddy, windswept North Sea, and just at a time when Great Yarmouth's steakhouse-based tourism boom was on the cusp of a drawn-out, forty-year decline. That instead of serving souvlaki to a throng of sun-drunk, big-tipping Scandinavians, she was here kicking the front-door draught excluder back into place and taking a lone order for spam fritters and a pint of Carlsberg.

The story of how Spam got its name offers an insight into a more innocent age of brand management. Desperate to revitalise his Minnesota-based firm's ailing range of Flavor-Sealed canned pork products, the Hormel meat company's MD announced to guests at his 1936 New Year's Eve party that all their drinks would have to be 'bought' with suggestions for a fresh name. 'Along about the third or fourth cocktail they began showing some imagination,' he later told *Life* magazine. 'Finally my butler came over with a slip of paper marked Spam.' That's my kind of focus group. Why couldn't British Leyland's management have similarly incentivised their production-line staff before the ballot that christened the Austin Maestro? Actually I know why: it's because they didn't fancy marketing the Austin Cockhouse.

Spam, like the Maestro, was a product of its time – a time, you would think, which had long since and deservedly passed. As a reminder of grim austerity, Spam should survive only as a special-interest foodstuff, purchased either by tittering culinary ironists or by old people who leave a forlorn and accusing tin on the kitchen table when relatives visit, in the hope of being taken out for a guilt-fuelled slap-up lunch. But somehow, I was astonished to discover, thirteen million tins are still sold in the UK every year.

My own previous experience of spam fritters dated back nearly thirty years, to a time when strict regulations ensured that educational establishments served dishes proven to be both repulsive and unhealthy – that's to say not just nutritionally barren, but actively deleterious to well-being. Those battered roundels of mechanically recovered meat absorbed whatever it was they were fried in with rapacious efficiency: you pressed one with the flat side of your knife and a shiny, viscous puddle seeped out across the plate. To look at, and if it came to that to taste, a spam fritter seemed less like a human-grade victual than a discarded filter from some lard-powered canal dredger.

I'd figured on priming myself with at least two pre-fritter pints, but the food turned up before I'd raised the first to my lips. The waitress laid the plate down with a slightly helpless smile, as if to say: 'You asked for 'em, you got 'em.'

The spam used to create my last fritter had emerged from a gigantic cylindrical tin, hewn from the flaccid pink bollard within by a fat-armed dinner lady. The fritters nestling in a bed of chips and peas before me had been cut from a different cloth – a much smaller, squarer one. A pair of crusted oblong pouches, like Brillo pads would look if you used a lot of magnolia emulsion in your cooking. Other than that it was pretty much business as usual: I prodded one with my knife and it wept grease. That spectacle was enough for the waitress, who retreated swiftly back to the kitchen.

It was just me, the maroon-walled gloom and the fritters. I gripped the cutlery with purpose, then systematically dispatched everything on the plate that wasn't spam or a spam covering. I downed the pint. I wondered how long a man could live by spam fritters alone (answer Googled up later: six a day would fuel you nicely for three months, at which point scurvy would kick in, and do for you within the year). At length I bisected the first fritter, and was contemplating its oozing layers of badness when the waitress emerged. She went straight to the door and turned round the 'closed' sign, taking a sideways look at my plate en route and allowing herself a 'told you so' hike of the eyebrows. I seized the moment. 'Sorry, have you got any mustard? English mustard?' She nodded, and I knew then that everything was going to be all right.

If the Lord had wished us to shun terrible food, he wouldn't have given us condiments. Especially not the fearsome, vengeful condiment-god that is mustard, proper acid-yellow, nose-twitching, palate-flailing English mustard, as manufactured by Colman's of Quite Near Great Yarmouth. The agent orange in any war against bad flavour, laying waste to the most menacing gustatory jungles. A generous smear did for the fritters, shouting down their many provocative tangs and textures with a long, strident, fire-breathing roar. I might have seen evil, even heard evil bubbling greasily out when I punctured the fritter's crust, but with a savage angel trying to pull my tongue out through my nostrils I wouldn't have to taste it. In a moment there was nothing on my plate but a yellow skidmark. I looked at it and sensed I might be eating a lot of mustard in the weeks ahead.

'Bee's knees?'

The waitress placed the bill before me and smiled mildly; I creased my brow. 'You come to Yarmoat for bee's knees or holly die?'

The moment Craig's former keeper had asked what I'd be using his treasured car for, I realised that any local curiosity regarding the nature of my trip would need sensitive handling. Honesty was probably not the best policy if I wished to avoid ushering in offence and its hand-maiden, the ugly scene. It had all gone swimmingly when I'd fielded the very same question from the Star's receptionist, so I now delivered the very same dead-batted, non-committal answer that he had wordlessly accepted.

'Oh, right: well, a bit of both, really.'

'Yiz?'

'Yes.'

If I'd been paying cash that would have been that, but instead I was committed to a protracted three-way ceremony involving me, the waitress and her little handheld card terminal.

'What bee's knees?'

Before setting off I'd toyed with various cover stories, struggling all the while against a lifelong weakness for over-elaboration: when my teenage peers ran away from a ticket inspector, I would stand my ground and offer an explanation in made-up Hungarian. No, simplicity was the thing. That and yawn-enforcing dullness, a rationale that would instantly neuter any dangerous inquisitivity, indeed kill all conversation stone dead. What was the least interesting reason why an out-of-towner might be passing through an offbeat, downbeat place? The most obvious answer had suggested itself throughout my research, and with a growing silence to fill I now duly wheeled it out.

'I'm in sales. On the road.'

'So is no holly die?'

I muffed my PIN and at once began to slip into the old vortex of blathering cobblers.

'Well, this weekend is kind of like a reward, for, you know, regional achievement, in sales.' 'PLEASE RETURN TERMINAL TO VENDOR,' said the screen. I did so and delivered the *coup de grâce*.

'Carpet tiles.'

'Oh, yiz! Like you mean Heuga, like you mean Tessera, I have many catalogue, we need replace old carapit here, maybe you advice?'

The waitress's kindly features brightened with expectation. My innards shrivelled.

'Right, well, yes, though I don't deal so much with the actual tiles as . . . carpet-tile . . . adhesive.'

'Ah, which best: is spray or liquid?'

'Carpet-tile adhesive . . . removal products.' The terminal spooled out my receipt. 'Spillage and soiling issues. Nasty stuff.'

I retrieved the card with hot fingers, then fairly leapt to my feet, plunging arms into coat sleeves as I did so. The waitress proffered a little curl of paper and did her best to recap.

'So you are carapit-tile adessive removal product selling-man.'

'Of the year, East Anglia and Home Counties, 2009. Thank you!'

I was fairly blown back to the Star, past the Poundlands, the Cash Generators and charity shops, past all the boarded-up foyers and the signs reading WE HAVE MOVED! and ENTERTAINMENT PREMISES TO LET – INCENTIVES AVAILABLE. Past the Troll Cart, a pub which looked pretty much as it sounded, wide-necked bouncers stationed at every door but facing inward at the lairy, stumbling patrons, the scene almost visibly simmering with pent-up alcoholic violence. Why did Saturday-night Britain always have to be this way? I wondered, then promptly discovered it didn't.

Buffeted off down a side street by a rogue Arctic gust, I found myself before a little café that leaked bright light and happy noise. Through the steamed-up window I could make out a sea of bobbing heads and raised glasses; I located an unfogged corner and peered through with hooded hands. The chalkboard menu on the back wall was composed in a language that I eventually decided was Portuguese, a conclusion compatible both with the cheery, dark-haired throng beneath it and with a news story I'd read a few weeks previously, which revealed that Great Yarmouth was home to a five-thousand-strong Portuguese community, most employed in food processing. Well-paid, stimulating and wholesome: just some of the adjectives you would not choose to describe such jobs. These were people who spent long days shot-blasting the flesh off pig skulls for £5.80 an hour, people who had surely earnt the right to punch away their cares in the Troll Cart of a Saturday night. Yet here they were, in a strip-lit, overcrowded café, showcasing the kind of convivial and carefree Latin merriment you don't often see outside advertisements for cook-in pasta sauce. They had mastered a skill that had once been a very British preserve – making the best of a bad lot. When did we mislay that national trait? A few minutes later I walked past the Star's reception area feeling rather ashamed. And a few minutes after that I was back down there, demanding ice cubes and extra pillows.

Chapter Three

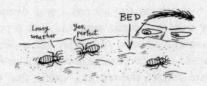

As long as they're not in the room with you – it happened to me once in Jersey – there's something rather wonderful about being woken up by seagulls. And if the shrill cries of freedom and briny adventure were a sensory call to arms, then so too was the smell of freshly fried smoky bacon. I greeted the gawky black lemon in the car park with a wave and a repulsive belch, replete with a cooked-to-order full English that augured well for breakfasts ahead. Misleadingly so, as it transpired.

Great Yarmouth seemed a little sorrier for itself by daylight. It looked sorrier still when a gust of fat raindrops clattered the windscreen, with the glowering overhead prospect of many more to come. Nothing paid more fulsome tribute to Craig's manufacturing ancestry than his performance in foul weather. The footwell rugs were soon blotted with damp, and squishily waterlogged before we bypassed Norwich. The arthritic wipers shrieked and juddered across the windscreen, smearing it with arcs of damp mud that the impotent, dribbling washer jets weren't about to shift. All the while I had to remind myself that I was asking Craig to do something he hadn't been designed to do: cover a very large distance without falling to pieces.

At least the conditions were taking the shine off his alarmingly pristine appearance. Without wishing to cause Craig excessive offence, it was frankly embarrassing to be thought of by all who saw me as someone who cared that much about something so very silly – a bit like having a Cliff Richard tattoo. I still remembered my neighbour Sha's expression as he watched me parking up on my return from Slough, and the words that emerged from his gaping jaw: 'Good God.'

Britain is rather larger than many people appreciate, particularly those who've never driven around it in an Austin Maestro. After setting to work on the sat-nav I was dismayed to find that Hull, my next overnight stop and just a pootle up the coast in my mental road atlas, in fact lay 222 miles off. Though admittedly not via a direct route, as ahead lay a far-flung festival of fail. The road skirted the big wet square that is the Wash, and dead-flat, grey-green Norfolk evolved to dead-flat, grey-green Lincolnshire, with nothing to leaven the persistent vista: a churned arable plain sporadically marked with a muddy cairn of harvested sugar beets. It was the sort of drive that screamed for musical distraction, a raucous singalong through a medley of old favourites. Instead, hell's own jukebox coughed up the Rolling Stones' horrifically dull 1986 album *Dirty Work*, the rent-a-riff sound of cynical has-beens with nothing left to say taking the cash to say it anyway. Critics at the time generously concluded that Mick Jagger had kept back the best material for his forthcoming solo album. As I was about to discover, he really, really hadn't. After a cheery blast of Benny Hill's 'Ernie' – now there's a proper, honest-to-badness novelty hit – a turgid twang of steel guitar was joined by a familiar cocksure drawl. It was forty-nine long minutes before either of them shut up.

If *Dirty Work* represented the Rolling Stones' creative funeral, *Primitive Cool* was the embarrassing uncle who ruined the wake. Not the most ear-bleedingly awful music I'd endure – *Q Magazine*'s readers had after all found seven worse albums to vote for – but perhaps the most dispiriting. Part of my love for the band – the real band, the pre-jumpsuit, pre-opiate Rolling Stones – died with each over-produced, under-written five-minute drone-a-thon. The entire album was like a soundtrack to the most awful scene in the most awful 1980s buddy-cop film. The DA's in cahoots with the mob, my girl's kicked me out, and that maverick sidekick of mine just traded his badge for a bottle of Jack: cue music! I heard myself ask Mick a simple question, repeatedly and increasingly loudly. Why? Why? WHY, YOU TREMENDOUS BUM-FUNNEL? Then the rain intensified, and we were both drowned out by the rubbery screech of double-speed wipers.

Old Leake, Wrangle, Friskney Tofts: the village names told their own tale of deepening isolation, places where there was nothing to do but watch potatoes grow and take unnecessary risks at unmanned level crossings. The landscape seemed to hunker down further still, readying itself for submergence. There'd be no dramatic cliffs or river deltas when I hit the coast, just one damp, flat surface giving way to a slightly damper, flatter one.

I'd be hearing a lot of 'Agadoo', the pineapple-pushing million-seller performed by bleached-mullet serial cack-merchants Black Lace. The song made the upper echelons of almost every poll I'd sourced my playlist from: it made the top five in dotmusic's Most Annoying Songs, and took gold in a *Q Magazine* vote to nominate the Worst Song Ever. Because of an administrative failure on my part, double entries of this sort were not culled. I think in the end I listened to 'Agadoo' four times. Yet after the ponderous, complacent guff my ears had just endured, I found chirpy cheese hard to hate. How can you despise a song whose Wikipedia entry includes the sentence, 'It was produced by Barry Whitfield, who also appears in the video as a pear'? Yes, it's inane and crass; yes, any public occasion, from school disco to wedding reception, is damned to death the moment that chorus bursts out of the speakers. But there's a reason why 'Agadoo' sold a million copies, and why *Primitive Cool* failed to dent the top forty, and that reason explains why I'm not ashamed – not too ashamed – to admit that I sang loudly along, and even pushed the odd pineapple when road conditions permitted. At any rate, as a paean to tropical beach-life cooked up in Castleford, West Yorkshire, it seemed a fitting welcome to Skegness.

It was a personal pick. No one had said anything particularly bad about Skegness, other than a throwaway reference to 'the UK's Devil's Island', and that was probably more to do with its position on a stretch of the most barren and thinly populated coastland in Britain. I couldn't even call upon any first-hand experience to justify its inclusion on my itinerary. I'd simply decided that a seaside resort in south Lincolnshire must, by definition, be both grim and ridiculous. Its grim and ridiculous name didn't help, even before the locals shortened it to Skeggy, an appellation with all the come-hither holiday allure of a hoof-rotting livestock disease. To paraphrase the prancing fatso who put the place on the map, Skegness sounds SO ghastly.

It didn't look that bad, though, especially after the sun came out on my final approach. The fields around here were once considered the richest grazing land in the country, and they certainly looked the part with a rainbow stretched over them, their resident cows nose-down in glistening green. Like so many of the places along Britain's Scandinavia-facing coast, Skegness is of Viking origin. As my Icelandic wife likes to remind me, her adventurous forefathers can claim naming rights over anywhere that ends in ness, by, wick or any of the brough/borough/burg variants. Skegness, then, means either 'forested headland' or 'pillagey rapeville', depending on whether you're more interested in etymological fact or winding up the in-laws. Still, as an unappealingly named fishing village of four hundred hardy souls backed by vast flat tracts of rural nothingness, Skegness seemed an unlikely resort-to-be when the railway arrived in 1875. Fittingly, its success is the legacy of an unlikely duo.

The Earl of Scarborough was the dominant local landowner, and a man who saw something in the lonely dunes around Skegness that others didn't. Spurred on by architects and builders with guinea signs in their eyes, in fifteen years the Earl boldly blew the family fortune in laying out promenades, gardens and a new main street across the windswept foreshore. He built houses, a church, and a pier that strode far out into the cold grey sea. To friends, relatives and anyone else hoping for some action in the Earl's will, the whole scheme must have seemed an act of hubristic folly. For thirty years, it was. In contravention of the *Field of Dreams* maxim, he had built it, but they didn't come. No one came. I picture the Earl of Scarborough standing alone on his weed-decked pier, stovepipe hat clutched to chest, mutton-chop whiskers belaboured by the chilly gusts, cocking his ear at a lonely call from the distant, empty promenade: 'Nice one, Granddad, you div!'

Finding themselves saddled with an unprofitable branch line, the Great Eastern Railway shared some of the Earl's pain. The company's early attempts to capture the would-be resort's appeal produced what may be the most anti-magnetic tourism slogan of all time: *Skegness – Nottingham by the Sea!* Crestfallen at its failure, in 1908 GER changed tack, paying illustrator John Hassall 12 guineas to depict the town's appeal. Hassall, who had never been anywhere near Skegness, felt curiously inspired to anthropomorphise the place as a fat old fisherman, skipping campily along an empty, puddled beach with a pipe in his teeth and an overbearing leer in his mad, mad eyes. Unveiling this extraordinary character to GER's publicity executives should have procured a long, uneasy silence, followed in due course by anger, then legal proceedings to recover the 12 guineas. In fact, the board decided the only thing this deranged and alienating image needed was a matching strapline. Those pools of standing water were a start, but they didn't communicate the south Lincolnshire coast's full spectrum of holiday-hostile deficiencies. 'Think, chaps, think – I'm getting scary weirdos, I'm getting bleak, I'm getting rain . . . But come on, I need wind, I need cold, and I need them now.'

Skegness is SO bracing! It should have been the stillborn resort's epitaph, but somehow the twin promise of fat nutters and terrible weather proved irresistible. 'The Jolly Fisherman' singlehandedly put Skegness on the holiday map: almost overnight, day-trippers pitched up in droves, and within five years, the town's population had more than quadrupled. The Earl made millions, then millions more when he sold up after the First World War. In 1936, the grateful townspeople finally gave John Hassall a reason to visit Skegness, hosting a ceremony at which he was presented with the freedom of the foreshore, and a silver model of his camp creation. 'The reality of Skegness has eclipsed all my anticipations,' he told the assembled crowd, in an address with all the sparky authenticity of a prepared confession at a Stalinist show trial. 'It is even more bracing than I had been led to expect.' He never returned.

If Great Yarmouth had slunk off into hibernation, Skeggy seemed like a resort in a state of seasonal denial. At half twelve on a bright but very bracing Sunday in late November, the pavements were thronged with weather-resistant families in varying states of undress: chilblained young girls in halter-necks and short skirts, Jolly Fisherman-sized fathers in football shirts. There were a few pound shops and 'fashion clearance outlets' along the Earl's high street, but not a single boarded-up economic casualty. The whole place exuded an almost palpable sense of civic defiance, hardy locals sticking two fingers up at the weather, hardy shopkeepers tweaking the nose of recession. It was all rather infectious, though enthusiasm levels dipped a little after I parked Craig up by the pier and experienced the elements first-hand. It was a battle to heave open the door, and another not to berate the red-haired fibreglass clown I then found myself confronted by. 'Have you no respect, Mr McDonald? This is a British seaside resort, I'll have you know, the very cradle of terrible greasy crap. Now be gone, sir! Though, um, not until I've nipped into your place for a wee, and had half an hour's free parking.'

Eyes slitted, trousers a-flap, I leant into the wind and struggled along the promenade. Gale-torn half-snatches of bored bingo lingo blew out from the 'Skeg-Vegas' arcade's Tannoy: on its own, number legs, clickety-eight. The pier, rationalised by fire, storm and commercial reality, was now little more than a stub that stopped well short of the tide line. Puddles shimmered in the wind. Benches and bins cast long shadows across a deserted beach pock-marked by the morning's rain. Way out into the excitable grey sea, a white forest of wind turbines rotated as if set for take-off. I braced myself against a handrail and looked back at the town. A sign that read HEATING!

in a snack-bar window, the warning beside me detailing the fatal risks of tidal conditions and areas of sinking sand – everything screamed out Withnail's forlorn words to a neighbouring Lake District farmer: 'Excuse me, we've gone on holiday by mistake.' All this, and yet the scene was a-buzz with happy families, red of cheek and blue of limb, queuing at the six-for-a-quid doughnut stall and striking comedy poses by the Jolly Fisherman statue near the clock tower. There was an almost perverse, bring-it-on dedication to having a great day out despite everything. The Windbreak Generation's forgotten tribe, a people who didn't just weather the storm, but went out in it with a towel and a grin. Along with the trouble I had making myself understood at the doughnut stall, all this made one thing very apparent: I was now in the north of England.

Skegness gave way to huge fields of static caravans, geometric ranks of white on green, like war cemeteries. In a moment of weakness I shut down my in-car Radio Awful and twiddled along medium wave in search of football commentary, but out here Five Live sounded like Alexander Graham Bell doing a bungee jump in a cave full of angry bees; the only decent signals were being pumped out in Dutch and German. That meant a deep sigh and *Tin Machine II*, voted the worst album by a great artist, doing for David Bowie's reputation what that clown in a goose-drawn barrel did for Norfolk's bridge engineers. If my spirits rose, it was only because the view did: after hours and hours of pan-flat nothingness, the landscape was now rucked up into plump, green, sun-kissed hillocks. It felt like driving across a giant Windows XP desktop.

I was going to North East Lincolnshire, which as well as being the third worst place to raise a family (after Reading and Waltham Forest), also bagged a bottom-three slot in the definitive quality-of-life survey carried out by Channel 4's *Location, Location, Kneecap* (sorry, I've cracked already). But what with North East Lincolnshire being a whole county, I'd put my trust in Google: I typed those three words into their map search box, clicked return, and zoomed in on the little red marker flag that confidently popped up just below the Humber's gaping mouth.

So it was that I now found myself driving up Wellholme Avenue, Grimsby, deemed by computer algorithm as the unhappy county's epicentre.

The town's opening syllable seemed to set out the civic stall, and my sole previous visit had dutifully suggested Grimsby as a place that had seen better days, and would only see worse. Perhaps it hadn't helped that I'd gone there in a wet gale, and saw little of the town beyond its inevitably discouraging container docks. There are also powerfully negative associations with the manner of my farewell to Grimsby, and the three days that followed – a storm-tossed cargo voyage to Iceland that left me a yellow, wizened husk of a man.

Anyway, it was still a pleasant surprise to find Wellholme Avenue reveal itself as entirely unobjectionable, indeed rather agreeable – a long, straight road of trim, red-brick, late-Victorian terraces, with arched windows, stucco trimmings and a Spar on the corner. Half a dozen boisterous kids in filthy football kit were disgorged from a mum-driven people carrier, a pizza-delivery moped buzzed past and a tubby old man in a flat cap walked by with a tubby old Labrador – just a normal, whole-some Sunday afternoon in a normal, wholesome British street.

My neighbour Chris was born and raised in Grimsby, and while explaining to him some months previously just why I'd acquired the shaming, ridiculous vehicle that now besmirched the street we both called home, I saw his features sag into a kind of defeated wince. 'All the worst places?' he said flatly, when I was done. 'So I take it you'll be going to Grimsby, then.' This was before Google Maps finessed my itinerary, so as things then stood, I wasn't, and told him so. His face lit up and I pictured it now: grateful, reprieved, maybe – like all my neigh-bours – just a tiny bit in love with me. So though I'd driven into Wellholme Avenue feeling a little guilty, I drove back out of it smiling. I could knock firmly on Chris's door and treat him to a happy-ending confession.

If I'd then motored out through Grimsby with my eyes shut, everyone but my insurance company would have been happy. As it was, I watched the town go to pieces around me. First the side streets devolved into a hotch-potch of pebble-dash and ramshackle uPVC porches; the dogs grew stockier and scarier, and the men walking them younger, wearing hoods instead of caps. Shops were shuttered up, then bricked up. The traffic melted away as I approached what would have been Grimsby's bustling port-centred heartland, back when Wellholme Avenue was laid out, and the prosperous streets were a-throng with trawlermen and stevedores. Instead, the townscape fell away, leaving an eerie, brownfield vacuum, with only the odd marooned hulk to betray a once crowded commercial skyline. Worse still, it had evidently been this way for years, long enough for a pre-fab Allied Carpets warehouse to have sprung forth from the stony soil, struggled to establish itself, and failed in turn. It wasn't alone. I turned off the main road and drove past umpteen retail hangars of recent construction, with weeds sprouting from their chained and empty car parks: the phoenix had risen from the ashes, then starved to death and rotted.

Yet in alarming reality, Grimsby is a regional success story. It's Britain's busiest port by tonnage, with a hefty fish and frozen-food processing industry that inspired the local authority to saddle it with the ungainly title of Europe's Food Town. Round one corner I was presented with a stirring, iconic vision: the bow of a huge grey ship, looming majestically over a Homebase. Give or take the odd step up the production chain, Grimsby is more or less doing what it's always done, and doing it rather well. It just so happens that these days you don't need very many people to unload a ship or make crispy pollock fillets: it's pretty much just Captain Birdseye and a forklift truck. Grimsby was simply built for a larger population than it can now support. I drove away from the town sensing there'd be similar stories in the weeks ahead, but with much sadder endings.

Exhausted by the effort of hauling itself aloft, the countryside soon lay flat down on its back again. The muddy plain separating me from the Humber was briefly but memorably filled by a pair of prodigious oil refineries, throwing up fumes and fire as if in the midst of an endless rolling catastrophe. Then

Ozzy's nasal haranguing bullied me off down a series of soggy, narrow lanes, and presently up to the banks of the Humber, and the town of New Holland. Almost everyone I'd discussed my forthcoming journey with had volunteered their own private hell, and here was Chris's.

When a town dies, it's typically a lingering affair. Industries are slowly undermined by changing consumer tastes, superior technology or cheaper foreign labour, and the commercial life-blood ebbs gently away. Not so New Holland, killed stone dead at midday on 24 June 1981.

A town with a simple, solitary function, New Holland was the staging post between Grimsby and Hull, a place where goods and people en route from Lincolnshire to Yorkshire got off a train and got on a trans-Humber ferry. There was a station, a jetty, and – the focus of Chris's unhappy memories – two big pubs, each named after one of the coal-powered paddle steamers that plied the route. The crossing was a twenty-minute job in theory, but tides and shifting sandbanks played merry hell with the timetable, often marooning Chris and his many brothers in those pubs for long and uncomfortable hours. More than once their big night out in Hull had got no further than New Holland, degenerating into an embattled ordeal in the company of restless and increasingly drunken dockers.

I'd assumed the town had been named in honour of the Dutch engineers who helped reclaim so much of Lincolnshire from its watery encroachments. In fact, rather wonderfully, New Holland is thus called after the Dutch gin that was ener-getically smuggled through here in that spirit's Hogarthian heyday. True to this heritage, both pubs were still in business. I was welcomed into New Holland by the Magna Charta, its stout cream-coloured flanks decorated with images of the eponymous paddle steamer that inaugurated the route in 1820, and waved out of it by the Lincoln Castle: not just the last ferry to cross the Humber, but the last paddle steamer to operate a scheduled service in Britain. (That vessel and its last sister ship, the *Tattershall Castle*, both live on as floating pubs, one on the Thames and the other at Grimsby docks. It's what the gin-smuggling, boozed-up Chris-taunters would have wanted.)

Linking the two themed inns was a shabby and forlorn quarter-mile ribbon of red-brick terraced cottages, built for the ferry and railway workers, and hence now sparsely occupied. Many were for sale, and most of those that weren't had an unloved Craig-era Astra or Escort out front. It was 4 p.m., and the only other soul on the streets was a helmetless youth on a trials bike, demonstrating a fitful mastery of the wheelie. I rumbled to a halt on a squalid patch of threadbare cobbles and tarmac, and opened the window. It was all puddles and weeds and a creepy Sunday silence. The petrochemical billowings to the west had coalesced into a dense cloud of butterscotch, being eased towards me on the stiff, cold wind.

What a horrid place, I thought, then said aloud, neatly filling the silence between 'So Macho' and 'Remember You're A Womble'. Beyond the Lincoln Castle lay a moribund Victorian warehouse, a rusty railway line overseen by a derelict beach hut of a signal box, and the silos and lofty conveyer belts of a bulk-goods terminal. Somewhere behind this lay the Humber, and somewhere up that soared the mighty suspension bridge that had whipped the rug out from under New Holland's feet. The ferry and the railway station both closed at the precise minute it opened, and that was this place – certainly the dullest, deadest and dankest I had yet visited, the town I was most heartily relieved not to call home – done and dusted.

The fresh-faced two-wheeled lawbreaker buzzed back into view, flicked me a dispassionate V-sign, and buzzed away behind the warehouse. His suggestion appealed instantly. Scrapping my plan to share Chris's pain with a pint in the Lincoln Castle, I heaved Craig into first, and with Mike Batt urging me to remember-member-member my true heritage, fucked off.

Plans for a suspension bridge over the Humber were first drawn up in the 1930s, at a time when clipping fifty miles off the road-trip between Grimsby and Hull made compelling economic sense. The Humber numbers probably still worked when construction finally began in 1972, though they probably didn't eight years later, when my Geography teacher Mr Brooks reluctantly selected the project as an O level case study. Largely involving us watching Mr Brooks connect hexagons on the overhead projector, this sought to demonstrate how the bridge might benefit a fictional bakery on the south side of the Humber, dispatching fictional bread to customers on the north. We were fifteen-year-old London boys who had never been anywhere near Humberside, but we'd heard of the Cod War, and Margaret Thatcher: fisherman and fictional baker alike would soon have nothing to deliver. Like its close contemporary the Austin Maestro, the Humber Bridge was a decent British idea whose time came and went somewhere along the long, long road from drawing board to final completion.

Yet as deluded as those projections of exponential traffic growth and associated regional prosperity so plainly were, no one objected as Mr Brooks mumbled out the data. Largely because we just wanted him to whip through it all and return to what he loved about geography: the mighty peaks, cliffs and chasms of its physical incarnation. This was a love we shared, for Mr Brooks always illustrated the related phenomena with a slideshow of self-timer portraits from his solo field trips – the most compelling body of images, with predictable exceptions, that any of us had yet been exposed to.

Mr Brooks was a painfully retiring fellow, who looked at the floor when he spoke, and tackled classroom disorder by slowly shaking his head. The one suggestion that a very different Mr Brooks might lurk within was his beard, a wild and hefty moustache-less bush that strayed way beyond standard-issue 1970s Geography teacher territory and deep into the realm of the Amish elders. When the lights went out and the projector clicked on, we saw this other Mr Brooks: a man who gestured confidently at drumlins and batholiths, a man whose massive beard framed a brilliant, fulfilled smile. And a man – now I see that head begin to slowly shake – who spent his summers in wellington boots, a lumberjack shirt and a pair of incredibly tight denim shorts.

The maelstrom of face-wetting, wrist-biting, desk-clawing hysteria thus unleashed, and the failure of Mr Brooks' hands-off, mouth-closed approach to restraining it, should have made that first slideshow the last. Yet so blind was the man's passion for glacial erosion and longshore drift that it never took much to get him eagerly rooting out the Kodachromes. 'I think I understand the principle, sir, but what does terminal moraine actually *look* like?' Blinds down, lights off, and there it all was again: the beard, the beam, the boots, the shorts.

Anyway, I thought of Mr Brooks as just outside New Holland the top half of the Humber Bridge showed itself, two massive concrete ladders supporting God's own clothes line. I've always had a thing for epic civil engineering, though it proved tricky to settle into a mood of sombre awe with Chas and Dave's 'Rabbit' as a soundtrack. Here was the last hurrah of newsreel-voiced, look-at-us Britain, when the future was always bright, nature was there to be conquered, and speed was the answer to everything.

The 1982 opening was accompanied by a fanfare of gosh-inducing statistics: the world's longest single-span suspension bridge, with a main cable long enough to stretch twice round the globe, and a toll booth constructed entirely from crushed puffin beaks. But even then the instinctive, hexagon-based misgivings of my youth were hardening into proper, grown-up facts. The simple truth that the Humber was still, in 1981, ferrying passengers in a paddle steamer seems a fairly potent suggestion that economic progress might have stalled round these parts, and sure enough, when those trans-Humberian bakers finally stood up to be counted, there just weren't enough of them. Traffic has never come close to the predicted levels, not even halfway. Two thousand cars now use the bridge every day, which might not sound too awful until you work out that's barely one a minute. I've lived on busier suburban back roads.

The Humber is now only the fifth longest suspension bridge, its conquerors betraying the shift in the economic balance of power: one each in Denmark and Japan, the most recent two in China. It's still a record-breaker, though: the longest bridge in the world that one can cross on foot, and thus a powerful magnet for those weary of life. I'd only spent ten minutes in New Holland, but it was still probably for the best that my route drew me away from the bridge, and a handrail that's now vaulted once a fortnight.

The day was dimming, and I had something to see before it went the way of all days. In a triumph of hope over experience I put my foot down, which had little influence on the speedometer but made it very hard to hear Jonathan King's 'Una Paloma Blanca', especially once I began to bellow out a rather brilliant rework of its chorused title. 'You're just a fucking wanker!' I roared over the clatter of labouring pistons, hands juddering on the wheel, willing Craig to make a blur of Lincolnshire's wide-open spaces.

We don't really do big country in England, but this stuff was pretty sizeable. Lincolnshire is our second largest county in size, but just scrapes into the population top twenty. On the bedspread-sized laminated map of Great Britain and Ireland that fills the wall behind my PC monitor, the county is a white void sparsely veined with trunk roads, its far-flung habitations labelled in tiny lower case. On all sides but the big blue one it's surrounded by regions crazy-paved with major road routes and dense with capital-letter cities. All in all, it was perhaps inevitable that when the Ordnance Survey's cartographers were asked to nominate the most boring spot in Britain, they found themselves drawn to this county. Though, in fact, they eventually stuck the pin half a mile off its edge, in the East Riding of Yorkshire.

I inched towards grid reference SE830220 in the throes of a sunset that poured gold across the flat fields in a dangerously compelling fashion. It even cast an almost fetching gloss over Britain's most inexplicable holiday destination, a vast muddy hollow filled with static caravans. The interestometer flickered crazily as we passed into the splendidly named Hatfield Chase, an age-old royal hunting ground that spent much of its time beneath the surface of the many large rivers that ran through it. Until 1626, when Charles I contracted Cornelius Vermuyden, superstar of Holland's thriving land-reclamation scene. Vermuyden masterminded the extravagant network of dykes and drainage canals that would spare SE830220 and its neighbours from repeated inundation, and swiftly establish Hatfield Chase as one of Britain's most productive but least fascinating arable regions.

Ousefleet, near the point where the Trent meets the Ouse to form the Humber, was one of the farming villages that emerged from the flood plain. Just outside it I carefully recalibrated the sat-nav, and bumped gingerly down a lumpy track that trailed off into the yawning cultivated prairie. This was it, the proverbial middle of nowhere, the square kilometre selected as the cartographic final answer to a cheerfully pejorative debate amongst Radio 4 listeners. 'We ran a computer analysis of each of the 204 maps in our widely used Landranger series,' commented an Ordnance Survey press officer, doubtless in a soporific nasal drone. 'Of the 320,000 squares, this one contained the least information. No ditches, streams or buildings are shown on this particular scale, though I should add that there is an electrical pylon in one corner, and that people edge away from me at parties.'

Nobody rushed to stand up for SE830220, which given its absence of inhabitants shouldn't have surprised anyone, but apparently did surprise the media. Ever keen to make mountains out of molehills – not a huge challenge, you'd have thought, in a landscape that's pretty well done the job already – the press tracked down the landowning farmer and tried to rouse him to a spirited defence of his maligned tract. Yet Tom Ella nobly declined to play ball. 'Look, it's just a field,' he told one reporter. 'If people want to come and look at it, I don't mind, but they're wasting their petrol.'

I got out to see what I'd wasted my petrol for. The darkening sky was unblemished, save a few painterly streaks of grey and orange smudged around the sinking sun, and a distant puff of industrial vapour. Below it: nothing, but in such extraordinary amounts that boredom was comfortably transcended.

The stripe of crispy brown bracken and grass lining the lane gave way to a fat, 360-degree layer of furrowed brown and green, which would have seeped away for ever had the blue-grey horizon not cut it off. The whole still and silent panorama had a sweeping grandeur to it, rural yet abstract, a Constable by Rothko. I'd imagined that pylon, part of a column marching away to Scunthorpe, as SE830220's scene-stealing cameo performer; in fact, it seemed a spindly intrusion. Even the odd skeletal tree and the distant huddle of tiles and whitewash that was Ousefleet just got in the way.

It was a beguiling, oddly magnetic scene, somewhere you could hide in plain sight, see everything without being seen. Extrapolating from the clutch of dented old cans I now spotted in the dead bracken, I could imagine SE830220 hosting a bit of lager-with-Rosie action of a summer evening. I suddenly found it easy to imagine all manner of remarkable and contra-tedious chapters in SE830220's super-aquatic history: the shoot-out between rival gangs of gin smugglers, the dispute over a prize beet that set Ella against Ella, that terrible business with the pylon repairman and the milking machine. And then I looked around again, and noted that the sun had finally called it a day, and that this little square kilometre, with all its epic vistas and made-up mysteries, was now just a cold, dark and very lonely place. Not somewhere you'd want to get stuck for the night, as I had cause to ponder during an ill-judged three-point turn that threatened this very fate upon me. Fifteen hectic and very sweary minutes elapsed before Craig slithered away from SE830220, wheels steaming and flanks splattered in Tom Ella's brown gold.

The road took me up to the Ouse – a theoretical entity that lurked behind a hefty embankment – and through a series of sleepy, unkempt villages, where no front yard seemed complete without a windowless caravan. The evening river-mist seemed laced with something thicker, and I presently identified the moreish whiff of domestic coal-smoke wafting in through the many gaps in Craig's bodywork. It was to become a defining odour.

From Skegness to Scunthorpe, Lincolnshire can blame the

Vikings for the unbecoming names that burden its habitations. No such excuse for the nineteenth-century Yorkshiremen who built the Aire and Calder canal, and founded a town called Goole at its confluence with the River Ouse. And if Goole doesn't sound bad enough in its own right, consider its etymology: the name is derived from the Anglo-Saxon word for 'open sewer'.

This unfortunate history provided irresistible inspiration for the many journalists who came to the town after it was exposed as the home of Britain's youngest heroin addict, an eight-year-old boy. 'Goole was named after an open sewer – and now that sewer is metaphorically choked with drug dealers, and no doubt actually choked with their horrible druggy poo.' That sort of thing. Further research revealed that Goole suffers more fatal heroin overdoses per head than anywhere else in Britain – around seven every year in a population of just eighteen thousand. Also that the town's pensioners are regularly arrested for intent to supply, and that a regional 'culture of injecting' encourages jaded locals to shoot up everything from valium to whisky when their class As run out. Some pictures paint a thousand words, but a photo I came across restricted itself to a pithy seven: a boarded-up Ford garage daubed with the legend, *Welcome to Goole – we kill smack dealers*.

As it was, I found myself driving into town past a big dockside shed bearing a less diverting salutation, *The UK's premier inland port*, which had an underwhelming, defensive ring to it, as if Goole couldn't quite make a claim that wasn't much of a claim in the first place, along the lines of 'Great Yarmouth's leading pet crematorium' or 'New Holland pub-of-the-year finalist'. In fact, the half-hearted adjectives were misleading – Goole is by any calculation our largest inland port, and despite being 50 miles away from the salty sea, has all the trappings of your actual bona-fide marine port. Three million tons of cargo a year, proper lighthouses all the way along the banks of the Ouse and the Humber, and ready access to uncut, fresh-off-the-boat, overdose-strength skag.

I actually gasped at the townscape that sprang up the moment Craig crested the box-girder bridge over the Aire and Calder.

Squinting at the fuzzy, sodium-lit skyline, all I could see was a scrappy void occasionally punctured by a twisted section of gantry, or a gasholder, or a silo, or a water tower. It was like some tableau crafted from C.S. Lewis's definition of hell, as a desolate twilight city upon which night is imperceptibly sinking. These weren't the outskirts: this was downtown Goole, in fact this was the whole of Goole. My mind chose this moment to retrieve an entry I'd come across in a regional internet forum, contributing to a collation of fond local memories. 'I married a lass from Goole. Sadly, she died in an industrial accident at the luncheon meat factory some years ago.'

I bumped over a series of level crossings and was offered a glimpse of inert high street, devoid of humanity and lavishly puddled with the morning's rain. Then it was off down a road of boarded-up, bring-out-your-dead terraces, past disembodied walls bearing ancient hand-painted promotions for drapery stores and distemper treatments. Even the inevitable post-industrial retail invaders – Netto, CarpetRight – looked more like dumpy little prisons, each a windowless, metal-shuttered fortress sitting in its razor-wired, flood-lit tarmac compound.

It felt like driving through a town-sized advert for the heroin marketing board, yet I came out of Goole with a smile on my face. The world outside might be a dank, foresaken wasteland with a permanent touch of flu, but Craig was a deafening singalong party on wheels. It had started when Timmy Mallett, children's TV presenter cum living incitement to blunt-force trauma, launched into a cover version that I came to interpret, with alarming gusto, as 'Itsy Bitsy Teeny Weeny Yellow Wart-Encrusted Peenie'. This segued into the opening bars of an album that I shouldn't really have included in my playlist: it was an American production – so American that it featured the eighteen-year-old Jon Bon Jovi's recording debut. However, the revelation that the lead vocal artiste was an Englishman by the name of Anthony Daniels gave me the excuse I needed. Because this was the super-bad, over-proof hard stuff – not just a stand-out album in *Q*'s roll-call of the damned, but a top-ten entry in a *Daily Telegraph* poll of worst record covers. I'm looking at it now: a kindly old gent with a big white beard and pebble specs sits by a glowing fireplace, surrounded by half-finished toys and a number of – wait for it – androids. Prominent amongst these is Anthony Daniels, imprisoned in the golden carapace that made him famous, though evidently not that rich. Welcome to *Christmas in the Stars*, a 1980 festive production featuring the 'original cast of *Star Wars*'.

Well, what a tonic the ensuing thirty-three minutes proved to be – just what the methadone clinic doctor ordered. Beneath the goodwill-to-all-droids theme ran a curious sub-plot in which C-3PO laboured to talk-sing his little dustbin chum R2-D2 into whistling a tune, a feat finally accomplished on 'Sleigh Ride' ('Oh, R2, I knew you could do it! Again!'). That hit the spot, and hit it hard. My fascination, dangerously hysterical as it was, only sagged during 'R2-D2 We Wish You A Merry Christmas', which didn't have nearly enough C-3PO, and instead had far too much Jon Bon Jovi, giving it his youthful, huge-haired all above a high-school choir (the album was recorded in the studio where his uncle worked, and where he had a part-time cleaning job). Then we were into the unforget-table highlight, an ensemble number that propelled me shrieking on to the M62: 'What can you get a Wookiee for Christmas, when he's already got a comb?' I was vocally and emotionally drained long before the final track delivered the underwhelming answer to this conundrum (a brush), and almost asleep at the wheel when at around 7 p.m. I passed a huge roadside billboard that read CLOSING DOWN. Thus I found myself welcomed into Kingston upon Hull.

The grand old man of sad old dumps, the dad of bad, Hull ran away with the top spot in the popular publication *Crap Towns*, and came a solid second in the more scientific survey commissioned by *Location, Sedation, Castration*. It's been dubbed Britain's obesity capital, and seen both its police force and its education authority rated the worst in the land. A survey of local drinking habits found that 95 per cent of Hullensians under twenty-five drank to harmful excess. I imagined the entire city being sat down and given a talking-to by the college dean from *Animal House*: 'Listen, son: fat, drunk and stupid is no way to go through life.'

Hull is almost synonymous with unloveliness, deprivation and failure – literally so, if you take the city's winningly outspoken council leader at his word. 'Until recently it was difficult to find a story that didn't mention Hull and crap in the same sentence,' he said in 2008, committing the sin himself. 'We've had the shit kicked out of us for thirty years.' His next word was naturally a 'but', though this sadly presaged the pump-priming, morale-boosting achievements of Hull City Football Club, then enjoying what proved to be a very short-lived stay in the Premier League, and an even briefer period of solvency.

Ozzy f-f-fucked me off the motorway and into a shadowy zone of wasteland and distribution centres. I spotted my first white telephone box, for as every civic-trivia buff will know, Hull is home to a telecommunications network that uniquely in Britain remained independent of the General Post Office and British Telecom. I was so diverted by this sighting that it took me a while to note that I was in the red-light district. Craig's evidently unpromising appearance had the lone kerb-dwellers slinking off into the shadows as I approached; I looked in the rear-view mirror and saw them slinking back out, peering at me suspiciously. What sort of man kerb-crawled in an immaculate black Austin Maestro?

I spotted my destination just before Ozzy crudely informed me of its proximity. The Stop Inn: a hotel masquerading as a mid-rise, mid-Sixties council block, and burdened with a feebly comic name of the type associated with hairdressing salons. 'Stop Inn? Move on!' So began a typical review, one of the torrent that described the hotel in the most damning terms. Lice, swearing, gouges, threadbare, damp, peeling, hairs, 'Sunday towels and a haunting stench' – the complaints went way beyond simple disgruntlement, coming across more like the urgent, rasped words of a man whose dying wish was that others be spared his ordeal. 'Please, please do not stay here under any circumstances . . . Avoid – just avoid.' This man could die happy, for as I gathered from the small heap of mail gathered behind its locked glass doors, and the security-firm logo that implied the premises were patrolled by an armed lion, the Stop Inn had bidden farewell to its last unhappy resident. Across the street, next to a vast cinema-turned-bingo-hall, sat a trim new Ibis, no doubt the straw that broke the Stop Inn's hairy, damp back. I admit I was briefly tempted: whatever a Sunday towel might be, you surely wouldn't find one there.

But surveying that bland, corporate frontage, smug with the promise of a louse-free, odourless overnight experience, I felt my brain stem begin to shrivel. Bumhats to the Ibis, uniform, dependable and deeply, deeply dull, the hotel equivalent of the Kinder Bueno in Angela Merkel's handbag, a two-year-old Ford Mondeo 1.6i Edge nosing into car park 5B at Bluewater, Tim Henman watching *Countdown* in his cords. I was on a quest for the local, the unpredictable, the non-globalised and non-homogenous, the thrill of the unknown that had once made travel an adventure, even here in my homeland. The fear and excitement that went with never being quite sure that you'd ever get to where you wanted to go, let alone what you'd find there if you did. The mysteries that once lay in wait behind every hotel-room door, inside every menu, under every bonnet.

The zeal thus unleashed ebbed away somewhat over the following hour, during which I established that the Stop Inn was merely the freshest corpse in the hotel mass grave that is Hull. After taking Craig on a tour of the city's many roofless former guest houses, I presented myself at the reception of the Ibis's only surviving competitor, fewer than 200 yards up the road: the Royal Hotel.

A period attachment to Hull's railway station, the Royal was graced with an ominously regal gold-lettered façade, all arches and pilasters and newly scrubbed Victorian limestone sheathed in pigeon-netting. I needn't have worried. The reception area looked out across a grandly proportioned hall supported by marble columns, but a half-eaten sandwich sat on the nearest Chesterfield, with a half-drunk pint on the discoloured carpet beside it.

Perhaps she saw my tense features sag in relief as my gaze alighted on this still life; perhaps she'd spotted me parking Craig on her CCTV monitors, and wanted to distract me before I tried to consume it. Either way, the chirpy young receptionist's words of welcome betrayed a psycho-sociological prescience beyond her years. 'Good evening,' she said brightly. 'Could I interest you in our deal of the day? A single room plus dinner and a half bottle of wine.' She paused for effect. 'For £36, including breakfast.'

As many as ninety seconds later, I'd taken a seat in the expansive dining room. There was plenty of choice – my sole fellow diner was an elderly Japanese man engrossed in a paperback copy of *What in the Holy Name of Fuck Am I Doing Here?*. Picking my way past the trio of waistcoated staff trying to thread a string of fairy lights round a squat plastic tree, I'd plumped for a table that looked directly out on to the station concourse.

It was pleasingly peculiar to be right up by the platform action, to see incoming locomotives loom up towards me over WH Smith's, to hear the bing-bongs and deafening but entirely unintelligible snatches of Tannoy. How excited we all used to get about the technology of travel! So proud were the Victorians of their rail-based achievements that they could think of nothing better than sitting down with a cup of tea to stare at trains. They grandly dubbed this station Hull Paragon, and endowed the en suite hotel with its regal appellation following Queen Victoria's sleepover in 1854. It didn't stop there. In the Twenties, new apartment blocks across the land were tricked up like ocean liners, and in the Thirties every urban dual carriageway was lined with houses, allowing a privileged front-row view of the petrol-powered future. In the Sixties, no airport was complete without a viewing gallery, where families might spend a happy day watching planes take off and land. If we don't do that kind of thing any more, it's not because we're all grown-up and sober and now realise the short-sighted, environmental folly inherent in celebrating such progress. It's because there is no such progress to celebrate. On cue a feeble little

Sprinter-type affair wobbled away from platform 4, farting out a puff of diesel exhaust. I glanced up at the richly decorated, cast-iron arches that vaulted impressively above it, and thought: We've literally run out of steam.

'No, Sandra – he's on the wine!'

A stout waitress, approaching my table with a menu, turned to look at the receptionist, who'd arrived to assist the tree-dressers and had delivered this arresting announcement.

'Are you, love? Are you on the wine?'

The waitress's tone was kindly and confidential, but it was aimed at me from a distance and at stentorian volume. I noted the old man looking up from his book.

'The wine deal?'

I nodded cravenly.

'Which one, love?'

'The one that makes you and everyone else in here shut up, straight away,' I should have said. Instead I just looked at her helplessly, like the helpless alcoholic I was.

'See, we've different menus for each deal. There's the half-bottle . . .' she began, now standing beside me yet raising her voice to the level of an extremely enthusiastic circus ringmaster. I tried to cut in with a confirmation, but my words were lost in a sudden reverberating blare from without, informing passengers of the neck stain tour egg impolite Fermat's theorem. Belatedly I understood why the strident bellow had become the default manner of in-restaurant communication.

'. . . and there's the unlimited deal – you know, where you drink as much as you want.'

As I mumblingly put her straight, I saw the old man's eyes widen in a manner that suggested a deeper familiarity with the language than I'd lazily assumed. Then he shook his head very slowly, and shot me a look laden with foreboding and dismay, a look that said: as much as you want, or slightly more than you can?

My first course arrived just before the high-noon bedfellow pomade eater, and my pudding just after the departure of the minor drawstring Toulouse Colgate buffs elbow. The meal may well have been rather swish – I recall artful swirls of jus – but both food and wine were dispatched with a shame-fuelled haste that left little imprint. Not since completing further education have I drunk so fast, a performance unlikely to have persuaded my fellow diner to reappraise his opinion. In tandem with the sleep-defying feats of an over-zealous motion-activated security light outside my window – calling all units, pigeon pecking at cold chip in car park! – this half-bottle haste very unfairly landed me an unlimited-sized hangover.

Chapter Four

Iwas heading ever further north and into the year's final month: from here on, no walk would be a stroll. The local breakfast TV weatherman predicted a vicious Arctic gale, in a tone better suited to revealing that Hull had just been awarded the 2016 Olympics. Just walking out of the Royal I felt my freeze-dried lips chapping up. On the plus side, the cobwebs of crapulence were blasted clean out of my living soul by the time I turned the first corner.

The streets around any main-line station are a sure bet for action, even if it's the sleazy crack-and-kebabs variety. This is emphatically not so in Hull. Right opposite the Paragon's taxi-drop-off side entrance stood an abandoned hotel I'd somehow missed the night before, a once-noble Victorian edifice with mature shrubs sprouting from the gutters, begging to be put out of its misery. The first pedestrian I encountered, 100 yards up the road, was an old man in carpet slippers, shuffling vacantly out of a hostel of some sort, a filthy plastic bag in one hand and a bloodstained rag in the other.

Adelaide Street, Canberra Street, Ice House Road: the addresses betrayed a cosmopolitan and bustling mercantile past, but the ice houses and warehouses and whorehouses were long gone. Instead I trudged down a mile-long stretch of Soviet-pattern tenement blocks, fourteen-storey concrete megaliths laid out in drab grey ranks under a drab grey sky. It was an eerily bleak environment to encounter so close to the centre of a city, and the scale of these estates suggested that some drastic and abrupt calamity had cleared the way for them, rather than any drawn-out commercial decline. In fact it was a bit of both.

As well as jutting out provocatively towards the Luftwaffe's airfields, like an overconfident boxer's chin, Hull had thoughtfully sited itself on an estuary so navigationally conspicuous that a drunk badger could have flown you there. It was Britain's third busiest port, and its most feebly defended. The city's principal anti-aircraft measure was a battery of seventy-two barrage balloons strung out across the Humber, which claimed its first victim in March 1941, when a dirigible broke loose and demolished the Guildhall clock tower. Between then and the end of the war, the barrage downed a total of four aircraft. None bore a swastika. Given an almost free rein, Goering's boys set about literally wiping huge areas of Hull off the map. The city endured Britain's first daylight bombing raid, and was the target of the Luftwaffe's final attack. In between, a dumbfounding 95 per cent of Hull's housing stock was destroyed or damaged, and over half of the 320,000 citizens lost their homes. Twelve hundred lost their lives. A single raid in 1941 destroyed no fewer than six cinemas (the shell of the National Picture Theatre still looks out onto Beverley Road, one of the last surviving Blitz-wrecked buildings in Britain). My wife's grandfather, an Icelandic trawlerman, was a regular wartime visitor to Hull, and recalled looters doing a busy trade in the dockland shadows, hawking jewellery snatched from the city's endless mounds of smouldering rubble.

Everyone knew about the London Blitz, but Hull's greater traumas were blue-pencilled by the censors. Each pocket apocalypse that flattened another swathe of it was blandly reported as 'a raid on a northern coastal town'. Peace laid bare the scale of the civic devastation, but also a harsh commercial reality that had been lurking since the 1920s, when three hundred years of uninterrupted growth first faltered.

Hull had earnt its prosperity as an adaptable port, always

quick to follow the money: from wool to wine, from sail to steam, from Flanders to the far-flung colonies. The dockers hauled ashore the raw materials that fuelled the Industrial Revolution, and loaded the ships back up with its manufactured bounty. (I'd always assumed that local MP William Wilberforce was inspired to abolish slavery by terrible scenes witnessed on the city's docksides, but in fact Hull was never significantly involved in history's most shameful trading enterprise.) I turned left, and found myself walking down a survivor of these happier, wealthier times. Coltman Street was a long, long road of fine nineteenth-century terraces, interrupted by the odd chapel and church: a model Victorian thoroughfare, as long as you ignored the occasional Goering-ordained gap. The street's prodigious length made it plain that these were homes for a broader demographic than the merchant class, yet their dimensions and optional architectural extras – a columned portico here, a fancy fanlight there – set them distantly apart from the two-up two-down brick hutches that would have been the comparable accommodation stock elsewhere. This was the Hull that struck it rich and spread the wealth around, the Hull that in 1814 had opened one of Britain's first people's dispensaries, a clinic where the poor were offered free treatment and medicines.

'Lust?'

I looked up from the tiny and useless map of Hull I'd been given at the hotel, and found myself presented with a fellow pedestrian whose bulk and genial ruddiness instantly called to mind the Jolly Fisherman, in a turquoise shell suit. You could get through an awful lot of aimless wandering in London without attracting attention, let alone concern, but despite Hull's travails the Yorkshire spirit of kindly nosiness had evidently prevailed. So too had the local dialect, which processed vowels in a manner that even fellow Yorkshiremen found challenging.

'Curled out this marnin, intit?' he said, rubbing a huge pair of hands together after I'd told him I was trying to find my way to the docks. 'Like the Nerth bloody Pearl! Reckon sner's on the way. Foller this rerd and yerl it docks, what's left of them.'

I thanked him, bowed my head into the bitter wind and headed for the Humber.

For most cities the Depression was a blip; for Hull it proved a tipping point. In 1935 one of the biggest docks was filled in, and by 1939 almost half of the sixty-five local railway stations designed by George Townsend Andrews, architect of Hull Paragon and the Royal Hotel, had been closed down (fewer than a third now remain). When the time came to rebuild the war-shattered city, it was clear that with both the Empire and British manufacturing already in retreat, finding dockside employment might be an issue for the tens of thousands who would call those new council blocks home.

The local fishermen had a history of falling victim to their own success: after an insanely lucrative thirty-year whaling boom – the oil and baleen from a single carcass could net a Victorian skipper £2,000 – Hull's harpoon-happy fleet set off for Greenland in 1850 to discover there wasn't anything bigger than a walrus left for them to catch. (A hardy few kept doggedly at it. In 1910, an expedition set out to see if the population of bowhead whales had recovered: it hadn't, so to make the best of a bad job they shot 242 polar bears.) Serendipitously, or so it seemed, seven years earlier a trawler blown way off course in a storm lowered its nets into unknown depths 60 miles off the Hull coast. The crew hauled them back out with some difficulty, having chanced upon the fishing grounds of the Dogger Bank, the richest that had ever been found in British waters, or indeed ever will be. So vast was their catch of cod and herring that they returned to Hull with their boat's flanks thickly encrusted with gleaming fish scales. The area was duti-fully nicknamed the Silver Pits, and just as the whaling gold rush died, along came another. Such was the demand for crew that over half the apprentice trawlermen had to be recruited from workhouses as far away as Manchester and London. Such were the riches on offer that more than one of these fish-fingered Oliver Twists retired as millionaires. The railway arrived to take away cod to the nation's chip shops, and deliver coal for the new steam trawlers. By the end of another insanely lucrative thirty-year boom, the Silver Pits were already in steep decline.

The overfishing precedent was there, and not only there: Great Yarmouth and its abruptly redundant herring fleet lay just down the coast. Yet, Hull went on to base its entire post-war economy on intensive deep-sea trawling, and the concomitant assumption that the cod was not as other living creatures, in that it didn't breed, but rather spewed forth in unending profusion from the mouth of a magical undersea cavern. Guess what happened next? That's right: an insanely lucrative thirty-year boom. Hull's trawlermen did so well out of North Sea cod in the Fifties and Sixties that they were known as 'three-day millionaires', a reference to their pools-winner spending habits on those long weekends ashore. Tubby old skippers in canary-yellow drape suits and snakeskin shoes were driven about the city in cabs with seventy-two-hour fares on the meter, trailing crowds of children screaming for 'scrambles': a rather unedifying pastime wherein handfuls of cash tossed out of the window unleashed an apparently hilarious feeding frenzy. In 1975, a third of all Hull households were effectively dependent on cod and its batter-bound brethren.

By then, the skippers of Europe's largest fishing port were having to sail an awfully long way to bag a decent netful: the Baltic, the lonely Barents Sea, and most fatefully the waters around Iceland. Having no wish to incite the wifely wrath of Odin, I'm happy to state that the Cod Wars of the mid-Seventies were the inevitable consequence of intolerable bullying and provocation, and their outcome a just and noble victory for the plucky underfish. In reality, the Cod War was missing an 'l': the presence of a huge and strategically vital NATO base near Reykjavik had a decisive bearing on how things panned out to Hull's considerable disadvantage, particularly once the Icelanders announced an intention to defend their newly enormous fishing limits with a fleet of Soviet Mirka-class frigates. The British government's decision to respect these limits was probably less to do with any dutiful acceptance of Iceland's right to its own marine bounty, and more down to a short and very loud phone call from Washington.

Anyway, the consequences were devastating and immediate. In 1975, 150 trawlers were registered in Hull; today there are three. The local fish-processing industry collapsed almost overnight, and this time there was nothing to replace it. A website devoted to the city's history concludes with this sad round-up of 'late-twentieth-century local industries': 'Oilcake is made in Hull. So are plastic bags and caravans.' Hull had gone into the economic egg-shop with just the one basket, and tripped up on the way out. Since the war, the city has shed a quarter of its population.

Feeling my limbs growing rigid with cold, I juddered robotically up to the waterfront. The first dock I encountered was lined on one side with long-derelict warehouses and light-industrial workshops; the other had been gentrified along the model pioneered in London, with the old wharfs and shipping-company offices hollowed out, tarted up and reinvented as bistros and fancy handbag shops. Little knots of well-groomed women squinted at menus or window displays, the cobbles gleamed: it was all entirely agreeable, as long as you ignored the striding, hair-gelled battalions of self-important young-executive bellends, and kept well away from a fountain that the wind had transformed into an annoying elder brother with a garden hose. And as long as you didn't turn to face the dock itself, there to confront the structure that emerged from its waters on stilts. An information board identified this as the Princes Quay centre, a shopping mall that opened in 1991 and bore noble tribute to Hull's marine heritage by virtue of calling its floors 'decks', and looking a bit like a ship (I paraphrase).

It did look a bit like a ship, but it looked a lot more like a temporary pedestrian bridge at Gatwick Airport. Judging from the flimsy, glazed superstructure's slightly ramshackle demeanour, and its streaks and scabs of premature decay, such a construction had provided not only the architectural inspiration, but the raw materials. What a sorry contrast with the weighty domes and towers that stood in ageless, stolid majesty along the imperial-era downtown skyline behind. And with what had gone on here before: a hive of eager, cosmopolitan economic production reduced to a tawdry little shrine to parochial consumption. The interior lived down to expectations, the usual study in soulless, cheerless retail geometry, a place where shops were units, arranged above the inevitable food court and around the inevitable atrium. JD Sports, The Disney Store, Clinton Cards. The 'shopper's map' by the lifts betrayed the one conspicuous feature: almost all of the larger 'units' had been covered with a sticker marked VACANT. Fortunes were once made in this dock, but they clearly weren't now being spent here.

I peeled one of the stickers back far enough to reveal a familiar red logo, which caused me to sigh aloud, and so attract the attention of a security guard who delivered a half-hearted ticking-off. Thirty years ago, he'd have got me in trouble with my parents; thirty years hence, with my children. Committing petty acts of vandalism without serious redress must be one of the principal advantages of middle age, and I made a note to do it more often.

The logo directed me to a long and very closed unit, its departed incumbent identified in ghostly negative by the dust silhouetted around absent lettering. Woolworths: our ultimate retail institution, an idiosyncratic and stridently native presence on every high street (um, even though it was originally American). Defiantly, definitively British for one hundred years, from the days when that meant energy and innovation, then into the complacent good times, the complacent bad times, and finally via belated scatter-gun commercial desperation to a pitiful, whimpering death. It was all very Austin Rover, I supposed, right down to the humiliating post-mortem efforts to resurrect a brand by then so toxic, so synonymous with shoddiness and failure, that no sensible business would have anything to do with it.

I pulled up my collar and jogged towards the dual carriageway that now separated Princes Quay from the grown-ups' pool, the Humber Dock. This was where the deep-sea big-boys had once been relieved of their exotic contents; rebranded Hull Marina, its quaysides were now bordered with swish warehouse conversions, and – miles away at its Humberside extremity – one of those big glass hotels that seem to be obligatory in such developments. I half-closed my eyes and tried to picture the scene in a more flattering light; there was a café that might have looked the part with tables outside and the sun on its face. Instead a grim alchemy now turned the lead skies to iron, as a rogue shaft of celestial light picked out those vast petro-chemical plants on the Humber's opposite bank, their chimneys lined up like a smouldering bar chart.

How absurdly deluded this whole project seemed. Did those who aspired to the yachting lifestyle really picture themselves bobbing out across the dun-coloured waters of the Humber Estuary, dodging container ships and hail storms and sucking in deep lungfuls of neat cancer? I shook my head, crossed the road, and found that at least some of them evidently did: the dock's dark, wind-rippled waters were home to a pick-and-mix flotilla of small yachts, perhaps a hundred in all, masts swinging like metronomes.

Nonetheless, it seemed a shame that a dock which made millions as the exhilarating interface between honest Yorkshire toil and hessian-bagged spices of the Orient should find itself scrabbling around for the odd fifty-quid mooring fee, beholden to plump and insufferable retirees in stupid caps with anchors on, and the wit of a cardboard dog. What kind of world is it where pleasure craft can be named *Why Knot* or *Fishful Thinking*, without those responsible being stuffed into a sack and battered with shovels?

I struggled on into the wind, ever more bemused by the weird dissonance that had persuaded the city's authorities to decree that Hull's future lay in leisure, not labour, without stopping to ask themselves how its residents might go about spending money they hadn't earnt. Whoever called those ware-house conversions home, or pottered around in the galley of *Sir Osis of the River* or *Fuh Get A Boat It*, it's a fair bet they didn't clock in at the oilcake plant or the caravan factory.

Across into the off-wharf hinterland, where patches of old cobbles showed through the threadbare tarmac, I found myself presented with the most moribund, bankrupt vista of my tour to date: a snaggled hotch-potch of workshops and small ware-houses of varying ages and in varying states of decay, from fresh corpse to bleached skeleton. All the shutters were down, and some had long since rusted off their hinges. At any rate, none were ever going up again. The only other living being in a broad radius was a man in overalls and a high-visibility jacket, decorating lampposts with laminated notices explaining that the many resident wholesale fruiterers had now relocated to some new industrial estate. He nodded an acknowledgement as I approached him.

'End of an era,' I said. 'Sad.'

'Yer jerkin,' he replied, yanking a cable-tie home. 'This earl area's been a turtle dump long as I can remember.' A damning statement indeed, once I'd decoded it, coming from a man of about my own age. He pulled another notice from a reflective satchel around his shoulder. 'Some giggles durn ear as a lad, mind. We used to come up this rerd after skerl and chuck rotten fruit abert.' He smiled distantly, then refocused. 'So what brings Europe ear?'

I made a querying sound that conveyed, as politely as possible, a desire for this sentence to be constructed afresh.

'What yer dern appear in Ull?' He pronounced his hometown as more of a brief noise than a word, like wool without the w. But his question was more or less clear, and I was ready with an answer. Too ready.

'Bit of both.'

'Eh?'

'Sorry – business and pleasure. No: business and . . . further business. Just business.'

'What line of work yerin?'

'Salesman,' I said before I could stop myself. And then: 'Pencils.'

My companion whipped out a roll of gaffer tape from his bag, and tore off a strip that would have done very nicely for my mouth. Instead he used it to affix a notice to an adjacent set of blistered shutters.

'More fun than it sounds?'

'Absolutely not,' I said.

'Well, it's work, intit? Birruva shirtage of that rurn dear.' He extracted another notice and sniffed wearily up at the awful sky. 'Only two kinds of purple in Ull: them who can't find a job, and the burn idol who dernt even try.' We exchanged glum nods and he trudged off to the next lamppost. I watched him for a while: last man off the stage in the final act of Hull's rise and fall, the centuries of breathless, slapdash growth, the long decades of decline and depression. A century before, when Hull was home to the world's largest shipping lines, every square inch of this area had been vibrantly, vitally important. Now none of it mattered at all.

The waterfront offered a snapshot of the old maritime grandeur, with a parade of smart and stately buildings that were home to the port authority headquarters and a couple of law firms. This was Hull in its Sunday best, the well-scrubbed face with which the city once greeted the world. Its subsequent decline was neatly projected by the faces now doing that job, belonging as they did to a bench-bound group of weathered winos, silently contemplating the broad and mighty Humber, that very brownest of rivers. Beyond them stretched the jetty that had welcomed the ferries from New Holland, and was thus now doing its bit to bolster the mood of aimless unemployment. The gloopy silt heaped up at its feet was slowly absorbing the weekend's happy-hour haul of traffic cones and uprooted signage; a clutch of crispy, cellophane-sheathed old bouquets wedged in the railings told of a dare too far. The view across the Humber was fittingly lifeless. 'Where sky and water and Lincolnshire meet,' in the words of poet Philip Larkin, the famously miserable git whose Eeyore-like tendencies blossomed in the thirty years he spent in Hull. (Asked why he had chosen to live there, Larkin would always cite the geographical loneliness that so effectively deterred unwanted visitors: 'Hull's a difficult place to drop in on,' he once said, through the letterbox.) Even at midday the streets felt haunted. In the open areas behind them towered piles of rubble that had clearly lain there since the Blitz, absorbed into the derelict landscape with a sense of monumental permanence. This was hairy-chested, hard-bitten urban decay, brownfield wasteland with tattoos and attitude. Regenerate THIS.

It's a strange fact of modern life that every town, county and nation now feels obliged to sell itself through a slogan, and that such slogans are always underwhelming, inane or deranged. An investment of £120,000 recently saw Nottinghamshire rebranded as 'N'. In 2007, the director of the Scottish tourist board authorities silenced a press conference when she explained that the giant projected message up there wasn't just an introductory screen-saver: six months and £125,000 really had been spent on coming up with the words: *Welcome to Scotland*. One assumes similar amounts of cash and mental energy went into the likes of *Peterborough: think, learn, live!*, *Because Mid-Wales is as unique as you are* and *New Holland – Past Caring and Proud of It*.

Inevitably, this curious syndrome is most prominent in blighted and benighted cities, which seem incapable of setting out on that long road to regeneration without at least a couple of emboldening mission statements. Hull, I saw, was running three at once. At the outskirts I'd been ushered into *The Pioneering City*, a slightly half-arsed attempt to trade on former glories. *Stepping Up*, the prominent slogan around the desolate docklands, acknowledged that Hull found itself in a hole, but was at least trying to climb out. Crossing back over the dual carriageway and into the old town, I passed a flank of glossy civic billboards that welcomed me into *Real Hull*. Real Hull, so I was pictorially informed, was home to some real boats, a real footballer, and a real waitress carrying a tray of real drinks. It looked like a pretty nice place, if not quite as captivating as Surreal Hull, a city of screaming clockwork moths governed by a giant brass slipper.

The Hull and East Riding Museum, deep in the old town's cobbled-alley core, introduced *Living in the Past* as a further civic theme, and ran with it, over the hills and far away. *The Story of Hull*, I gathered from a wall-filling tableau thus labelled, began with the Big Bang. I couldn't dispute that this was literally the case, but it still seemed a trifle presumptuous: I pictured some robed deity effecting nucleosynthesis between his giant fists with a cosmic roar: 'Let there be Hull!' The story arc did not steepen, and seeing the third chapter in the making of Kingston upon Hull headed *Earth's Crust Forms*, I involuntarily emitted a loud and disparaging noise. There were no other visitors around to hear it – none, indeed, in the entire museum – but a man in a name-badge quickly appeared. He gave me a cold look, and followed me at an indiscreet distance into the next room, in which Hull was exposed to carboniferous life-forms, and struggled against glacial erosion. Indeed, he went on to shadow my entire tour, making theatrical attempts to appear nonchalant and distracted whenever I glanced over my shoulder, rubbing at a spot on a glass case or flicking imaginary dust off a mammoth's knee. He was there when something unique and definitive finally happened in the East Riding (four thousand years ago, when local traders set out across the North Sea in 45-foot plank-built craft: the excavated survivor on display is the oldest boat in Europe). He was there when a native British mosaicist copied a Roman pattern-book image, shown below, and when Northern European urban civilisation set the standards for Hull's emergent merchant class, see left. He was especially there, right by my elbow, in fact, when I interacted with a miniature diorama portraying the 1643 Siege of Hull, in which many blue LEDs outlasted the encircling red ones. That was the final exhibit, and when I'd pressed every button twice he all but stomach-barged me through the exit.

Old Hull revealed itself as a pleasant little maze of tight lanes that occasionally threw you out into a bijou cobbled square, with a church at its heart and a border of gable-fronted houses betraying the city's age-old links with the Low Countries (ferries still run to Zeebrugge and Rotterdam). The irresistible street names told Hull's tale rather more evocatively than the museum had managed to: Whitefriargate, Bowl Alley Lane, Three-Crane

Wharf, Land of Green Ginger. Some of the sympathetically renovated red-brick mills and warehouses that lined them were home to design agencies and the like, but a fair few were home to no one, which along with the vast and empty bike racks spoke of a well-meaning make-over that had stalled. I'm guessing sensory deterrents may have played a role in this. The River Hull, the modest Humber tributary that runs through the old town, had done a grand job as a mercantile artery back in the day. But as a picturesque aquatic backdrop – its current civic duty – it proved a truly horrible failure. With negligible river traffic, and hence no dredging, the upstream estuary's silt monster had for unchecked decades been spewing its big brown guts out all along and sometimes right over the banks. Sometimes caked and crevassed, sometimes as moist and slurried as the loosest of loose stools. The gathering stench proved an unfortunate complement. I'd been told that Hull smelt of chocolate, but my wrinkled nose suggested otherwise, a suspicion later confirmed by my eyes when I Googled up details of the nearby ADM Cocoa Mass factory. Cocoa mass is to chocolate what magnolia emulsion paint is to gold-top double cream. It's actually nothing more offensive than ground-up cocoa beans, but it sounds grim, and my word it smells grim, like plasticine fried in linseed oil. This difficult odour has hung over central Hull for generations, but naturally enough won't be troubling local nostrils for much longer: a couple of months after I passed through, management announced plans to close the factory.

The miasma dispersed as the lanes opened out into the broad granite streets of imperial Hull, all Victorian heft and confidence. I noted with dismay, if not surprise, that almost every one of the grand old civic institutions, with their columns and domes and roof-mounted statues of Britannia in a chariot, had been Wetherspooned. The big banks had been first to succumb, and the magnificent general post office was now two bars and a snooker hall. I couldn't find it, but Bevin House – formerly the regional headquarters of the Transport & General Workers' Union – is apparently a casino. Isn't that just beyond parody? Old Ernest must be spinning faster than the roulette wheels.

I spent the rest of the afternoon hiding from the Yorkshire winter in Hull's many municipal museums. All were free, which in my book is half the battle won (no children in tow, no giftshop-crap-related bribery – and so the remaining half is won). At the same time, every single one of these museums was entirely deserted, which meant some awkwardness at the less captivating amongst them. A nice old lady at an entrance kiosk would welcome me in with a grateful smile, then I'd walk straight into a room filled with old buckets and ironing boards, or a gigantic gallery of full-length portraits of Edwardian harbourmasters. Stripped of the getting-my-money's-worth factor that would have otherwise stubbornly detained me, it was tricky to know just how long to mill about before I could slink out past the kiosk without earning a look of disappointment or betrayal. Answer: never quite long enough.

By far the best was the Maritime Museum, which with poignantly impeccable timing emerged from the magnificent old Docks Offices in 1975 – the very year that the local fishing industry died and Hull's marine associations became a past to remember, not a present to administer. I spent a happy hour poring over its maps alone, amongst them a contemporary depiction of the River Hull's docksides in their copperplate pomp, a dense compaction of activity you could almost hear and smell: timber yards, coal staithes, cooperage works, breweries, cotton mills, sugar mills, corn warehouses, bonding warehouses, and a sperm candle manufactory that dated it to the city's whaling boom, and doubtless entertained the school parties. And there were humbling reminders that whatever the downsides of the dole queue or a career in oilcake, the locals must at heart be very glad not to call the sea their workplace. I learnt that in 1830, nineteen of the whaling ships sent out to the frozen Davis Straits did not come home. The terrible winter of 1968 claimed fifty-eight fishermen's lives. Between those two dreadful years, a trawler and its crew were lost on average every two months.

Tales such as these didn't do much for my existing terror of the open sea, so it was a soothing pleasure to find the museum's first floor almost entirely devoted to model ships in glass cases, which I happen to love. Especially when, eighty-six years after they were made, a restorer finds a note stashed under a funnel, and that note reads thus:

Oct 6th, 1913. To whom so ever find this may know that this is placed inside of the model of the *Imperator*, H&A Line, 828ft long, 87ft beam and 48ft depth. The model is built to scale by the writer in Fuhlsbuttel Hard Labour Prison with very odd and rough tools. Despise it not on account of roughness, it is a labour of love and helps to pass the time. I am here now two and a half years, having been sentenced in Leipzig to seven year for espionage for the dear old English Government. I am an English man and a ship owner residing in Coltman Street, Hull, Yorkshire, England. Wife a Hilton good and true, five children. Max William Schultz.

What a wonderful story, made more wonderful as I'd walked right down Coltman Street that very morning. Admittedly not quite so fab for Max, who was finally let out at the end of the war but died in Hull just six years later, aged forty-nine.

I'd left Craig outside the Royal Hotel, and picked out by a late, low shaft of sun he looked as good as he ever would, black coachwork against burnished Victorian limestone, every inch the British Leyland brochure cover. I imagined the strapline: *The Austin Maestro – because you're not worth it*, or, *Come on – it's got four wheels and everything. Please?* Who *was* Maestro man? Not for the first time I wondered why anybody at all had ever bought one. Ford and Vauxhall, British Leyland's American-owned rivals, had for some years been making cheap family cars that were demonstrably more reliable and better equipped, so I could only assume that the customers who stayed loyal to BL did so out of dogged national pride. All the same, it was a little sad to realise that even the kind of people predisposed to engineering romance would be left entirely cold by the quirk-less, gawky, anti-charismatic machine sitting there before me. No prisoner would ever feel inspired to construct a lovingly detailed scale replica of an Austin Maestro, or if they did Mr Barraclough would inadvertently sit on it, to much canned laughter.

I'd read that half of Hull's 250,000 inhabitants live in the 105 most deprived metropolitan areas in the country, a statistic that sounded dreadful but was quite hard to make sense of. Aside from the uninviting parade of windswept council blocks behind the station, Hull's class-leading awfulness had only manifested itself through ghostly commercial desolation rather than living, breathing fucked-uppery. Perhaps sensing this, Ozzy's chosen route out of town took me through Bransholme. Not so much a housing estate as a housing borough, even a whole county, an East Riding of Housing, Bransholme fanned endlessly out into the gathering gloom. I wasn't surprised to learn later that it's the largest post-war council estate in Britain. Every exit from every landscaped roundabout dispatched me into a little satellite Bransholme, all stubby cul-de-sacs of identical slit-windowed, wedge-shaped homes, laid out by the half-dozen in two-storey terraced slabs. Ozzy didn't like it at all: 'Turn around when f-f-fooking possible!' he'd yell; I'd do so, then a minute later find myself surrounded by rusty lock-up garages, earning another shrieked reprimand and some more heavy work on Craig's ever-reluctant wheel.

In between U-turns, I was scoring big points in my *I-Spy Book of Urban Meltdown*. Burnt-out car in playground? Tick. Pregnant teenager in tracksuit pushing pram? Tick. Smoking child idly flicking the Vs at buses? Mystery pile of mangled bar optics in middle of road? Knot of potato-faced hoodies by parade of boarded-up shops seeing man in stupid car taking pictures, then lumbering towards him en masse? Tick, tick, tick, eeek, screech, vroom, come on you useless crap-tent I said *screech, vroom*. The mood of ratcheting panic was fed by the in-car soundtrack, which now married Rolf Harris's 'Two Little Boys' to Ozzy's disorientated screaming. It was like karaoke night in Broadmoor.

Bransholme was built for the tens of thousands Blitzed out

of their homes, but half of them had died or moved away long before the estate was finished. Vast areas of Bransholme were ghost towns from birth, and as the population dwindled further so its streets grew ever quieter. Craig's clock said early-evening rush-hour, but my eyes said Sunday afternoon. People who definitely had jobs looked as vacant as those who probably didn't: two policemen drove by looking like crash-test dummies in uniform, and I saw a postman standing motionless with the flat of his hand against a pillar-box, as if being recharged. Even the conspicuous absence of graffiti seemed consistent with the general air of sloth, as if the young people of Bransholme couldn't be arsed to hate their surroundings enough to want to deface them. How tragic that these blank trudgers were the grandchildren of the dockers I'd seen scurrying around the holds of ships in the Maritime Museum's newsreels, the embodiment of time-is-money commercial hyperactivity. Now everyone had far too much time, and not nearly enough money. The best I could say, in relation to their hometown's table-topping achievements in over-indulgence and under-learning, is that nobody looked too fat or too drunk or too stupid, at least not all at the same time.

I wondered how long Hull could go on like this. You felt it was living on borrowed time as one of only six English cities deemed worthy of identification on ITV's national weather map. The recession stamped on Hull's fingers just as it put a hopeful hand up to haul itself out of the mire: from the start of 2008 to the end of 2009, more people lost their jobs in the city than anywhere else in the land. By 2010, advertised vacancies (oilcake taster, caravan-finder general) were outnumbered sixteen to one by jobseekers. And yet it could all have been so different.

In 1999, Hull council sold its stake in the city's telecom operator, Kingston Communications, for a more than tidy £263 million. Overnight, one of our most destitute and desperate regions found itself blessed with the wealthiest local authority in Britain. It must have felt like a lottery win, and was certainly disposed of as such. The council listened to the sober voices of reason advocating steady investment in the city's infrastructure, educational facilities and so forth, with a long-term view to creating jobs and otherwise bringing the regional economy back from the dead. Then it went out and blew £32 million on a state-of-the-art sports stadium, and another £45 million on an aquarium with the deepest fish tanks in Europe – I'd seen it marooned on the inert waterfront, angular and sinister, like a Stealth bomber that nosedived into the estuary mud. In a fit of morning-after remorse, councillors then vowed to do something for Hull's long-suffering poor and needy. The citizenry expressed loud relief that their elected local officials had belatedly come to their senses. Except they hadn't: Hull council promptly shelled out the balance of its windfall, an extraordinary £96 million, on double-glazing the Bransholme estate. Many of the houses thus enhanced had lain empty for years, and hundreds were subsequently demolished. In three mad years, they spunked the lot.

The mini-Bransholmes grew steadily more unsettling. One was entirely composed of boarded-up bungalows. Another had words like BELIEVE and FAITH signposted in the centre of every roundabout, creepily dystopian attempts to instil a sense of purpose and community by decree. It would have been about now that I recalled Hull's hallowed reputation for 'glassing': when the city's pubs took part in a two-year trial serving beer in plastic containers, the local NHS saved £7.2 million on eye-surgery costs. I sensed it was only a matter of time before my increasingly frequent and panicky about-turns would cause me to sideswipe somebody's careworn Astra van or smoking child, and thus interact with the glass-toting zombies of Bransholme in a scenario heavily weighted to my disadvantage.

At last I hit the roundabout-roulette jackpot, and presently found myself in the realm of dark trees and the national speed limit. The road rose away from the Humber's alluvial flatlands; I knew I'd definitely left poor old Hull behind when I passed a telephone box that wasn't white. I sighed mournfully, but pathos was never easy to sustain with Craig's jukebox up and running. Just past Beverley, Frankie Howerd launched into a rendition of 'When I'm 64', and I found myself greeting the black moors ahead with an expression of lobotomised disbelief that I must have picked up in Bransholme.

'Sunday morning – go for a ride?!' Frankie's throaty, swooping innuendo introduced the soundtrack to a musical production so provocatively obnoxious and ill-conceived it made *Springtime for Hitler* look like *Mary Poppins*. *Sergeant Pepper's Lonely Hearts Club Band*, a 1977 production financed with the profits from *Saturday Night Fever*, put a work of lofty musical genius into the hands of oafish has-beens and never-weres, and weaved in a storyline so shed-eatingly inane that after some deliberation I've decided I cannot bring myself to describe any part of it. Except for the happy ending: the trumpeting enormity of the film's box-office failure bankrupted its producers.

The cast of this ungodly travesty reads like a veritable 'Why Them?' of late 1970s popular culture: Methuselan cigar enthusiast George Burns, frog-eyed pocket whisperer Donald Pleasence, any number of shirt-averse period pretty-boys from Paul Nicholas to Peter Frampton. Earth Wind & Fire appear as themselves; legacy-shredding keyboardist Billy Preston as 'a magical golden weather vane come to life'. To put the project's comprehensive awfulness into perspective, the Bee Gees – the sodding Bee Gees! – repeatedly begged to be released from the film, and later sued the producer for $200 million. In a state of mesmerised horror I led a queue of impatient motorists northwards through the night, past Scarborough and Whitby, into and out of mysterious little coastal towns where silver waves crashed in under a full moon. George Burns fixed a hole where the rain got in; I gripped the wheel harder as the brothers Gibb read the news today, oh boy. The remaining tracks had all been fed through a vocoder, the 'Mr Blue Sky' voice manipulator that held so many period artistes in its idiotic thrall. This at least had the benefit of muffling the final contributions into an unintelligible stream of twangy robotic flatulence.

Things were getting bleaker, more serious. Every seaside

settlement was a mean and moribund ex-mining village; I drove down into one and found a huddle of pebble-dashed terraces staring out at a terrifying sea, black and white and furious. The shingle was bulked up with hunks of masonry and what I first took for lobster pots were balls of rusted chicken wire. I was, it now occurred to me, definitively in the north-east: where the wind was always cold, the people largely unintelligible and the front gardens – a nation-besting 47 per cent of them – entirely paved over.

Just up the road I passed another jaunty seaside attraction: Redcar steelworks, home to Europe's largest blast furnace and the dominant local employer for a century and a half. Though not for long: the day after I drove by, Tata Steel announced the plant's imminent closure. It's now fairly clear that by this point I had evolved into something more than just a curious tourist on a last-chance-to-see trip around his nation's neglected nether regions. I was the very angel of death, dispatching chocolate factories, wholesale fruit markets and any number of venerable hotels with my life-sapping aura. Sorry, Britain.

I approached Middlesbrough with a level of expectation appropriate to its table-topping position in the *Erection, Erection, Erection* chart: the very worst place to live in all of Britain. On cue, a thin, gritted sleet began to spatter the windscreen, scraped into cloudy mush by Craig's flapping rubber twigs. The roundabouts were embellished with sculptures paying dour tribute to the area's metallurgical heritage – molten iron pouring forth from a giant bucket and so on – and the night was distantly bordered with gleaming, steaming petrochemical cathedrals. In twenty-first-century Britain you'd imagine poor air quality as something you'd need a white coat and a big machine to detect, but when I creaked down the steamed-up window an inch for a better view, a gust of soured brimstone smacked straight into the back of my throat.

Local lad Chris Rea once imagined himself standing next to a stagnant, poisonous river. In lyrics that I've been forbidden from quoting directly, he articulated these ponderings in a tribute to the Tees, whose concrete-walled banks lay just to my right. That was in 'The Road to Hell', his biggest hit, a song inspired by pairing the M25 rush hour with this very stretch of the A66. Though it might just as easily have been a premonition of *The Road to Hell – Part 2*, the follow-up album whose opening track now appositely burbled from Craig's under-dash speakers.

Chris Rea seems like a decent bloke who did pretty well for himself by appealing to the durable MOR millions – you know who you are – who like a bit of husk on their vocals, and a lot of slide with their guitar. *The Road to Hell – Part 2* duly kicked off with a good long minute of quavery axe-twang. But it was the dumbfounding minutes that followed – all seven of them – which explained why the album peaked at number ninety-six in the Swiss chart, and did much, much better than that in *Q*'s Worst Ever rankings. Random electronic bleeps, warbling lift-music saxophone, no fewer than twelve consecutive repetitions of one phrase . . . this was a work of startling, fanbase-bewildering lunacy, the sound of MOR going AWOL. Like his home town, Mr Rea struck it rich, then completely lost the plot.

It was difficult to tell when I'd arrived: Middlesbrough is less of a stand-alone city than the central chunk in the industrial agglomeration known as Teesside. One minute I was following signs to Middlesbrough, and then I wasn't. Last stop on the road to hell. The sleet had devolved to steady rain by the time I found the station, with its Hull-ish encirclement of dead hotels and empty streets. The taxi drivers queuing in the rank outside had their chins on their chests, and might have been lightly shrouded in cobwebs.

There was a curry house at the end of the road, next to a drop-in centre with a couple of doorstep smokers who jeered unkindly as they watched me secure Craig with the Autolok (this was always happening: I felt I should have some flyers printed out, explaining that the most commonly stolen cars are both old and crap). It was a tiny place with blotchy red carpets and a wobbly table that would shortly account for the top fifth of my pint of Kingfisher. A certificate by the bar read *2002 Middlesbrough Curry Chef: semi-finalist*, and the only other customer was an unsteady wobble-chops in a paint-spattered puffa jacket, awaiting a takeaway order. Hunger may well have diminished my critical faculties, but I'm nonetheless prepared to state on record that this unpromising environment yielded one of the finest meals it has ever been my pleasure to cram into a nan-crumbed, jalfrezi-smeared maw.

As a bonus, halfway through the unsightly dining process two glamorous and wealthy-looking young Sikh couples came in and were deferentially ushered into a curtained-off side chamber. While I dabbed the last rich and spicy sauces into my hot mouth, wafts of rich and spicy conversation lodged in my hot ears.

Wife B: 'Stubborn, angry depressive he was – typical Taurus. He ripped them off for four million.'

Husband A: 'I heard it were five.'

Wife A: 'We're bad, bad people, but we're not the worst. We're the best of a bad bunch.'

Husband B: 'You know, I *like* this town. It's not complicated. None of those Hartlepool mindgames.'

I came away enthralled and replete, and extremely pleased not to have been caught eavesdropping, which would have meant being bundled into a boot and driven away to Hartlepool for some complication. There was clearly more to Middlesbrough than met the eye.

On the other side of what I had to assume was the town centre, I at last found a hotel – a squat Travelodge that looked spanking new but did have an en suite Aldi, which for my purposes seemed a decent compromise. It was a predictably soulless establishment. The reception area – shiny white floor tiles, slightly overbearing illumination – felt like somewhere you might end up if you were apprehended trying to enter Norway illegally. I had the opportunity to savour this ambience at length, while a man in sweat-circled pale-blue poly-cotton arranged the loan of ironing apparatus with the moon-faced receptionist. Their negotiations were conducted with the brisk urgency of rustics appraising a half-finished drystone wall. There was the question of what time he'd need to return the board by, and who might be on duty when he did, and precisely where to leave the iron and in what position, depending on the temperature of its metal surface, with a run-down of all associated hazards to flesh and furniture. Cheerfully oblivious to my increasingly mobile proximity and gathering tuts of exasperation, the receptionist moved on to a ruminative tutorial on the iron's steam function, and how it was still a little temperamental despite the recent descaling. I've seen mortgages drawn up and signed off in less time. At last the man patiently coiled up the iron's flex and put the board under his arm. I surged forward but it was a false alarm: he had neglected to request instructions on how to adjust the board's height, a wrong that was now fulsomely righted. When, finally, I was allowed to pose the receptionist my simple question, it came out in a strangled voice pitched an octave or so above my usual.

A *room*? A room *for the night*? Her ample brow furrowed as if I'd asked for the name of Britain's smallest owl. After some consideration she turned to the PC monitor before her. A minute of tapping fitfully at the keyboard's down button procured a brief sigh and a single word. Shortly after I was slumped behind Craig's wheel, weighed down with chicken jalfrezi and hopelessness.

I'd given up on Middlesbrough by the time I found a bed. The Metro Inn Teesside lay across the river in Stockton, and just after 10 p.m. I spotted its illuminated sign while en route to a twenty-four-hour Asda, and the car park I was resigned to calling my home for the night. The hotel, a noun I could already sense the Metro Inn would not have dared claim for itself, was hidden away at the back of an industrial estate, its architecture very much in sympathy with its environment: a two-storey pre-fab with tiny windows, like a cardboard box someone had stabbed holes in with a biro. I parked between a rusty Transit and a stack of broken pallets, and pushed my way into the reception. It was dingy in the extreme, and smelt as if someone had wrapped a jumbo sausage roll in an old sock and wedged it behind a radiator. The avuncular but rather defeated chap at the desk gave me an apologetic smile and told me it would be £24.50, 'for up to three people'. Handing over my debit card I experienced an epiphany. The location, the design cues, the ambient odour and that quirky pricing policy . . .

'Did this place used to be a Formule 1?'

He winced, then replied in the tone of a man recalling a disastrous first marriage. 'Few years back.'

If you've stayed in a Formule 1 more than once, you're either a French lorry driver or a career skinflint whose grim enslavement to economy has flayed from his soul the last clinging shreds of dignity. I've stayed in five.

'I'll be taking breakfast in my suite,' I announced airily, scribbling the room's six-digit entry-code on the back of my hand with a flourish, then heading off to Staircase B.

I approached my room increasingly baffled by the reluctance with which the receptionist had confessed his establishment's ancestry. Apart from the sign outside, every fixture and fitting shamelessly flaunted its origins as a branch of the French-centred chain of ultra-budget motels. Blue carpets, red handrails, yellow doors: spartan but aggressively colourful, the mood pitched somewhere between the lower decks of a cross-channel ferry and a prison for Teletubbies. Many years of targeting the cheap-slob market had taken its toll. The corridors appeared to have hosted a keenly contested race between a drunken horse and a motorcycle powered by gravy. Opening my bedroom door I was confronted by a wall of stench, the nasal equivalent of finding out the hard way that last night's half-finished can of cider has been pressed into use as an ashtray.

Women don't stay at a Formule 1 (unless, as suggested by some of the more shell-shocked TripAdvisor reviews I later read, they've been paid to). These places are grubby monuments to a kind of anti-Gillette masculinity, a lowest-common-denominator celebration of the worst a man can be. As toilet attendants the world over can confirm, leave a man to his own devices and he will rarely do himself credit. In a budget hotel environment, it's men who steal the batteries from TV remote controls. They etch bed frames with terrible words and crude depictions of sexual acts. They get drunk and forget how to operate the electric radiator's control panel, then get more drunk and kick it off the wall. They spot the little sink in the corner and think: That's my en suite sorted out. And in a Formule 1, up to three of them share two bunks, egging each other on to new excesses of slovenly vandalism and alcoholic flatulence.

In fact, the Metro Inn's management had thoughtfully provided an insight into their painful experiences of a very British strain of male-pattern badness. It came in the form of a checklist by reception, detailing behaviour that would lead to the forfeit of a deposit (a deposit the receptionist hadn't asked me for – more fool him!).

1. Any inconvenience that is caused to other guests that would result in a refund, by means of noise level.
2. Any damage to your rooms, or any hotel property (external and internal).
3. Setting off fire alarms/interfering with smoke detectors.
4. Interfering with fire extinguishers without due cause.
5. Smoking in a non-smoking room.
6. Bringing illegal drugs on to the premises.
7. Any abusive or physical harm to any guest and any member of staff.
8. If removed by staff or the police you will also lose your deposit.
9. Bed wetting.

With the thankful exception of the last, each transgression had featured in the TripAdvisor reviews. How glad I am that I only read these after I left. Three separate guests reported that they'd woken in the night to find strangers stumbling about in their room.

Why did the British have to behave this way? As I knew from experience, the typical guest at a French Formule 1 was an unshaven boor who left smouldering cigarillo butts in the shower and felt uncomfortable wandering the corridors in anything more than pants and an Amstel T-shirt. He'd have the TV on too loud, and would consider it a point of principle to piss in the sink, but he wouldn't assault anyone or systematically destroy property. Violence, vandalism and drugged-up incontinence were our own gifts to the low-end accommodation market, and I couldn't help thinking that the parent group's decision to offload its UK outlets might be connected to them.

'Awake? Then sod off.' From the strip lighting to the bright blue walls, from the single plastic stool to the relaxation-proof foam mattress, a Formule 1 room is a seven-foot cube of joylessness, purpose-built to deter the lingerer. It feels like the result of some painstaking scientific study to establish the environment in which caged rats exhibited the most profound levels of unease, stopping just short of the point where they began to eat themselves. The Metro Inn variant added a patina of neglect and abuse that blurred this boundary. Huge and complex stains blotted my carpet. The malodorous air was also frozen, with the equipment to render it otherwise rendered impotent. Those unwholesome assumptions regarding the en suite sink took on the horridest possible significance when I ran the tap and watched the water immediately back up.

I pulled back the blind and peeked out through the little square window. Below was a patch of frosted grass bordered with rodent-baiting stations and the odd shoe, engulfed on all sides by a misty sea of tarmac bestrewn here and there with a skip or a stoved-in shipping container. I removed some clothes, reappraised the conditions, and put most of them back on. Then I flicked off the horrible strip light, and made a painful error of judgement by flomping back on the bed.

A dusty little telly hung from a ceiling bracket, craftily located in the one place I couldn't see when I lay down. The sound was no more than a forcefield buzz of interference, and someone had saved themselves the bother of levering off the battery compartment by having away with the whole remote. I wearily rose to switch it off, a movement that introduced my forehead to the edge of the top bunk. As I levered myself back into the chilled and stinking darkness, a tattoo of muffled thuds rumbled up from the floor below, crowned by a ragged, furious shout and a heavily pregnant silence.

Chapter Five

'So dark and quiet, always wind and rain; I was cold and I cried every night. I felt it was a strange, terrible place and I hope I never have to return.'

It wouldn't be fair to damn Middlesbrough on the histrionic say-so of a single Brazilian WAG, obliged to relocate to Teesside during her husband's brief stint with the town's football team back in the mid Nineties. But shivering by a deserted, mist-wreathed bus stop at the edge of the industrial estate, I was at one with Andrea da Silva. When at last my bleary, bloodshot eyes pulled the timetable into focus, I found that it wasn't a timetable at all, but a notice explaining that service information could be procured via a text message, at a charge of 25p per enquiry. This sort of thing irks me at the best of times, and on the back of a night interrupted by sheer cold and the encroaching sounds of drunken violence my reaction was intemperate. To passing commuters it must have looked like Sir Alex Ferguson addressing a player he has just watched lob his own goalkeeper from the halfway line, twice.

I knew I'd be in Middlesbrough all day, and didn't fancy wasting half of it parking, but abruptly decided – then loudly announced – that the overweight self-abuse enthusiasts who ran the bus company had left me no option. Turning on my heel I let the freezing fog have it all the way back to the Metro

Inn. Not for the first time Craig translated my righteous, right-foot fury into a pathetic sequence of staccato wallaby hops.

Once again Middlesbrough did its best to hide from me. There was no cathedral spire or other lofty structure to aim at, just a lot of demolition sites interspersed with more of those discouragingly anonymous retail halls that define so much of the British urban experience these days. Largely because of the magnetic lure of their attached car parks: by default I ended up at the Hill Street shopping centre, where I enjoyed a Gregg's breakfast roll as much as you can enjoy any experience that incorporates microwaved bacon. *Shopping brightens up your day!* yelled a desperate pennant strung above my head.

Greasy, bilious and wassailed by piped carols, I conducted a detailed survey of Middlesbrough's retail survivors. Let me tell you now they're a rum bunch. In a single parade I found no fewer than three tanning salons, and by the end of the day had become well acquainted with the city's curious two-tone populace: half the young women hewn from waxy lard, and half from a solid block of microwaved bacon. And while their girlfriends are broiling themselves under coin-op melanoma grills, the flower of Middlesbrough's manhood is browsing the peculiar plethora of novelty shops, devoted as these are to equipment facilitating the rapid and prodigious ingestion of lager: a seven-litre pressurised 'beer rocket', a 'Russian roulette beer bong' and the 'Extreme Beer Funnel and Tube', a grimly surgical device that looked as if it might have been used to force-feed hunger-striking suffragettes. And how did all those mobile-phone shops ride out the storm? In fact, how did they even ride into it in the first place? At one point I could count four, without even moving my head. Each was replete with young staff in crisp shirts, bobbing about looking dynamic and urgent – no mean feat in shops completely bereft of customers. Clinton's Cards: another mysteriously durable high-street success. In a just world, every branch of Clinton's Cards would be burnt to the ground at once by state decree, for the public good. Something is intrinsically wrong in a transaction that requires people to pay £2.15 for a folded piece of cardboard that might as well read,

'I have absolutely no taste and an appalling sense of humour. Happy Easter to a Very Special Nephew.'

The retail thoroughfare opened out into a broad grassed square crowned with a modest observation wheel, farthing to the London Eye's penny. This was evidently Middlesbrough's pre-eminent public space, but it was lined with civic and commercial structures of bullying concrete soullessness and engulfed by yawning, long-vacant plots (LAND FOR RESIDENTIAL OR COMMERCIAL USE – FRANKLY, AT THIS STAGE WE'D LISTEN TO FARMERS). Beside the wheel was a big glass box that identified itself as the new Middlesbrough Institute of Modern Art, bright and studiously contemporary, but in the circumstances no more than a bold gesture. *Middlesbrough – moving forward*, read the inevitable regeneration slogan above its automatic doors. I went through them to learn that all the galleries were closed, and later discovered they were still clearing away an exhibition of fanciful motoring art, curated by the hosts of *Top Gear* and filmed in their presence a couple of days before. 'We've been away in Middlesbrough,' I heard Jeremy Clarkson sneer at his studio audience a few nights later, 'and it's good to be back in England.' *Biographical note: Jeremy Clarkson was born and raised in Doncaster (see Chapter 13).*

MIMA, as of course it's known, presided over a lumpy sweep of green that looked suspiciously like a hastily turfed-over demolition site. To one side was a small lake whose ice floes were home to thuggish seagulls. I kept walking and at last spotted a proper throng of citizens, trooping in and out of an institutional edifice and gathering on the pavement outside. It's slightly more than twenty-five years since I last walked into a Job Centre, and walked out with a position in sanitary management at an IBM warehouse. I've no idea what forklift drivers eat for lunch, but I do know that it clearly isn't good for them. Still, cleaning those toilets was the making of me, or might have been had I stuck it out for more than six hours. The establishment I entered now announced itself as a Job Centre Plus, which offered the promise of additional on-site facilities: something wholesome and uplifting, perhaps a petting zoo. In fact, the subtitle simply acknowledged the sheer size of its customer base. The place had the feel of a busy multiplex cinema foyer, smartly carpeted and dimly lit, its open-plan acreage bestrewn with interactive screens. Young men in sportswear ambled about, chatting in low monotones, occasionally leaning over a monitor and tapping at it with the expression of unimpressed channel-flippers. The security guard notwithstanding, there was none of the brooding despair that defined the last Job Centre I'd been in, the sense that at any minute some donkey-jacketed Yosser might dash his forehead into something or someone. Here everyone just seemed profoundly resigned. I found a spare screen and saw why. Of the 211 job vacancies it offered me, five were local opportunities in retail security (£6.10 per hour) and food production (£5.85 per hour). The rest – page after page of them – were 'independent sales representatives' based in the lonelier parts of Scotland, from Inverness to Perth. All sounded comfortably more terrible than any of the fictional related positions that I'd been stuffing into my CV of late: successful applicants would find themselves hawking cosmetics or replacement windows on a door-to-door basis, in areas where those doors might be separated by a couple of glens and a loch. The reward for this activity was described as 'meets national minimum wage'.

Contaminated with aimless depression, I went out and trudged back up the street, past a church that was now home to a Money Shop pawnbroker's. Outside it stood a map of the city, which I perused for some time, dully transfixed by annotations that seemed designed to leach the life-force from all who passed. 'Middlesbrough Bus Station is a purpose-built facility providing a high-quality bus interchange with modern information systems.' I wondered if it was possible to construct a less captivating sentence. I'm still wondering now. In any case, I felt abruptly compelled to get back to Craig and drive.

Middlesbrough's suburbs proved soothingly suburban. No creepy, lobotomised Bransholmes here: just bland and blameless streets of inter-war semis, with the odd gaudy sheaf of pampas grass springing out above a neatly trimmed front hedge. Only the occasional glimpse of some distant clutch of silvered, smoking organ-pipes reminded me this was supposed to be the worst place to live in all the land. Pink-slippered housewives exchanged cheery words as they pushed their wheelie bins out onto the pavement for collection. A hale pensioner creosoted his fence. There was a touching preponderance of aged British cars, though one love still dare not speak its name: all these streets of pampered old Cavaliers and Rovers, and not a single Austin Maestro. I drove with one hand poised over the horn stalk, ready to give a reedy little toot of greeting, but it was not to be. This was Craig's natural habitat, and he was condemned to roam it alone, the last of his kind.

Middlesbrough's proudest civic emblem is 225 feet high and bright blue, but it took a lot of finding. In the end I hit the river and followed it downstream as closely as I could, weaving through ever more wasted post-industrial wastelands. And suddenly, in a celestial pool of late sun, there it was, a soaring lattice of struts and crossbeams, the ultimate tribute to Meccano engineering: the Tees Transporter Bridge.

I parked up and walked towards the little visitors' centre that cowered beneath one of the bridge's spindly legs. From afar it had looked frail and temporary, the scaffolding for a bigger bridge rather than one in its own right, knocked up out of floodlight gantries and bits of old oil rig. Up close it was fearsome, though my awe subsided rather when I watched it in action. In contradiction of my excitable and – let's be honest – witlessly unscientific imaginings, the structure's giddying height did not define the crossing experience. A modest yellow gondola, just big enough for half a dozen cars, was attached to cables slung from the top beam, and thereby hauled languidly across the water at a height of about four feet. The lofty clearance, of course, was down to what went up the river, not across it. The bridge was opened in 1910, when the ships were tall and the Tees was full of them. In the half-century before that, Middlesbrough had grown into the world's iron and steel capital from nothing – literally nothing. The settlement of that name was a four-cottaged hamlet in 1830, when an extension of the Stockton and Darlington line – the world's first railway – improbably hauled it into the vanguard of the Steam Age. A dock was swiftly built, and Middlesbrough became a serious player in the coal business, taking in the black stuff from the north-eastern coalfields and shipping it down south. Just as this trade peaked, the serendipitous discovery of huge local ironstone deposits sparked an extraordinary iron rush. Foundries and metalworks popped up all along the river banks and into the fields behind them, attracting job-seeking families from all over the north of England. In 1862, Gladstone, then Chancellor of the Exchequer, paid personal tribute to a town whose population had more than trebled over the previous decade. 'This remarkable place,' he portentously announced to the gathered locals, 'the youngest child of England's enterprise, is an infant, but if an infant, an infant Hercules.' Suitably inspired, the town adopted the stirring civic slogan *Erimus* – in Latin, We Will Be.

Middlesbrough reeled that future in with the manic haste of Norman Wisdom rehearsing the tablecloth trick. Trainloads of migrant workers arrived from right across Britain and Europe. The town became known as Ironopolis, and the Tees as the Steel River. Railways from Italy to India were laid with the fruit of its furnaces. Still the population doubled every few years, a rate of sustained urban growth never matched in Britain before or since. By the time the Transporter Bridge opened, the settlement that a dozen farmers had called home just a couple of generations before was a smoky, clanging city of 120,000. Amongst their number was Arthur Darwin, who made a posthumous name for himself by falling off the top of the bridge during the opening ceremony. Almost a century later his family was back in the news, courtesy of great-grandson John and a canoe-centred life-insurance fraud.

The town hit its industrial pinnacle in 1932 with the opening of the majestic Sydney Harbour Bridge, designed by local engineers and built from Teesside iron. A few years back I walked across its hefty span, and stopped halfway to survey one of the world's most becoming prospects. Standing with my elbows on the handrail, those glittering yacht-speckled waters laid out before me, I spotted the legend 'Dorman Long, Middlesbrough' stamped into a girder, and found myself abruptly filled with heart-swelling, eye-moistening pride: for the momentous achievement that was the British Empire, for the faraway men whose toil and genius had brought this mighty, fearless structure to life, for the fact that I could call these men my forefathers. It was all I could do not to throw back my arms and burst into patriotic song, though for the sake of my family and Sydney's police frogmen I'm glad I didn't.

The Transporter Bridge visitors' centre traced the city's subsequent decline, through a table that highlighted a steady dwindling in traffic, both down the river and over it. It seemed sadly apt that other than guest appearances in *Billy Elliot* and *Auf Wiedersehen Pet*, the only memorable incident in the bridge's recent history occurred in 1974, when Terry 'And June' Scott got confused driving home from a bear-baiting workshop, and drove his Jaguar straight off the end of the boarding platform. 'Luckily Scott's car landed in the safety netting,' explained a caption in the visitors' centre, whilst maintaining a diplomatic silence with regard to Terry's earlier whereabouts, perhaps because I just made them up.

I wandered out into an afternoon that was now bright but still bitter, and for half an hour drove around St Hilda's. This was the heart of old Middlesbrough, a place where heavy industry lived cheek by sooty jowl with churches, where the ironmakers' mansions were shoehorned in between streets of workers' cottages. A mid-Victorian print in the visitors' centre had shown a genteel market place that could have come straight off the Quality Street tin, ringed with bow-fronted haberdasheries and populated with promenading couples in extravagant headwear.

'Middlesbrough is a typical town in which to study the lives of those engaged in the making of iron, for it has come into existence for that purpose and for nothing else.' So wrote Lady Florence Bell, wife of a prominent ironmaster, in a period account of her city. It wasn't intended as a dire warning, but now began to feel like one, particularly as she'd then gone on to refer to the local foundries as 'a Titanic industry'. Its wrecks lay all around. Eroded stubs of black-bricked factory wall cast long shadows over street after street of ransacked, rubbish-strewn nothing. It had been evocatively named in honour of the Roman god of fire, but the furnaces along Vulcan Street had long gone cold. 'There is nothing here to appeal to a sense of art and beauty,' continued Lady Flo, 'yet imagination can be stirred – must be stirred – by the hardy, strenuous life of the north, the seething vitality of enterprise with which this town began.' I drove on through the un-seething, non-vital anti-enterprise with which it ended.

Travelling from Bolton to Manchester in 1933, J.B. Priestley was awed by the clamorous, filthy compaction of slums and factories he passed through. 'The ugliness is so complete it is almost exhilarating,' he wrote. 'It challenges you to live there.' I could imagine walking about St Hilda's that year, or at any time in the hundred years before, and feeling the same grubby wonderment. Now the whole place was a silent ruin. St Hilda's is dead in all but name; in fact, dead even in that – the first church thus called had been built here in AD 686, and the last demolished in 1969. The houses that replaced it are already being knocked down.

As I had just learnt, there were once a hundred public houses in St Hilda's. At length I found the solitary survivor, the Captain Cook, opened in 1840, a great scabby mansion of a pub surrounded by defunct engineering works and a partly demolished, wholly abandoned post-war council estate. From a primary school to a car park, much in Middlesbrough is named in honour of its most famous son, though James Cook was actually born in a village a few miles south of a town that didn't then exist, and wouldn't until eighty years after he was battered to death on a Hawaiian beach. The pub – Middlesbrough's oldest – succumbed in belated sympathy six months after I passed. 'The lads who drink here keep saying, "Where are we going to go now?"' the landlady told the local paper on the day she pulled her last pint. 'But there's nothing round here any more. Nothing.' From 'We Will Be' to 'Well, We Were'.

I drove until the road ran out, or more accurately until it was blocked by two young men of unpromising appearance, doing something under the bonnet of a battered Fiat Punto without any numberplates. Ahead lay a straggly void that had been the docks, huge empty basins surrounded by huge empty wastelands. The lofty old four-faced clock tower was still here, its dockside dial blank, as it had been since a Victorian boss removed it to stop his workshy stevedores clock-watching. Across the water stood a lonely jewel in the mud: the silvery Riverside Stadium, home of Middlesbrough FC. Football grounds are reliably huge, yet this one seemed dwarfed by the brownfield dishevelment around it. It was built in the mid 1990s, with the club confident that all manner of glamorous new leisure and entertainment facilities would swiftly follow in its wake. When they didn't, or so I'd read, the directors had been reduced to wooing prospective continental signings with a tour of the picturesque and not especially nearby market town of Yarm, encouraging them to take it for downtown Middlesbrough. One player supposedly thus deluded was Brazilian star Emerson, whose wife would later deliver her damning revenge.

The Riverside was financed through the generosity of club chairman Steve Gibson, a local bulk-liquids-transporter made good. They'll probably be naming car parks after him in decades to come. But surveying Gibson's gleaming endowment and the sprawling, post-industrial mess in which it lay marooned, I couldn't stop thinking of the tireless and more straightfowardly edifying Victorian philanthropy described in the Transporter Bridge visitors' centre. Every public building in old Middlesbrough had it seemed been financed through donations from ironmasters and shipping merchants. Charity was almost a competitive sport, and one they were still playing beyond the grave: bereaved relatives smiled wanly as wills revealed that the family pile was to become a lunatic asylum or sanatorium. Prussian-born Henry Bolckow, Middlesbrough's premier industrialist and its inaugural mayor, indulged the citizenry like no other: he built the first proper school, the first proper hospital, and the first proper city park, named in memory of his fellow German, Prince Albert. Bolckow died without an heir, and bequeathed the vast bulk of his fortune to sundry charitable concerns. Within thirty years the magnificent ancestral home was a ruin.

Back then, do-gooders did good. Now they build football stadiums, and pay ungrateful Brazilians £80,000 a week to play in them. I dare say we've only got ourselves to blame.

I about-turned through the puddled potholes, and drove back to the highest point in St Hilda's, a low hill crowned by the barricaded relics of Middlesbrough's first town hall. The ox-blood rendering and Portland stone arches were crumbling and idly spray-tagged; the semi-tiled roof supported a clock tower whose four faces each told a different version of the wrong time. I steered Craig over a stretch of weeded pavement and eased up to the steps where Henry Bolckow, in contemporary portraits a Gordon Brown with big sidies, first stood in his chains of office. It seemed almost unkind to imagine confronting Henry with the present panorama. As a captain of industry – in fact more of a rear admiral – he would surely at least have approved of the Transporter Bridge. 'A thrill to see from anywhere', in the words of architecture's Mr History, Nikolaus Pevsner, who clearly hadn't looked at it from up here. Nor indeed since 1983, when he died. Today, and from on high, the bridge was doing its best to impersonate the girder-roofed structure left alone on the Hiroshima skyline on that terrible dawn in 1945. I was reminded that at the height of the Cold War, Middlesbrough retained sufficient economic heft to rank number two on the Soviets' UK nuclear hit-list.

That morning I'd read a newspaper report on the closure of the Redcar steelworks. 'It's horrible,' said one quoted local. 'This place is on the bones of its arse as it is.' It was a strangely compelling phrase, and one that now sprang unhappily to mind. Here I was in Middlesbrough's arse, and all around me lay the bones of that arse. Even those would soon be gone. The residential crescent in front of the town hall was being stolen faster than it could be demolished: the gutters and drainpipes had vanished, most of the roof tiles, even window frames and the odd wall. One of the few remaining front doors bore the daubed legend, *Leave us alone*. I tugged at Craig's heavy wheel and headed away. It was a journey that demanded a sombre, elegiac soundtrack, almost certainly Elgar's 'Nimrod'. Instead I found myself obliged to recall the happier times in our nation's proud history – specifically 1981, when Buck's Fizz won the Eurovision Song Contest.

The sun had tucked itself up in fat grey clouds by the time I drove past Ayresome Park, formerly the home of Middlesbrough FC, now an insipid Bovis-pattern estate with streets called The Turnstile and The Midfield. Surrounding it was a grid of narrow cobbled streets flanked by tiny red-brick terraced houses – the kind of streets that a patronising London-based tosspot finds it impossible to drive down without humming the old Hovis ad, even if he's in a car that's calling the kettle black. At the end of one, a grand pair of gates stood guard over a sweep of greenery and skeletal wintry trees. I parked up and walked into Albert Park, past a monumental sundial inevitably donated by H.W.F. Bolckow. It was marked up to display the time in Middlesbrough, Melbourne and New York; I couldn't stop myself recalling the global reach of Trotter's Independent Trading Company, as advertised on the side of Del Boy's Reliant Robin.

The park's large open spaces were lightly peopled with the hardy regulars you might expect to find in such a place on a December afternoon: lone dog-walkers, red-faced and smoking, plus the odd huddle of hoodies up to things I didn't wish to investigate. At length, I came across a small bust of the hugely bearded, late-model Bolckow, surveying his creation through the bars of a vandal-proof cage. Henry was a modest man, who spurned all the many offers to have institutions he'd paid for named in his honour. Here, the trumpet he had been so reluctant to blow in life was yanked from his cold, dead hands and huffed into most forcefully. MIDDLESBROUGH'S FIRST MAYOR AND FIRST REPRESENTATIVE IN PARLIAMENT, read the weathered inscription beneath, CHIEF FOUNDER OF ITS INDUSTRIES AND PIONEER OF ITS EDUCATIONAL, RELIGIOUS AND CHARITABLE MOVEMENTS. Yet Henry's head and frock-coated shoulders were now hidden away and neglected, inestimably less conspicuous than the life-size bronze that dominated the park's most prominent stretch of grass. I believe Brian Clough built the Transporter Bridge with his bare hands, and personally taught every steelworker on Teesside how to read, though it's possible he might just have scored a few goals for Middlesbrough Football Club before moving on to a career in quotable rudeness. Underneath all Henry's facial hair I saw a look that said: I just don't know why I bothered.

Back at the gates I spotted an evidently recent information panel, detailing in its first paragraph how Henry Bolckow announced his intention to lay out Albert Park at a Temperance Society gala. I was trying to picture a more definitively Victorian moment when a local voice piped up right behind me. 'There's sixteen mystiques on that sign, man. Sixteen! It's a tootle bloody disgrease. These fork want to go back to school.' I turned to see a little old man in a splendid astrakhan hat and coat of matching trim, who now launched unbidden into an evidently well-rehearsed rundown of the panel's grammatical errors.

As a rule, the citizens of Middlesbrough are a placid bunch. When a local TV crew went out on the streets to record reactions to the *Location* survey, they encountered widespread indifference to the town's humiliating denigration as the very worst in the land. All one could muster in its defence was that 'a pint here costs 50p less than it does in London'. Even the local MP did no better than point out that Middlesbrough was 'near some good countryside, and less than fifty miles from York'. No, it's said that if you want to rile someone round these parts, there are only two sure-fire ways to do it: spell Middlesbrough with two o's, or Teesside with one s. By the time the old man reached the park sign's final outrage against orthography – a superfluous use of capitals in Sun Dial – I could very easily believe it. For good measure he then progressed eagerly into a withering character assassination of his own city.

'Run by daft buggers this toon, man. A bloody dump and all. No walk, no money. You live rune dear?' I raised a finger and opened my mouth, but had time to emit no more than a small cloud of vapour. 'You don't want to stay, man. See that rude?' He waved a dismissive astrakhan cuff at the plain and dreary thoroughfare outside the gates. 'Whole thing wants bloody nockerndoon. All you've got from one end to the bloody other is bloody teaker-wheeze. Not even a decent fission-chip. All teaker-whee bloody kebabs and bloody parmos.'

I'd spotted this mysterious word in the windows of many such local establishments, and seized the opportunity to ask for an explanation, and to sound like Prince Charles on a regional walkabout in doing so. 'Parmo? Bloody crap, man. Foreign crap. Some horrible bloody foreign idea with chicken and foreign bloody sweaty-foot cheese. Smells worse than bloody Billingham chemical works.' I was, of course, now duty bound to put this verdict to the test, and so some hours later pulled up in the dark outside a dazzling cathedral city of steam and light, with a horrible bloody foreign idea in my lap.

Even by the stunted health and safety standards of Victorian industry, a chemical plant was a particularly terrible place to earn a living. Work long enough processing white phosphorus – as many thousands did in match factories – and you would succumb to 'phossy jaw', a flesh-eating disfigurement which gave off an appalling stench and glowed in the dark. A chromium worker was readily identifiable by the misshapen hole in his face that had once been a nose. Opened in 1833, when workplace protection meant a baker's boy hat and the Lord's Prayer, Middlesbrough's first chemical plant produced sulphuric acid.

As you'd hope and expect, conditions steadily improved thereafter, but never to the point where a Teesside mother would weep tears of joy at the news that her son or daughter had begun a career at Wilton or Billingham, the two sprawling chemical complexes that by the 1950s had established them-selves as the town's dominant employers. As the chorus to a self-evidently unofficial 'ICI Song' of this era cheerily put it, 'Every day you're in this place, you're two days nearer death.'

It was perhaps with this in mind that Middlesbrough so recklessly embraced the escalope parmesan, a dish decreed by North Yorkshire Trading Standards to incorporate nearly twice the recommended daily allowance of fat for an adult male. So my subsequent research revealed, along with a potted history of this regional fast-food phenomenon, created by an American army chef who settled in Middlesbrough after the war. Swiftly abbreviated to 'parmo', Nicos Harris's recipe was a cheerfully dumbed-down take on an Italian classic: a veal fillet coated with batter and breadcrumbs, then deep fried, topped with béchamel sauce and parmesan, baked briefly in a pizza oven and laid on a bed of chips. Ignore the original garnish of choice – who on earth let creamed cabbage into the world? – and it doesn't sound at all bad.

I placed my order knowing none of this, nor the bit that described the half-sized dish I'd opted for as a 'ladies' parmo'. It was prepared backstage at one of the many Asian-run outlets that now dominate the local parmo scene by an unsmiling wobble-chops who left me alone for fifteen long minutes at the counter, there to contemplate the many other dishes I might have ordered from him in preference. In fact, there were none. I shall never understand how any competent and incorruptible health inspector can stand before a rotating bollard of animal matter, days old and defiantly unrefrigerated, without calling forth the proprietor and wordlessly executing him on the spot.

The pizza box I took possession of was almost too hot to hold. It was still impressively warm by the time I'd driven over the Tees, and right round Billingham to a lay-by beneath a gigantic overhead pipeline, broad as a Tube tunnel. I switched off the engine and heard a resonant gurgle from above; presently a complicated and very unhealthy smell eased in through Craig's air vents.

It's years since ICI sold off most of Billingham to other chemical firms, and I'd been told that the complex was now a shadow of its former self. Some shadow. For more than twenty minutes I'd skirted its perimeter, silently agog at the gleaming, steaming alien structures, with their silvery entrails and spires of flame, their gigantic metal spheres that gasped and wheezed with whatever terrible process they were striving to encourage or restrain. It was at once both exhilarating and dreadful, and I could very easily understand why Aldous Huxley felt inspired to write his creepily dystopian classic *Brave New World* after a tour around Billingham. It's also said to have provided Ridley Scott, raised in Teesside, with the visual template for *Bladerunner*.

That smell was rather a leveller, though, like Darth Vader towering above you with his light sabre poised for the *coup de grâce*, and then doing a blow-off. There's something just so stubbornly prosaic about bad odours. Scent is claimed to be the most evocative of the senses, but the most apocalyptic memory my nose could summon as I drove around Billingham was of youthful afternoons spent in the back garden, holding a stick crowned with a gently blazing carrier bag, raining fiery balls of molten plastic death upon a huddled platoon of 1/76 scale infantrymen.

And sadly for Middlesbrough, Billingham and Wilton have made the town synonymous not with a fearsome, futuristic grandeur, but with smelling awful. Teessiders are known across the north-east as Smoggies. The *Location, Slow-Motion, Damnation* survey laid heavy emphasis on Middlesbrough's abysmal air quality when justifying its verdict. In the medical journals, the region is identified as the UK's asthma black spot; on the football terraces, Boro fans are greeted with taunts of 'What's it like to smell fresh air?'

What indeed. I opened the pizza box a crack and was hit by a curdled waft that precisely replicated the challenging under-sock aroma described by the old man in the park. In haste I clamped it shut and wound down the window, welcoming in a roaring hiss and a chilled wave of pickled swamp gas. By judicious tinkering I established that a half-inch gap allowed the two stenches to cancel each other out. Then I eased the lid right back and there, prone on its nest of chips in the moody shadows of Craig's interior half-light, sat a flaccid, glistening dumbbell weight.

Underscoring the insidious dangers of long-term exposure to airborne toxins, those who work at Billingham or live near it must cope with the more tangible fear of being abruptly blown to pieces. The plant was opened in 1917 to synthesise ammonia-based artillery explosives, and is today the UK's largest producer of ammonium nitrate, a fertiliser whose fearsome combustibility has attracted the attention of many a terrorist, and whose manufacture and storage are fraught with hazards. The industry's most dumbfounding catastrophe occurred in 1947, when a ship full of ammonium nitrate caught fire and exploded on the quayside at Texas City, just south of Houston: 481 people were killed, including passengers in two passing aeroplanes whose wings were ripped off by the blast. The ship's two-ton anchor turned up, still too hot to touch, in a field over a mile and a half away. That shattering disaster led to a radical tightening in precautionary regulations, but ongoing demand for what remains the world's most ubiquitous fertiliser means vast and lethal bangs are never more than a discarded fag away: in the first decade of this century alone, related mishaps claimed five thousand casualties. In suffering no explosive deaths in recent years Billingham can count itself fortunate, though that's probably not a word you'd want to suggest to veterans of the many ammonium-nitrate-based excitements the plant has hosted. A former instrument technician at Billingham recalled a 1960s blast of such harrowing intensity that three shell-shocked colleagues resigned on the spot. In 2006, nearby residents were flung from their beds by an explosion that 'turned the whole world orange', and was heard over 20 miles away.

My stinking lapful of ladies' parmo was beginning to look like an encapsulation of Middlesbrough's every deficiency. At this stage it wouldn't have been a huge surprise if it had blown up in my face. But I hadn't eaten since breakfast, and felt sure that a parmo's bark (smell and appearance) could not possibly be as bad as its bite (taste). I grasped the warm and yielding roundel; it promptly divided into soggy cubes, like a partly diced mango half. Then with a snatch and a snap of the jaws, my parmo virginity was sacrificed.

Sensations were instantly unleashed that seemed distant from anything Nicos Harris could ever have intended. Gone were the breadcrumbs; more significantly, gone, too, was the escalope. At the core of my mouthful sat a loose layer of puréed fowl. Outside that, a fat sheathing of oiled sponge, and outside that, a crusted ooze pairing the odour of century-old Dairylea with the flavour of exhumed whey solids. It was like a spam fritter left outside for a year in a land where it rained fondue.

I think we have now established that I will eat almost anything. I could not eat this. Another and much smaller bite confirmed the terrible evidence of the first. Even the chips, contaminated by leachate from what I would some months later hear a TV chef describe as 'the antichrist of cooking', proved beyond me. I tossed the box wanly into the footwell and drove away. Only then did I take note of the hour, and what it implied for my short-term accommodation plans. There was only one solution, and in a state of malnourished resignation I accepted it with no more than a slight lowering of the shoulders.

'Hello again! Listen, we're a bit full tonight. Would a view of the flyover be OK?'

Chapter Six

SMACK!

It was a shudderingly bitter morning, hazed with Billingham smog, and I walked stiffly out into it, still harrowed and damp from my ordeal in the Metro Inn's communal cleansing pod. Every Formule 1 shower comes decorated with an ankle-high frieze of van-driver pubes, marking the tide-line limit of the self-cleaning jets that dribble into action when you vacate the pod. Your bathing pleasure is compromised by the certain knowledge that gingery strays are plaiting themselves into your leg-hair, though only until you step into the drying zone, where they're blasted free by a million-watt jet of hot air. Not so at the Metro Inn, where I writhed pitifully before a frail and frigid wisp, like a Death Eater's final breath.

Craig sat frost-rimed and alone in the mist-wreathed car park, looking as if he'd frozen to death in the night. So indeed he had. The choke knob proved immovably glaciated, resisting my efforts to free it so doughtily that before long I had worn right through the tips of two glove fingers. Undeterred by the hard-lacquered remains of a lady's parmo in the footwell, despair and its foul-mouthed minions soon made themselves at home in Craig's Arctic interior. I gave the key a twist, thereby filling the world with hypothermic mechanical toiling topped with a squawked request to take my order. So began the parping litany of burger, fried chicken and pizza establishments that is 'The Fast Food Song', the queasily, cheesily appropriate E. coli of novelty hit singles.

In my twin capacities as tightwad and idiot, I spent an awful lot of my young adulthood on the hard shoulder, unscrewing the wrong bits of some stricken jalopy. It was a bitter-sweet moment when, at the age of twenty-seven, I opened the bonnet of my new (old) acquisition – a Citroën – and saw the entire engine hidden beneath a big cowl with DON'T EVEN THINK ABOUT IT, SONNY stamped on the top in seven languages. The age of clueless fumbling was at an end: my relationship with the motor vehicle would henceforth be agreeably more distant than the needy, dysfunctional, love-hate *folie à deux* it had become. I haven't bought a Haynes manual for two decades, let alone quickly reduced one to an oil-smeared, bloodstained and – don't ask – flaming mess.

The remedial skills currently at my disposal may be encapsulated in one simple maxim: if it ain't broke, don't fix it – but if it is, spray WD40 all over the bastard and give it another go. Get some under your fingernails and wave a socket wrench about and it even looks as if you know what you're doing. It's amazing how often this technique pays dividends: I strongly suspect you could employ it to good effect on head lice and sore throats. At any rate, it was with some relief that I now remembered the huge can of WD40 stowed in the boot, and indeed the scraper and de-icer acquired in a pound shop the day before and stowed alongside it.

But the boot lock was stubborn at the best of times, and this certainly wasn't one of those. I depressed the chrome knob and it stayed depressed, deep-frozen and obdurate. Nothing was going to coax it back out, though that didn't stop me pushing through my right glove's final fingers while trying. Could a man hate a silver button? I gave it my best shot. I sank to my haunches and stared at it coldly from point-blank range, then spattered its stupid little face with the fruits of a long and furious raspberry. That felt good; I inhaled deeply and did it again. I was drawing breath for a third when I saw I was being observed through the driver's window of a lorry parked outside.

Something had happened to Craig's insides when I got back in behind the wheel. Something bad: loud, hot rage had fast-tracked the parmo-defrosting process, releasing a retch-friendly stench that I correctly guessed would haunt the interior for many days to come. Even with the parmo snatched up and by some irresistible reflex hurled into a hedge – sorry, Stockton on Tees – the sour and sickly smell hung heavy, so thick you could almost see it, like the wavy lines above a cartoon Camembert. I wound down all four windows and sat there for a while, letting the faintly acrid smog creep in and 'The Fast Food Song' creep out. McDonald's, Kentucky Fried Chicken, Pizza Hut. Then I turned the key again and again and again, hearing Craig fire and die, fire and die. Pizza Hut, Kentucky Fried Chicken. And with the starter wheezing into its death rattle, fire – and hold. Gunning the engine crazily and thickening the mist with great billows of uncatalysed fumes, I peered hopefully through the crystallised windscreen haze and pointed the Parmobile north.

It is better to travel than to arrive, said someone who'd never gone very far in an Austin Maestro. The driver's seat had begun to fall in on itself, sucking my trunk ever deeper into the wire eggbox of its fundament. The steering made roundabouts a decent aerobic workout and parallel parking an iron-man triathlon, even with the front tyres so recklessly over-inflated they pinged when I flicked them. Bulgarian peasant-spec suspension meant that speed bumps and potholes weren't so much absorbed as battered into submission. Craig cornered on rails – rails made of warm licorice.

The whole car had a sort of Tesco Value feel to it: it just about did the job, but felt like it wouldn't for long. Shutting the door made a sound like kicking an empty Coke can, and more often than not caused the glovebox door to flop open. Closer inspection of the sat-nav screen's data revealed that my true rate of progress was hugely slower than that indicated by Craig's speedo, which read 70mph when I was actually doing 58. In their press releases, Austin Rover had made great play of the Maestro's 'homofocal' headlights – an apparently innovative super-bright design burdened, like the vehicle they fronted, with an extremely silly name. Maybe he had suffered electrical complications during a difficult two-stage birth, but I have to say Craig's homofocals were a useless liability. Heading through the Teesside fog I might as well have had a couple of IKEA tealights resting on the front bumper. Though it wasn't all bad, as I was thus spared the finer detail of the terrible urban wasteland we presently broached.

An also-ran in the *Location* chart at number twenty, Hartlepool didn't make the cut on my initial itinerary. Belated persuasion came via the dark insinuations of 'Hartlepool mindgames' overheard in the Middlesbrough curry house, and – read over an Asda Value breakfast – a newspaper profile of Peter Mandelson, for many years the town's MP. This reacquainted me with a notorious local tale: that of the ship's monkey, sole survivor of a Napoleonic warship wrecked off the Hartlepool coast, lynched on the foreshore by hysterical townspeople who took him for a Frenchman. What I found interesting about this shameful episode is that it never happened: there was no shipwreck, no monkey, no hanging. Even more interesting is how the townspeople went on to embrace this fictional humiliation as their defining symbol. In 2001, Hartlepool FC introduced a man in a monkey suit as their official mascot. H'angus, as he was known, quickly distinguished himself at away games by simulating sexual intercourse with match stewards, an activity for which he was regularly ejected by police. Undeterred by this CV, and a range of policies that began and ended with 'free bananas for schoolkids', a year later the people of Hartlepool elected him as their mayor. H'angus has since been re-elected twice – the first mayor in the country ever to be voted in for a third term. Perhaps it was their way of making up for electing Peter Mandelson three times, without lynching him on the foreshore even once. Or perhaps it was because they had simply gone past caring.

There were two questions I could be sure my friends and family would be asking when I visited them after returning home. The first: 'Sorry, but would you mind parking that round the corner?' The second: 'So, what *was* the worst place, then?' I drove through Hartlepool with my features set somewhere between confusion and disbelief, like George Bush being told about the twin towers, just as he was really getting into that story about the goat. I had an answer.

The drilled-metal grille, as welded over the doors and windows of long-abandoned buildings, was no stranger to me these days. But in Hartlepool, it had become the civic leitmotif, the must-have structural accessory. Entire misty streets, entire misty districts, bore this mark of the damned: Victorian back-to-backs, red-brick inter-war estates, Sixties mini-Bransholmes. The whole town had been earmarked for destruction, but the programme appeared to have been cancelled halfway through. There can be few sights more poignant, more disrespectful and intrusive, than a crudely bisected family home: a bathroom mirror gleaming out above the clinging shards of a pink-tiled splashback, an exposed bedroom wall still graced with a care-fully hand-painted depiction of the Hartlepool FC crest.

It was foggy, it was cold, and at 10.30 a.m. it was utterly deserted – the first and only gathering of townspeople I encoun-tered was a crowd of females, old and young, piling purposefully aboard two coaches parked outside a civic centre. It looked for all the world like the evacuation of the womenfolk, first phase of full withdrawal from a town deemed unfit for purpose. The men they were leaving behind, all six of them, seemed aimless and bereft. Two were walking stout little dogs across the empty car park outside a Massive Clearance Sale of Ex-Hire Formal Menswear. Two were wobbling around a playing field on what looked very much like their sons' mountain bikes, knees out, fags in mouth. And two had devised a pastime that shall define Hartlepool for me whenever I think of the town again. Why don't you give it a try? All you'll need are two baseball bats, two cricket balls, string, plenty of gaffer tape, and a fierce belief in pain as the only cure for boredom.

I'd asked Ozzy to direct me to Jutland Road, having chanced upon it in a local man's Facebook request for input into the Hartlepool Monopoly board he was designing. 'I know there are plenty of scruffy streets, but don't know what order to put them in.' There was one constant in the replies: anyone looking for an Old Kent Road need look no further than the street most knew simply as 'Jutty'. It didn't seem up to much at first: blameless, well-sized pebble-dashed semis, set back from the road, a Sky dish on every chimney. The first suggestions of a darker side emerged with the chicanes, elaborate deterrents to anti-social driving habits, there in essence to take the joy out of joyriding. Then I spotted CCTV towers pointing down at me from all sides, the cameras secured in heavy-mesh cages, above a medieval array of spike-tipped anti-climb deterrents. But when, at length, Ozzy announced that I had raiched my f-f-f-fookin dustinoition, the satellite-decreed centre of Jutland Road, I wasn't paying attention. Blocking the street ahead, oblivious to me or the watching eyes above, two stocky men in their thirties were lethargically belabouring each other with home-crafted maces, assembled from the components listed above. A swing, a yielding thwump of bodily contact, a low grunt of discomfort. Repeat.

Loath to alert them with a provocative toot of Craig's whiny horn, I watched and waited, in thrall to their vacant, workmanlike demeanour. No snarls, no sneers, no deranged cackles; one was even wearing a high-visibility jacket, which bolstered the impression that they were engaged in some tiresome blue-collar obligation, like welding window grilles onto an abandoned factory, or half-demolishing a street of houses, or pop-riveting a Londoner's nose to the bonnet of his Austin Maestro. Swing, thwump, grunt. It was simply the sort of thing people did in Hartlepool when there wasn't a fictional monkey to not string up. After half a dozen exchanges, one took a mighty blow to the neck, which had him holding a hand up to request a brief recuperative intermission. At this point his yellow-jacketed opponent noted my presence, and waved me idly through, as if I'd been waiting to drive aboard a cross-channel ferry. As I gathered speed I glanced in my mirror and saw his head pitch abruptly to one side and his knees buckle gently beneath him. It might not have been quite what the curry-house couples had meant, but I knew what I had witnessed: a skull-smiting three-pointer in the Hartlepool Mindgame.

The sky had spent all morning knitting itself into a heavy, grey blanket, and heading out of Hartlepool this began to leak weather that Craig's porous underpinnings eagerly blotted up. In this manner I was made aware that the sole of my left shoe now sported a hole. Having stopped at a petrol station to change into new socks, I was compelled to first tackle the conundrum of the unopenable boot in which they were entombed. Pleasingly, my cure-all remedy instantly sorted the boot, even if effecting it did mean having to buy another can of WD40 to supplement the one already in there. Duly inspired, I opened the bonnet and hissily lubricated the choke mechanism, more familiar to me as the entire engine bay. In the process I blundered across the dipstick: withdrawn and inspected, it bore no more than a black fingernail crescent at its tip. I felt exactly as I had when some student-era neighbours went away and I realised three nights on that I'd forgotten to feed their cat – in fact, worse, as I couldn't look back on seventy-two hours of wanton debauchery to offset the guilt. It required almost two litres of distressingly expensive lubricant ('Haven't you got anything for low-performance engines?') to get Craig back up to his mark. When I checked the manual I found I'd been working him like a pit pony: he'd been creaking through the agony with less than a litre of relief in his sump. It was difficult to know what was more impressive – my criminal neglect, or the dedicated incompetence required to design and manufacture an engine that after just 16,000 miles of social and domestic pottering was already burning oil like an aged tramp steamer.

It really didn't take much to top the charts in the mid Seventies. Here is Wikipedia's encapsulation of the 1976 world-wide hit that seeped dismally forth from the speakers as I headed away into the sodden coastal mist: 'The story within "Disco Duck" centres around a man at a dance party who is overcome by the urge to get up and "get down" in a duck-like manner.' Weave that epic fable around a studiously insipid rent-a-boogie riff, throw in some sub-Donald quackery and you had yourself a Billboard number one.

What you didn't have, being a Memphis-based DJ, is a song with any British connections whatsoever. My in-car jukebox promised death by a thousand cuts, but halfway through 'Disco Duck' I realised this was one little stab to the eardrum that I need never have endured. When a jab at the next-track button unleashed the plinky, parpy opening strains of 'I've Got a Brand New Combine Harvester', I felt like cranking the volume up to the max, winding down the window and filling the mist with a chest-swelling roar: Absent people of Cleveland and Durham's defunct mining settlements, this terrible, terrible music is ours and ours alone!

The fog thickened; I slowed down and clicked the high-intensity rear-light button, savouring the intrepid thrill that doing so unfailingly instils. 'Rear fogs activated, Captain. Steady as she goes.' For an hour or more there was nothing to see but the occasional misty reminder that up here the seaside was – or had been – a workplace, not a day-trip destination. A skip depot fronting a mountain of landfill rubble that loomed above the dunes; greasy, grey vessels on a greasy, grey horizon; a horseshoe sweep of sand bestrewn with old tyres and twisted sections of gantry. Then the weather closed in, hard, and it was just screechy wipers, Geri Halliwell and an oncoming convoy of battered lorries piled high with rusty scrap, as if the post-industrial wastelands ahead were being hastily dismantled and taken away before I arrived.

Somewhere out to my rain-lashed, fog-shrouded right lay Blackhall Colliery beach, the most thrillingly desolate and despoiled location in all of Britain. It was there that the 1971 classic *Get Carter* romped to its feel-good finale, one introduced with Michael Caine pursuing a Scottish gangster across the blackened sands. Caine, as Carter, presently batters his quarry to death and heaves the corpse into a coal-slag hopper; Carter then fulfils the film's entitled imperative by being got as he strolls breezily back across the shoreline, shot square in the forehead by a distant, faceless hitman. But even as the credits roll and the North Sea surf caresses Michael's gingery curls, the contemporary viewer is still struck dumb by the spectacle bridging the two murders: did I really just see that coal-slag hopper unload itself straight into the sea?

Indeed you did, and if you'd stood on any east Durham beach in 1971 you'd have seen conveyor chains of coal-slag doing the same, right around the clock. Several million tons of the stuff had rendered this entire stretch of coast one of the most polluted in the world by 1981, when Blackhall Colliery was closed down. Elsewhere in Durham the practice lingered briefly on. In 1924 the county had been home to 304 pits, employing 170,000 men. By 1969 that was down to 34 and 36,000 respectively. The graph-line had been heading one way fast for sixty years, and Margaret Thatcher's government did no more than usher it to the axis. Today not a single County Durham mine survives.

In thinning mist I drove now into one of the more feted casualties, a town that abruptly sprang forth from the tumbling coastal hillsides of east Durham in 1910, and on a wet December noon a century on was melting back into them, earth to earth, slag to slag, coal ashes to coal ashes. To enthusiasts of statistical calamity, Easington is notorious as the English town with the highest per-capita rates of obesity, unemployment and long-term sickness. Easington's pensioners are the poorest in Britain. Two out of five of its adult men claim invalidity benefits. By whatever basket of dispiriting data employed to arrive at the conclusion, it is the most economically deprived town in the United Kingdom. But to members of the Moore household, with all respectful apologies to its woebegone citizenry, Easington is known only as a place of glory and celebration. For it was through the front door of an Easington miner's home, as reimagined on a West End stage for the musical production of *Billy Elliot*, that my son dashed three nights a week for nine heady months in 2006, fixing the Equity-certified NUM strikers therein with a look of imploring horror, then captivating full house after breathless full house with a dynamic and flawlessly regional announcement: 'The police are coming down the street – they've kicked in Jimmy Milburn!'

The depth and vigour my son brought to the cameo role of 'Tall Boy' proved a mixed blessing. Victim of his own Day-Lewisian versatility, he was also called upon to portray the pivotal martyrdom of 'Posh Boy', accosted later in the production by the eponymous young Easingtonian, and slapped, kneed, headbutted or rabbit-punched, depending on which particular Billy was on duty. In any event, I felt something of a bond with Easington, though sadly one liable to earn me the Posh Boy treatment had I opted to reveal it.

Easington Colliery mine was one of the last to be opened in Durham; the coal seams here headed straight out under the North Sea, and tapping into them from the clifftop pithead required eleven years of grim and awkward toil. Specialist German engineers were called in to penetrate the watery strata using an experimental freezing technique: one worker fell down a shaft thus treated, and emerged three years later entombed in a block of ice.

A deep, dark hole in the ground is a compromised working environment, and there were few deeper and darker. Easington's miners would end up hewing coal from seams 1,700 feet under the seabed, 8 miles off the coast. But if Easington was never going to be a great place to work, in Edwardian Britain there were few better places for a miner and his family to live. By virtue of being built at a time when our industrialists could call upon an informed and sympathetic awareness of what was bad about old mining towns, and were blessed with the cash and philanthropic decency to put up a really good new one, Easington Colliery – attached to one of a cluster of blue-riband 'super pits' built along the east Durham coast – was assured of a gilded start in life.

Sited just down the hill from the old Saxon-founded village of Easington, the town was a top-of-the-range, state-of-the-art new-build, with the full set of optional civic extras: a working men's club, a miners' hall, even a cinema – an extraordinary embellishment for that time. The terraced houses were twice the size of their typical Victorian predecessors, and two imposing schools – one for girls, one for boys – went up side by side on Seaside Lane, as the high street was cheerily dubbed. Coal was king in 1910, and Easington Colliery was one of its grandest palaces.

Mindful of the many industrial towns that had swiftly outgrown themselves – Middlesbrough wasn't far away – Easington Colliery was future-proofed to soak up the inevitable decades of growth. I parked above the high street and looked out across what had clearly been intended as no more than phase one: lone columns of dark red terraces strode out up the wet green hills, north towards the allotments and pigeon lofts, east towards the fuzzy grey sea, still waiting for the cross-streets that would link them all together. The headstones were packed neatly into the distant far end of a huge cemetery, like the very early stages of a round of Tetris. Towering over all stood those his-'n'-hers school buildings, full-on, Harrods-turreted temples of academe.

It was hard to accept that the community huddled beneath these gigantic, neo-baroque edifices could ever have managed the frenzy of reproduction required to fill them. It certainly couldn't now. I hadn't passed a soul under the age of forty by the time I walked up to the schools' padlocked gates and looked through at the weed-pierced playground tarmac. No BOYS or GIRLS to walk in beneath the porticos thus grandly engraved, or stifle a ribald giggle by the door marked MANUAL INSTRUCTION. Easington Colliery pit closed in 1993; the two schools four years later. A survey taken twelve months afterwards established that only one in five former pupils of working age had found employment. And a decade on their schools were still looking for a job: as a weathered sign nailed high up the façade announced, the buildings remained a redevelopment opportunity.

Just a year after Easington hauled up its first buckets of black stuff, Winston Churchill, then First Lord of the Admirality, announced that the Royal Navy would henceforth be powered not by coal – bulky, labour-intensive, calorifically inefficient – but by oil. It was to prove a tipping point. Demand fell away, and the market for British coal in particular declined dramatically after the First World War, with the availability of cheaper foreign substitutes. Durham's coal output peaked in 1913, and Easington would never employ more than 3,200 miners, way below the projected estimates. The twin schools, built for 1,300 children, were never more than three-quarters full, and by the Second World War were more than half empty. To the plucky band of Billys and Tall Boys roaming its lonely corridors in the early 1980s, the place would have seemed almost godforsaken.

It felt a bit like that down Seaside Lane, home to an endless parade of small shops and perhaps half a dozen stooping female pedestrians. Easington Colliery's population peaked at ten thousand, but its local traders now had just 2,100 heads to coif, minds to feed, hearts to clog. The usual preponderance of bookmakers and undertakers was broken up with dusty, shuttered victims of steady economic decline or blindly irrational optimism: an appliance repair shop, a mortgage broker, a chiropody clinic. I struck off down a terraced side street and at last spotted some Easingtonian males: grey-faced Jimmy Milburns and Elliot pères in dockers hats and baggy tracksuits, tinkering with small, old, cheap-to-run cars, or walking small, old, cheap-to-run dogs. Born and bred miners to a man, living 100 miles from the nearest working pit.

I'd anticipated – OK, feared – that men like these might still be looking for someone to take it out on, their bitterness matured to violent perfection over twenty-five years. But the mood, as far as I could gauge it – from the null-and-void expressions, from the round-shouldered, silent shuffle with which everyone went about their non-business, from the way that long-abandoned premises were left to rot slowly where they stood, without the fast-tracking input of vandalism or petty theft – was one of profound resignation. The Bransholme Effect: people who'd never expected much from life, and weren't getting it. The spark had been snuffed out of a whole community, and how bright that spark had once burnt. When the inter-war collapse in profitability reined in the mine owners' philanthropic urges, the miners' pooled their own meagre free time and resources. They built a home for aged miners and a welfare ground with sports pitches and a clubhouse, and organised a communal doctors' surgery and a new bus service. Even by mining-community standards, Easington was a proud, defiant, all-for-one kind of town. You'll never guess what happened one summer's morning in 1984, when the colliery's striking miners discovered that a single scab had turned up to clock on with an escort of two thousand riot police. The Milburn-avenging re-enactment catalysed by my son necessarily underplayed events.

The 1984–85 miners' strike was by no means Easington's introduction to communal adversity. The town suffered horribly in the 1918 flu epidemic, and its miners endured a thirteen-week lock-out in 1921, as well as a very lean seven months during the 1926 General Strike. The colliery's practice of tipping red-hot ash from its boilers straight on to the beach (where else?) accounted for a number of recklessly curious youngsters, and provided a handy navigational beacon for the Luftwaffe, who killed nine locals in a bombing raid. Above and beyond all were the self-evident occupational hazards. Two other shaft-diggers had joined their deep-frozen colleague in the churchyard before Easington Colliery had even opened, and before it closed a further 191 miners would lie beside them. Almost half were killed on 29 May 1951, when a huge explosion sent walls of flame roaring through 9 miles of deep galleries. Britain has never since endured a more deadly mining tragedy, and doubt-less never will. At the end of the 1950s, annual fatality rates in the industry were half what they had been in Victorian times, yet still ran at around one death for every thousand workers. Those are not attractive odds. Would you go to a cup final knowing that eighty spectators wouldn't get out of Wembley alive? The miners, of course, didn't have the luxury of a choice.

The very real risk of being killed was just one chapter in the *Bumper Book of Mining Badness*. In 1937, George Orwell went down three Lancashire coal mines while researching his sociological treatise *The Road to Wigan Pier*, and offered a swift encapsulation of the underground working environment: '. . . the place is like hell, or at any rate like my own mental picture of hell. Most of the things one imagines in hell are there – heat, noise, confusion, darkness, foul air, and, above all, unbearably cramped space.'

As a man who spent much of his late twenties as a full-on tramp, Orwell was no whinging milksop. Rare is the novelist who can call upon an informed experience of what it is to shovel two tons of earth in an afternoon above ground, while assessing its subterranean counterpart. Yet nothing he had experienced – or would experience, in a life so rich with voluntary suffering that most obituaries found space for the word 'masochist' – could ever compare with the manifold horrors Orwell witnessed down the mines. The seams were often no more than 3 feet thick, obliging miners to hack and shovel for seven hours hunched in a squat. Still worse was the simple act of reaching the coal face, which involved creeping for long miles down black passages, usually bent double, sometimes on all fours. Every miner sported 'buttons down the back': permanent scabs on each vertebra caused by knocking against beams. Orwell got a good look at these, as the ambient temperature in many underground areas encouraged most miners to work in nothing but clogs and kneepads. 'By no conceivable amount of effort or training could I become a coal-miner,' he concluded. 'The work would kill me in a few weeks.'

I turned a few lonely corners and wandered up to the cemetery, trying to conjure a more positive rationale for the defeated air that hung over Easington. Perhaps it was just the December rain, I thought. Perhaps the citizens' spirits weren't crushed, just comfortably anaesthetised by the soothing beauty of their surroundings, horses gambolling across tilted pastures, the coastal walk that was such a bracing delight, or certainly would be once the last mountains of coal slag and discarded mining machinery had been cleared off the beach.

At the churchyard I gave up conjuring. The polished new headstones honoured dearest fathers and beloved husbands struck down at 49, 52, 50, 53, 42 . . . The statistics had forewarned me, but it was still a shock to witness the reality. It felt like a scene from some personal remake of *It's a Wonderful Life*, being shown how things would pan out if I went ahead and made that fateful decision to do nothing but eat crisps and smoke. Mining was an old man's game by 1951 – the average age of those who died in the Easington disaster was forty-three, with twelve victims into their sixties. But looking around the graves I grasped that if there's one thing worse for your health than working down a mine, it's not working at all. The shadow of death that hung over every mining community had been lifted, yet the graveyard was filling faster than ever. When the pit closed, 1,400 Easington men had nothing to do but grow old and die. It wasn't much of a job, and sixteen years on they were all opting for early retirement. I drove away in a mood of sombre reflection that Cliff Richard's 'Millennium Prayer' came worryingly close to complementing. Thanks be to Cliff's buddy upstairs that I wasn't a miner, or an ex-miner, or a miner-to-be: one day, you can be sure, we'll have to prise off Easington's little pithead memorial in a desperate search for the 8.4 million tons of fuel that still lie down that very deep hole, but when that day comes I'll be at peaceful rest in a rather shallower one.

I spent the balance of the morning pressing deeper into the unknown, that huge swathe of upper northern Britain only previously experienced through the window of a train or the windscreen of a much faster car. Craig-pace afforded me a ruminative drive-by of the Angel of the North, wings out on a neighbouring brow; I assessed it with an enhanced appreciation for the message inherent in its rusted majesty, and prayed that its head wouldn't fall off under the influence of my malignant forcefield. Other than that all was deeply, defiantly traditional. The sun came out and varnished the timeless wet hillsides. Every other pub was called The Shoulder of Mutton. Doyenne of novelty hits 'Lily the Pink' oompahed out of the speakers, nestled in my discography's timeline just behind David Bowie's youthful stupidity 'The Laughing Gnome' – the oldest track in there, and such a durable magnet for Bowie-baiters that in 1990 he scrapped a public telephone vote that had been set up to decide the playlist for his forthcoming tour.

Grange Villa, another erstwhile mining community, had been included in Sky 3's *Britain's Toughest Villages* by virtue of an apparently ugly record of leek-envy allotment riots. December clearly wasn't a hot-spot month for such activity, but the allotments I drove past – hundreds of them, like some sprawling shanty town of sheds and greenhouses – were still dotted with stooped potterers. Nurturing vegetables to prizewinning enormity was a pastime self-evidently honed to obsession in the time-rich forty-two years since Grange Villa's nearest mine closed (and since 'Lily the Pink' topped the UK charts). The village had indeed become defined by its leisure pursuits, if not in the way Sky 3 wanted me to believe: I was bidden farewell from it by a rather fetching roadside bas-relief of a racing pigeon rampant above a trug of gargantuan produce. (I've always rather liked the whole peculiar concept of racing pigeons as a hobby, if not its guano-steeped reality – it's just one of those things I'm glad somebody does, as long as it's not me, like clearing gutters or giving a prostrate derelict the kiss of life. In any event, I was pleased to discover that the Royal Pigeon Racing Association still issues over a million identification rings a year.)

'Bulldozers are due to start the demolition of Gateshead town centre today.' It's difficult to imagine a more damning admission of civic failure than that reported by Newcastle's *Evening Chronicle* back in 2007. Not just a few offices or shops, not even a couple of streets – a town that 190,000 people called home was to have its entire heart ripped out, and just forty years after the last transplant.

It was twilight by the time Ozzy stuttered out the news of our arrival. Never before had his valedictory imprecation sounded so heartfelt. Squatting thuggishly atop the bluff that crowns Gateshead, Europe's ugliest public building loomed over all it surveyed like a medieval fortress. The twelve slitted storeys imparted an air of narrow-eyed, thick-set menace, and the service shafts attached to opposite corners made convincing fortified observation towers. In the sodium streetlight I could see its flanks streaked and pock-marked with scabby decay, like a beached whale after a fortnight on the sand. I saw what the *Chronicle* had meant: Trinity Square car park might be defined as a single building, but in scale and in bearing, it was the whole town centre. Imprisoned behind blue-painted building-site barriers the car park now stood vacant, but two years on those bulldozers still hadn't dared to confront it.

A slashed canvas smeared with pus and swastikas, atonal cries of fury: I'd have no issue with a Brutalist movement in art or music, safely confined as its artistic output would be by gallery walls or headphones. Brutalist dance I might even actively encourage. But you can't take or leave architecture. It's rather forced upon us. We have to look at it and walk around in it. It's there to be lived in, worked in, shopped in, parked in. As such, I will never understand how an architectural movement that dubbed itself Brutalism was ever allowed to exist, let alone thrive as it did in Britain for two fateful decades. 'Kids, wait till you see our new flat. It's so brutal!'

With an effort I can just about forgive the forbidding and repetitive flanks of raw concrete that went up all over Britain in the 1950s. Cities needed rebuilding, and there was no cheaper, quicker way of doing it. Heck, I'll even cut some slack for those architects and planners who convinced themselves that such grimly functional structures embodied the progressive, honest and classless fresh start the nation needed after the war. Their hearts were in the right place, even if their brains – and eyes – weren't.

But that rationale was wearing thin by 1969, when Gateshead council finally declared the Trinity Square complex open. It was partly their own fault for taking six years to get the thing built, six years in which Brutalism's brave future had curdled into a dour and cowering present. Because as it turned out, people didn't quite feel at home in an abstract environment of bald cement. Reinforced concrete, which aged so gracefully in Le Corbusier's pioneering Brutalist blocks in Marseilles and

India, wept tears of rusty mould when asked to cope with north-European winters. Those tempting blank canvases didn't cope much better with north-European vandals. 'Britain's first major free-standing multi-storey car park to incorporate a shopping centre,' trumpeted the original Trinity Square proposal, words that in 1964 might have dampened pants across Geordieland. By 1969, they effectively translated as, 'People of Gateshead, look upon me and despair.'

The first calls to have the car park knocked down rang out before it was even finished. After opening, Trinity Square wasted no time in acquiring the ambience that came to define its breed: that heady air of lawless neglect, scented with solvents and urine. The building had yet to celebrate its second birthday when the *Get Carter* crew arrived to film some of its more iconic sequences, but already bore the ravages of 'spalling' – a fragmentation of concrete surfaces typically seen in structures that are very old, and have been burnt to the ground. Its upper storeys were soon declared dangerously unsound and closed off; the glass-walled rooftop cafeteria, as smarmily patrolled by a corrupt property developer in the film, would never find a tenant.

You've got to hand it to the *Get Carter* location spotters, who perceptively connected the north-east's doomed and desolate past with its doomed and desolate future. Blackhall Colliery is no more, and – finally – nor is Trinity Square. It's rare to find a local with a good word to say about the film, though, as its belated discovery by *Loaded*-reading New Lads kick-started a noisy campaign to save the '*Get Carter* car park'. Gateshead council had first proposed knocking it down as early as 1981, with outline consent for demolition finally granted in 2000. Three years after that, Trinity Square came in at number seven in a national poll set up to find candidates for Channel 4's self-explanatory 2003 series *Demolition* (I won't spoil the suspense by revealing the winner, or the life-changing adventures I was soon to enjoy in its considerable shadow). One internet forum voted it the ugliest public structure in Europe, and another declared the car park 'Britain's most hated building'.

Yet *Get Carter* enthusiasts successfully shouted down much of this accumulated opprobrium: one cheerleader went as far as to claim that 'Trinity Square is to Gateshead what the Eiffel Tower is to Paris'. This procured a local online response heavy on phrases such as 'pathetic middle-class gangster wannabes' and 'Mockney cockhouse', along with multiple offers to help re-erect the car park 'in their fucking back gardens, if they love it so much'.

I found a guest house which in daylight might have afforded a view of Trinity Square. It was a stout old Victorian building run by a stout old landlady, with gloriously horrid orange carpeting and fire doors that parted with a drawn-out, abandon-hope creak. I was about to enter my room when the door next to it flew open, releasing a cloud of thick soot. Through this emerged a young man in overalls, looking like the survivor of a cartoon explosion. 'Areet,' he said, teeth agleam behind blackened lips. Then he inhaled hugely, plunged back into the room and slammed the door behind him.

Somebody had thoughtfully cleaved a jagged hole through the partition wall that this miniature mining disaster shared with my room, about the size of a firmly swung fist or rifle butt. But when I lowered my face to it, there was only blackness and the unmuffled sounds of masonry and joists putting up a decent fight against the blunt and bladed tools of destruction. The heftier blows forced a coil of sooty dust through the hole. I decided the sensible thing was to wodge newspaper in it and go out.

It probably didn't help that I experienced Gateshead's after-hours scene on a Wednesday in December, and from the gutter of a dual carriageway that I'd somehow ended up walking down. But my, it was dead. I'd girded myself for the Mockney-cockhouse showdown that seemed inevitable in any pedestrian encounter that required me to open my mouth (preparatory mantra: never *New*carsle, always New*cassle*), but even when I scrambled across a concrete roundabout and six lanes of tarmac to a proper street with a proper pavement, there were no pedestrians on it to encounter. Regional-degeneration FACT: the north east is the only area in the UK with a shrinking population, and no other town within it is leaching citizens faster than Gateshead.

Crossing the River Tyne felt like crossing from East Berlin to West in the 1980s, or passing through some strange portal on the International Date Line that took me from Wednesday to Friday night. At the Gateshead end of the High Level Bridge I walked past a pub whose doors emitted a desultory, decrepit, old-man mumble. Its counterpart at the Newcastle side was a heaving, riotous Babel of life and young laughter. Even halfway across the bridge I knew I was set to reacquaint myself with almost forgotten urban excitements. Gateshead bid me farewell with a notice urging would-be jumpers to telephone the Samaritans; Newcastle said hello with a breathtaking vista centred around the floodlit Tyne Bridge, Middlesbrough-built sister of the Sydney Harbour crossing. It was all bright lights and bustle and the beckoning promise of boozy, big-city fun. Who was I to resist?

My evening explored the overlap between happiness and bemusement, as pub crawls are wont to. What a heady thrill to walk down streets where the shop windows were filled with cashmere and porcelain, rather than dead flies and some crack-head's old microwave. Where watches sometimes cost more than £4.99, and parking bays were sometimes fully occupied. Where the festive illuminations were kookily naive as a knowing act of arch post-modernism, rather than just being really old and crap. Where the buildings were scrubbed and the pavements a-throng with bands of hearty merrymakers, some laughing, some singing, and, OK, some trying to smash in a glass door with a dustbin.

I dutifully went in search of terrible places, but it wasn't easy. The bar-lined cobbled oblong that is Bigg Market seemed a good bet: whenever the *Daily Mail* runs a photograph of a girl with one shoe on slumped in the gutter, that gutter is generally outside a Bigg Market binge-barn. Hopes were raised by a rash of promisingly catastrophic encitements in the relevant windows (*All house doubles £1 every night until 10 p.m.!*

Have two large glasses of wine and get the whole bottle free!
Spend more than £15 and wet yourself in an unlicensed
minicab on the way home!), but when I put my head round a
few doors I saw just a light smattering of restrained and
thoughtful drinkers, resembling young librarians on a staff night
out. The music didn't even seem especially awful, though
having only hours before endured Duran Duran's covers album
in its soul-stabbing entirety I was in no position to judge.

It was an odd experience to turn corner after corner and not
once find myself frowned down upon by some towering eyesore:
Newcastle naturally suffered lapses of post-war architectural
judgement, but owned up to the worst and had them removed
from the skyline. Westgate House featured alongside Trinity
Square in the *Demolition* series, an enormous concrete phone
directory wedged into a shelf of regal old leather-bound façades
on the city's showpiece thoroughfare: possibly the single most
unsympathetic urban development ever approved in Britain.
Now it was just a hole in the night.

A gold-framed restaurant review posted proudly in the
window of a curry house caught my now practised eye:
'Tandoori night proves a qualified hit' ran the headline, an
actually rather generous summary of the experience described
beneath: 'Our house special side-dish went back largely
untouched . . . the service was not what it could have been.'
Yet I went in and found the place packed; a waiter told me I'd
have to wait at least an hour, then eased forward my trouser
waistband and tipped a plate of leftovers into the gap.

In the end I settled for an all-you-can eat buffet warehouse
called Gekko's, in a food court atop a busy but bland glass-
walled mall that styled itself as *Newcastle's premier leisure*
and entertainment centre. The two-for-£3 cocktail menu swung
it: there between Leg Spreader and Monkey Brains was Bloody
Awful, which I felt duty bound to sample. It certainly didn't
disappoint, revealing itself as an ingeniously repulsive blend
of sambuca and something called Red Aftershock, which had
the ring of a petrol additive for boy racers, and the taste of
Benylin's foray into the liqueur market. The young East

European waiter raised one eyebrow when I ordered a brace, and the other when – after a tiny, face-crumpling sip – I summoned the cider chaser that at the time seemed the only sensible way of washing the stuff down.

The 50-yard flank of stainless-steel tubs that comprised the Gekko buffet had at first glance seemed brimming with bewilderingly random comestibles. But approaching it with a bellyful of strange alcohol, the whole set-up made perfect and beautiful sense. Sweet and sour pork, balti chicken, glistening towers of chips: here, in steamy profusion, was all that a young man desires to feast upon when drunk. Around me, whole convivial tablefuls of just such people were doing precisely that, interspersed with rather quieter pairings, a girlfriend wanly nibbling naan while her partner belched seven shades of Worthington over some pick-and-mix heap of spiced fodder. With Red Aftershock nudging the doors of perception ajar, I looked about and realised I'd been wrong to fear a Newcarsle shoeing. Geordies weren't so much hard as incorrigibly debauched, to the point of reckless derangement. They get unbelievably drunk and do unbelievably stupid things, like surfing trains, jumping into rivers and taking their shirts off at football matches in the depths of a hard winter. They are, in essence, Paul Gascoigne. For the Geordie male, life is one long, out-of-control stag party. Though obviously not that long.

As the first of my many trips to the Gents made plain, Gekko's was not a place where decorum stood tall. At one point the self-service cutlery station ran out of knives and forks, but rather than complain or wait, the punters simply shrugged and bullied their bhajis to bits with fists and teaspoons. Content that no one was interested in whatever I might get up to – after my second cider, even the waiter seemed to forsake me – I set about indulging to unsightly excess. I returned to the silvered tubs again and again, first with eager vigour, latterly with the grim, stumbling resolve of a contestant at a 1920s dance marathon. Ciders came and went. For a while I neutered their effect through sheer calorific input, a dam of carbohydrates to keep the alcoholic flood at bay. Modern technology permits me to reveal that this defence was breached at precisely 8.18 p.m., when I chose to take a phone-camera self-portrait. Focus and composition issues make definitive analysis a challenge, but it looks very much as if that's a prawn on my shoulder.

Out in the street I found myself in a whole city full of new friends: debonair, attractive, happy people, my people. They were there in that lovely bar with the light sculptures and the big glass something or other, a wonderful and cosmopolitan establishment I simply don't recognise in the review I've just read that damns it as 'over-priced and full of pretentious gits'. They were there – hello again! – in a pound-a-pint Wetherspoon pub. They were even there in some Seventies club on Bigg Market, where I nosed into inebriation's ugly end-game by very nearly dancing.

Cold night air is well known for its sobering properties, and I went through a couple of thousand lungfuls while getting hopelessly lost in the coal-smoked, terraced back streets of Gateshead. Finding my guest house had proved remarkably straightforward, but swaying gently beneath its porch-mounted baskets of plastic flora I'd checked my watch and noted it wasn't quite ten: way too early to have got into this state, let alone to consider going to bed now that I was. I found myself seized by an urge to round the night off with a visit to the Pear Tree Inn, a Gateshead pub that irresistibly counted a horse amongst its regulars. ('I called in to attend a bank holiday karaoke,' ran one online memory, 'and there he was at the bar, drinking beer out of a bucket.')

A vague idea that the Pear Tree lay somewhere close at hand was hardened into a cidery, cast-iron conviction that it was precisely here, just up this empty, dark street of identical little Victorian houses, and left at the end. OK, maybe it was right. Oh, I get it: I'm remembering the map upside down. It's back across here and down this empty, dark street of . . . hang on.

After a lot more of this, I discovered I was not after all alone in Gateshead. A group of old men were gathered under a street-light, and I all but grabbed the nearest by the collar. Perhaps it was the befuddling revelation that this collar, and all the others, was attached to a long black frock coat, and set off with a Homburg and a full grey beard. Perhaps it was no more than the amnesia of the drunk and weary. For whatever reason, I now found myself badgering a huddle of elderly orthodox Jews for directions to a pub whose name I no longer remembered.

'Excuse me,' I began, filling their worried faces with Red Aftershock. 'I'm looking for the, ah, that, you know, that pub with the horse.'

In silence I watched fear evolve into something else. There were mutters and scowls, and suddenly I knew what it was: disgust. I rewound my question and came to a horrid conclusion. Turning around and going away would have been a good choice at this point, but Mr Cider would have none of it. 'No – not the *whores*, the *horse*! Hor-*sssss*: neigh, neigh! Like a big pony. They put down a bucket by the bar and the whores – the horse! – comes in and drinks out of it.'

Every face but one was now pointed at the pavement. It belonged to the youngster, whose beard still bore the odd fleck of black. 'I cannot help you,' he said, faltering and guttural. 'Down there is nice restaurant. Maybe you ask.'

How extraordinary to discover, as I did the next morning, that Gateshead is revered by Jews around the world as one of their faith's most feted centres of learning. Its trio of Talmudic colleges draw students and religious educators from across the globe, and are accepted as the most important outside the US and Israel. The first Jewish refugees arrived in Gateshead from Eastern Europe in the late nineteenth century, and the local ultra-orthodox population has since swelled to 1,500: many decamped from Newcastle and Hartlepool, disillusioned with the religious laxity of their local congregations. Gateshead was, and for most still is, a town where young Jewish men and women do their shopping at different times of the day, to forestall unsupervised mingling of the sexes.

And yet this ultra-orthodox community co-exists in harmony with a healthy local Muslim population, to the extent of advising drunken out-of-towners to seek directions from a kebab shop, as I presently discovered the nice restaurant to be.

'Is pub of young generation?' All things considered I doubted it – a horse is no youthful plaything – and told the kebab man as much. 'OK,' he said, wiping his hands on his apron as a prelude to much pointing. I set off fairly certain that his gesticulations would not lead me to the Pear Tree Inn. Sure enough, a while later I heaved open a door handle girdled in tinsel, and found myself inside the Nursery House Working Men's Club.

I strove to exude a sense of entitlement as I approached the bar, a gait and bearing that said: here is a man, a man who works. With every sticky step across the beer-steeped carpet swirls I expected conversation to stop dead and dominoes to clatter to the table, the oily palm placed firmly against my chest, the grubby thumb jabbed wordlessly at a notice over the bar: MEMBERS ONLY. ALSO, NO PONCES. But the half-dozen drinkers, mostly retirees with big moustaches, just mumbled on good-naturedly to each other. One or two even acknowledged me with tiny nods. All the same, I heard myself order a pint of lager from the young barman in a pathetic murmur stripped of geographical giveaways. After a moment's reflection he placed before me a large bottle of Newcastle Brown Ale and a very little glass. I had a stab at a grateful smile and passed him a fiver.

At a small table in the corner I sipped bitter-sweet amber and slid gently into a matching reverie. My gaze drifted from the wall-mounted telly broadcasting silent coverage of a Spanish league match and up to the low-slung ceiling, its polystyrene tiles spattered with the ghostly stains of past exuberance. Around me, my fellow drinkers idly discussed motor caravans and the perfect Sunday dinner, punctuating every contribution with languid nods and deep, approving murmurs of 'aye'. I sat there and savoured the low-key masculinity of it all, just happy to be accepted for what I was – a drunkard who didn't want any trouble. How uniquely soothing was the sound of old men agreeing with each other. Or rather, how affectingly, unbearably poignant. That's alcohol for you.

In 1976 there were over four thousand working men's clubs

in Britain. Now there are half that, with two closing down every week. The Nursery House and the way of life that went with it were clearly not long for this world: my arrival lowered the occupants' average age by some margin. On a wall outside the Gents, a massed group photo of a 1960s club coach outing told of a thriving past, as did the yawning battery of urinals within. Until 2004, the Working Men's Club and Institute Union operated its own Tyneside brewery, an arrangement that allowed members to imbibe at heavily subsidised prices. That year the CIU sold up to a duke who made his fortune filling in decommissioned mine shafts with a patent hard-bonding slurry of kidnapped racing pigeons and bits of Hartlepool, and the plant now manufactures solid-gold top hats. In fact, it produces brown ale on behalf of Scottish & Newcastle Breweries, but the point stands. I'd no doubt be appalled if I had any idea what my bottle would have cost in 2003, or indeed any memory of what I paid for it in 2009.

I certainly don't remember much about the reasoning process that now persuaded me to finish off my stay at the Nursery House with a large glass of ruby port, and a good old chinwag at the bar with the young man who doubtfully placed it before me.

'Quiet tonight,' I began. 'Had thirty urinals to myself.'

For whatever reason this failed to break the ice, as did further attempts to kick-start chats about his town centre's stupendous ugliness, and the coal mine in my guest house. Losing patience with the barman's tiny nods and his sudden interest in Athletico Madrid v Espanyol, I elected to redress the conversational imbalance in the only obvious manner.

'I'm in seals, me,' I announced, wiping a rivulet of fortified wine from my chin. 'Footwear. On the rude, like.' I was speaking Geordie, and if the dominant part of my mind was to be believed, doing so with fluent ease.

For some time, I fear, I held forth upon the canniness of wor life as a travelling shoe and boot salesman, gannin up and doon the A1, a hinny in every Dolcis. Then, quite suddenly, I succumbed to a terrible leaden fatigue and in a triumph of determination over coordination made my way across the bar. At the threshold I wheeled round to hoist a farewell hand at my fellow working men. 'Howay the shoes!' I cried, before noisily and repeatedly attempting to exit through a locked door.

Chapter Seven

It was a busy night at the guest house. At some point someone stealthily entered my room, threw clothes all over the floor, and left both taps in the sink running. Towards dawn they busied themselves tuning everyone else's television to *GMTV* at maximum volume, before creeping back into my room and redecorating it in a particularly effusive shade of brilliant white. Still their work was not done: the elderly couple who shared my table at breakfast couldn't speak highly enough of their full English, but mine had quite obviously been fried in cod liver oil.

A turn of Craig's key let forth a Satanic roar, and a far more terrible noise: the bleated, helium-huffing croak of a man pretending to be a plastic green duck. The reflex convulsion thus unleashed introduced my knee to the MP3 stalk, briefly separating it from the power supply in a manner that caused the track to recommence from its awful beginning. My groan tasted of old beer and young eggs. 'Orville's Song', perhaps my deepest excursion yet into the darkest heart of Maestro Man crap culture, an age when a middle-aged, mullet-permed ventriloquist called Keith could bag his own primetime show, and front it for eight straight years. To get an idea of just how far Britain had sunk by this time, one need only note that Keith Harris recorded 'Orville's Song' at Abbey Road studios, and that it sold 750,000 copies – one each for every Maestro owner, with enough left over to build a monumental vinyl statue of John Bull and Britannia kneeling down with their heads in an oven.

With Orville turned down to a sickly whisper I drove away very slowly through a gathering drizzle, back towards the town centre. It was plain from a distance that a good night's sleep and a shower hadn't done much for Trinity Square's looks. Every metaphor of structural ugliness tolled through my dull mind as its bullying bulk rose up: the Tony Montana of scars on the horizon, the Rorschach of blots on the landscape, the Cyclops and lemon juice of eyesores. Matron – the screens!

An entire town dominated by a car park? How very stupid we all were in the Sixties and Seventies. I supposed this was our final temple to transport, just as Paragon station in Hull had been one of our first. An appropriately hideous mausoleum for the childish fixation that compelled us to design whole cities around the motor vehicle, elevating a rather handy means of getting about into the very basis of society.

Demolition work finally began eight months after I passed through. Trinity Square is now no more, though it's hard to call an ending happy when it involves a 100,000-square-foot Tesco. Don't get me wrong: I like big Tescos. I'd grown to like them especially over recent days, with their cheap petrol and free toilets, and their unrivalled range of stupid Christmas crap for hungover absent fathers to cram tearfully into their car boots. But seductive as the rationale most surely is, the simple fact that I happen to really like something isn't always enough to justify its endless proliferation. I nobly accept, for instance, that some street corners might not benefit from a Mustard World superstore, and that paisley button-down shirts aren't for everyone. I'm not saying Trinity Square should be mourned, or – before anyone in Gateshead starts loading up the trucks – re-erected in my back garden. But as wrongheaded and hideous as the place most assuredly was, at least it had character and a kind of integrity, the product of public-spirited artists who confidently and genuinely believed they were creating something beautiful and good. Flimsy, faceless, off-the-shelf, conceived and designed by Excel spreadsheet: this is your basic massive Tesco. It's ruthlessly cynical, but worse than that, it's just so brain-drainingly dull. Tedium is insidious. People, almost by definition, just put up with it. The provocative ghastliness of Trinity Square stoked the fire in Gateshead bellies, forced the locals to come together and take a stand. Hatred is so much more energising, so much more *fun*. These days every new building in Britain, every new anything, is run through an endless blandification mill of public inquiries, community consultations and focus groups. Edges are knocked off, controversies neutered, any flavour but vanilla spat out. The result is an inexorable convergence towards the middle ground. These days you don't get ugly, offensive, ridiculous cars, or towns, or even music. Everything looks the same, sounds the same. Everything's boringly competent. Everything's one big massive Tesco. I glanced at the doomed Trinity Square in Craig's rear-view mirror, and felt a pang of melancholy for what it represented: a fallen dynasty of magnificent wrongness, our golden age of crap. Then I hit play, discharging an unsteady wail of late-era Billy Idol, and the moment passed.

I motored inland, north-west up a dual carriageway lined with some desperately dour moorland. It was as flat and featureless as Lincolnshire but very much yellower, all sickly and peat-poisoned, with the discouraging, boggy look of a land where it never stopped raining. All morning a sky the colour of last night's mushroom soup wrung itself out in Craig's face. After passing through so many man-made black spots whose ugliness had been thrust upon them, here at last was an area of outstanding natural disfigurement.

Hell's jukebox chipped in with a work by metal-mouthed, python-owning skinhead Goldie, quite certainly recorded, released and marketed by people who were simply too scared to call any of its manifold deficiencies to his attention. The track began and ended with the kind of breathy, synthesised noodlings that might play under documentary footage of a coral reef, interrupted by a bewildering burst of manic, staccato drum 'n' bass thrumps and furious shouting. It was like being yanked out of a coma with a massive espresso shot injected straight into your heart, and then dying. This experience went under the name of 'Mother', and endured for sixty-one minutes.

I pulled over just outside Wall, a village named in honour of the ancient imperial Pict-thwarter that passes by it. Courtesy of Craig's cardboard floorpan my feet were sodden even before I got out to follow a heavily reconstructed stub of it up a very wet hill. All around was lumpy mud and leaf mulch, not much fun in damp shoes but a lot less in imperial-issue sandals. Hadrian's Wall was the Roman Empire's grimmest outpost, so dependably inhospitable that its guardians were the first legionaries permitted to wear socks. Over 15,000 soldiers came up here to build it, and almost as many were required to patrol the 84-mile fortifications: it's estimated that one in six imperial legionaries would have done a tour of duty on the wall. Every one of them would eagerly have nominated it for demolition, then thrown up their cold blue hands in despair when Londinium-based *Get Caesar* fans launched a campaign to save it.

England mustered itself to a last surge of undulating greenery and village churchyards, then a light sleet speckled Craig's glazing and everything went bleak and bald and windswept. I was welcomed into Scotland by low hills and lower clouds, and a large red van which pulled straight out in front of me from a lay-by and then proceeded in a manner consistent with the transport of plutonium in open vats. I was still crawling along behind it when we wound into Hawick, famed for knitted socks, being pronounced hoick and 'really spoiling the Borders'.

Hawick's impressive rap sheet was gleaned from an article in the *Scotsman* and plentiful online discussions headed things like 'Worst shithole in Scotland?', all of them keenly debated by natives with something close to pride. The town's Borders-spoiling assets ranged from 'truly horrible pubs' to 'the unfriend-liest rugby club in Scotland', with special mention for a survey in which the Hawick ward of Burnfoot and Mansfield pipped many more notorious national rivals as the very worst place in Scotland to rear children.

If the pubs had been open and I'd found the rugby club it might have been different. As it was Hawick seemed blameless, though I did see two old men emerge from a metal shed advertising 'horse carrots', chewing hard. A legacy of the days when the sock was king, the gracious sandstone banks and public buildings on Hawick High Street were holding their heads up despite the parade of to-let signs and charity shops that faced them. If the people hurrying past looked a little grumpier than I'd become accustomed to, that was surely just down to the sluicing, relentless rain, and being Scottish. It's also an enduring truth that any small town with a big river running straight through it – particularly a half-tamed, semi-Alpine tumbler such as the Teviot showed itself to be – can never attain true ignominy.

In the spirit of dedicated enquiry I tracked down Burnfoot and Mansfield, in fact no more than a handful of streets bordered by overgrown wasteland that I guessed had once been home to riverside textile mills. Hawick clearly wasn't an ideal place to grow up: the council-sponsored downtown 'youth café' betrayed a plaintive quest to find wholesome remedies for juvenile boredom. Still, I wasn't sure what to expect in Burnfoot and Mansfield's finely demarcated concentration of wayward husbandry: shoeless bairns bobbing for horse carrots in an open trough of Irn Bru, perhaps, or duelling with Hartlepool maces on the roof of a burnt-out ice-cream van. Instead, I piloted Craig down quiet and well-kept rows of semi-detached pebble-dash and Victorian granite. There was a cluster of starkly horrible three-floor 1960s tenement blocks that no one would want to call home, but then no one now did: all were boarded up and primed for demolition. I figured Burnfoot and Mansfield was a statistical victim of its own tininess: the entire survey sample could have been corrupted by a single hungover Burnfoot Begbie telling a doorstep researcher to stick his clipboard up his bahookie.

It was a long haul across soggy, open heather to Forth, a town of three thousand just a few miles south of Scotland's dominant conurbations yet which somehow didn't get electricity until the mid 1930s, and still hasn't got gas. Stuck on a barren South Lanarkshire hill and forgotten about, Forth had by all accounts gone a bit funny. Beyond the predictable online comments about inbreeding and tumbleweed, a constant theme emerged amongst those haunted by the place, sometimes after no more than a single drive-through encounter many years previously. 'There's something eerie about it'; 'an odd town'; 'it's just not quite right'. Forth was Bad: 'I used to take deliveries up there every night, and the amount of fights I saw was surreal. They're all fucking nuts.' And Forth was Mad: 'We fancied a pint after a local league match at Forth and someone directed us to the British Legion – found the place and it had closed down years before. Ended up in the Masonic Lodge, watching Gretna v Dundee on the telly.' The windswept streets of Scotland's strangest place were naturally enough roamed by a race of giants: George Gracie, one of many Forthians to have topped out above 7 foot, was for a while Britain's tallest man. No extruded, glandular beanpole he – at 32 stone, Gracie was just a properly enormous bloke. His party piece at fairgrounds in the late Fifties and Sixties was to hoist a massive leg up on the roof of a Mini, like a mighty child trying to squeeze into an infant's pedal car. Photographers captured this pose with care: Gracie always wore a kilt.

The final approach made it plain that Forth was not an obvious magnet for human settlement. WARNING: BOG ROAD, read a sign at the last junction. As the lonely roofs of the town took shape on the misty brow ahead, so too did the energetically rotating blades of what was once the UK's largest inland windfarm. The winters here were evidently hard even by regional standards, and so were the inhabitants: such a proximate eyesore was an almost thrilling retort to the nimby trend. My back yard? Fuck my back yard.

Pebble-dash, or roughcast, is as old as the Romans. From their time until the Great War, architects and builders employed it as a widely admired decorative finish. Today, of course, pebble-dash is simply a devastatingly effective means of wiping 10 per cent off the value of your home. The rot set in when developers put roughcast to work as exterior Artex: with half the nation's bricklayers cut down on the fields of Flanders and Picardy, there were suddenly plenty of poorly finished new houses – and crumbling old ones – in need of a quick and cheap layer of slap. This trend reached epidemic proportions in areas where the material's low-maintenance durability promised additional benefits: 'In remote and weather-beaten places,' writes one architectural historian, 'pebble-dash seemed both sensible and stylish.' Slathered from head to toe in the stuff, Forth was a one-town rebuke to this verdict. Almost every home I drove past sat mired in that death-coloured porridge of sand, cement and gravel. Style may come and go, but there didn't seem anything sensible in the dark patches of damp blotting almost every roughcast surface, nor the hefty chunks of it that had fallen off. You could imagine the letters dropping through local letterboxes: 'Congratulations: as the resident of a poorly built house in a remote and weather-beaten place, you have qualified for South Lanarkshire's compulsory pebble-dashing programme. Close your windows and stay indoors.'

It was a town laid out without love, and built without care. Only one of Forth's undulating heathery panoramas was topped with a windfarm, yet almost every house turned its back on the view, instead staring out at its mouldering, roughcast clones across a cheerless square of patchy grass and a NO BALL GAMES sign. Barbed wire was strung right around the roofs of lock-up garages, perhaps the legacy of unusually determined burglars, perhaps of George Gracie on the rampage. Here atop a lonely hill they'd somehow managed to recreate the ambience of a truly horrid urban housing estate. *Welcome to Forth*, read the banner my mind slung across this vista. *We live here so you don't have to.*

The ironworks that was Forth's principal *raison d'être* shut down in 1940, followed in due course by the local coal mines, the railway station, the cinema, the brass band, the police station, and George Gracie's overworked heart. Yet Forth wouldn't die. In fact, its population is still growing. Nothing about the place made sense. The high street was a long, grey straggle of grimness, all grubby second-hand car dealerships and takeaways. Only the tanning salon seemed to be thriving: a group of homebound schoolkids were shuffling about outside while their mothers filed in for a Tango top-up.

There are now eight hundred tanning salons in Scotland, more than the national stock of chip shops, which is saying something. If there's a health-hazard bandwagon to jump aboard, the Scots will push everyone else off and drive it whooping over a cliff. These people just can't do bad things by halves. The appeal of ultra-violet tanning seems to echo an inter-war builder's attachment to pebble-dash: a cost-effective way to conceal shoddy exterior work, especially in weather-beaten places. The comparison works in the longer term, too, as neither technique has proved durably stylish or at all sensible. More Scots die from skin cancer than Australians, with at least 150 annual deaths attributed directly to tanning salons. In fact, Scottish women now endure the highest incidence of malignant melanoma of any demographic group in the world, up three-fold in a generation, entirely as a result of their addiction to coin-in-the-slot sunbeds. One deeply creosoted sufferer told doctors she'd notched up three thousand sessions in twelve years.

I bumped on to the petrol station's forecourt past a local-paper newsboard reading, VICTORY FOR VANDALS, and filled Craig up in the cold wind. This establishment had been severally identified as a hot spot of Forthian oddness: one motorist recalled how the attendant had insisted on trying to guess his name from the initials on his bank card, only to turn nasty when he failed.

'Is it Donald?'

'Er, no.'

'David?'

'Look, it's Douglas. My middle name's Alexander.'

'I don't *need* to know your middle name.'

But the cheerful girl at the counter processed my card without a glance at its details, a source of some relief given that the least embarrassing of my two middle names is Sebastian. She was still smiling when, a while later, I handed back a wooden heart the size of a medieval shield, and the lavatory key to which it was attached. 'Och, so how did that go, then?' In my haste to leave I left Craig's filler cap on top of the petrol pump.

Almost at once the clouds scurried away to the distant horizon. The sun burst forth and the golden moorland around was suddenly framed in more rainbows than I've ever seen sharing the same sky. 'Pump up the Bitter' gave way to 'Leap Up and Down (Wave Your Knickers in the Air)', Ozzy yelled out the big swears and all was right with the world as I'd come to know it.

I arrived in Cowdenbeath after darkness, which this far north in December kicked in well before *Countdown*. My familiarity with the town was limited to hearing its football team name-checked at the tail end of Radio 5's Saturday-afternoon results. Somehow I always pictured the footballers of Cowdenbeath, in fact every footballer in Scottish League Division Two, plying their trade on a sloping rectangle of coarsely mown heather in some windswept Highland outpost. In fact, Cowdenbeath FC and almost all its rivals are squeezed into the M8 corridor, the short, fat belt of almost unbroken development between the opposing firths of Clyde and Forth that almost everyone in Scotland calls home. I have before me a map of Scottish football clubs: imagine a shooting target fired at a great many times by an expert sniper, and then – ah, go on, sweetheart, just a couple of quick rounds – by his four-year-old niece. (Bang! Inverness Caledonian Thistle. Bang! Elgin City.) Suffice to say that stags on the pitch are not the problem I'd imagined them to be at the very urban likes of Falkirk, Stenhousemuir or Airdrieonians.

Cowdenbeath FC were once known as 'The Miners', but unsurprisingly now aren't. The town that dubbed itself 'The Chicago of Fife' when a modest late-Victorian colliery-linked boom raised the population to twenty thousand is clearly well schooled in the ironic arts, and have accordingly re-nicknamed their team – average home attendance 421 – 'The Blue Brazil'. I didn't find the ground, even though there wasn't much to Cowdenbeath – certainly a lot less than there might have been in 1949, when 25,586 turned out to watch The Miners take on the might of Rangers in a League Cup quarter-final, more than double the entire current population. My quest for accommodation took me up and down the narrow high street, railway bridge across one end, flaky-fronted old cinema-turned-bingo hall at the other. The dominant retail outlet between was festooned with a banner that read, *Fife's Largest Furniture Charity*. After a lot of driving about I found a pub that looked likely to contain people who might understand me, or at least not get too annoyed if they didn't, and went inside to ask for help.

It was a whisker after five but the trio of old chaps at the dim and silent bar had clearly been in situ for some time. Each had a pint and a whisky chaser on the go, yet all seemed genteel and respectable; three smart overcoats hung from pegs by the door, and they nodded at me courteously when I walked in. Then a barmaid of middle years breezed into her station through the hindward saloon doors, elaborately made up and exuding a dangerous waft of thwarted, resentful boredom.

'Och, it's your lucky dee,' she said, brightening in response to a new face. 'We've a few wee rums upstarers.' That was splendid news, and I told her so, adding that I'd just need to go and move my car, which was outside on a double yellow. 'Nae bother, we've a car park oot the back,' she said, smiling now and fiddling with a spray-crisped lock of Dark Intense Auburn. 'So what have you done wrong to desererve a night in Cowdenbeath, you knotty man?'

'I'm in marketing. Face-to-face roaming retail.'

The nearest of the old Shankleys at the bar half-turned and spoke in a gravelly growl. 'That like travlin sales?'

'Well, yes,' I conceded with an airy and indulgent half-laugh, trying to sound like James Bond being asked if he was a policeman. 'Yes, I suppose in a way it is.' Doubt and disappointment snagged the barmaid's powdered features. 'Exclusive luxury merchandise,' I went on, quickly. 'Not, you know, carpet-tile adhesive or shoe-pencils or whatever.'

'You mean like collectables?'

'That is *exactly* what I mean. High-class collectables.'

That was more than enough to be getting on with, but I felt powerless to hold back the flood of idiotic cobblers that had built up in my head during those long, long hours with only bleak moorland and novelty hits for company. 'Animals,' I announced confidently. 'Animal figurines. I'm talking top-end kit here. We do a crystal rabbit for £7,000. It's massive, like this high.' I held a hand out by my shoulder. 'Just sold three to Barry Whitfield, who produced "Agadoo", and also appears in the video as a pear.'

'Oh aye,' said the barmaid gamely, as if giving me the benefit of a Grampian-sized doubt. 'Well, just wait here a wee minute and I'll make some space oot back. Should be able to squeeze yerself in by my Fiesta.' She raised a pencilled brow and chuckled suggestively – all the Shankleys looked up at that – then sashayed out into the cold. She was back in before the door had time to close.

'That you with the hazards on?' Gone was the sashay, and the smile. I nodded, and she nodded back, fixing me with a brief but horribly withering stare. How dare you, *how dare you*, come flouncing in here with your promise of adventure and excitement and not being seventy-four years old, driving . . . driving . . . ? oh, you pathetic little man. And with a great clicking of tall and tiny heels, out she went through the doors behind the bar.

The landlady caught me just as I was about to go outside and move Craig, perhaps as far as Carlisle. She was a slightly harassed woman with a number of young children in tow, many of whom accompanied us on a tour up to and around my room. Being the size of a snooker table this certainly made for a memorable experience. Not much else did, once I had the place to myself. It was over-lit and under-decorated. Mildew seeped into my nostrils. The net curtains billowed as a Baltic gust barged its way in around the tall, narrow window frame. Someone next door was trying to cough up a fur ball. Suddenly very aware that I wasn't even supposed to be in Cowdenbeath, I put on two pairs of gloves and went out.

You might imagine the inhabitants of Lochgelly having strong words for the London-based national newspaper which decided that as the home of the UK's cheapest houses, their town deserved to be condemned in print as 'the last place in Britain people want to live'. But as I'd already discovered, there's nothing a Scot enjoys more than kicking his town when it's down. The *Observer* found plenty of locals happy to agree that an average property price of £55,000 made their former mining town precisely seven times worse than Henley-on-Thames, where the houses – Britain's dearest – were seven times more expensive. 'I'll tell you why Lochgelly is cheapest,' a retired steel fitter told the reporter, 'because it's like Beirut.' The online comments that ensued were more damning still. 'I grew up there and, by God, they're right: the place corrodes your very soul . . .' 'It's a pity Osama bin Laden wouldn't pay Lochgelly a visit and put us all out of our misery . . .' 'Everyone just sits at home in front of their two-bar electric fires, drinking Kestrel and watching Sky telly . . .', 'Since the bypass opened, no one at all has any reason to come here, except the drugs squad and the occasional sociologist . . .'

And me. Cowdenbeath was merely my staging post, the nearest place to the Beirut of Fife that promised a bed for the night. The towns lay no more than three miles apart: a five-minute drive or a twenty-five-minute wait for a bus, if you've undertaken to spend a long evening in Lochgelly and have contemplated its entertainment options in advance. With the aftershocks of Red Aftershock still rumbling through me I could muster little enthusiasm for alcohol. But the alternative didn't even bear thinking about: going alone into a Scottish pub and ordering four hours' worth of soft drinks in a London accent.

The bus ride was all condensation, diesel and swearing. Scotland appears to have carried through a major devaluation of profanity's dominant currency, the Fuck. In the ten minutes before the doors hissed me back out into the cold I heard the word casually piped, murmured and drawled three dozen or more times, by smooth-cheeked young bairns and well-kempt old men. And never with the slightest malice or aggression: the Scottish Fuck is sprinkled liberally into everyday humdrum conversation as no more than a mild intensifier. As a linguistic condiment it's salt and pepper, not Three-Alarm Wasabi Tabasco.

'All right there?' intoned an elderly voice behind me. 'How the fuck are you doin'?'

'No bad. Aw, but this bag is fucken killin' my shoulder.'

A while later, from two rows in front: 'Aye, I saw that last night. What a fucken belter. Fuck me.' It was the pleasantly lilted, home-spun discourse of *Dr Finlay's Fuck Book*, or *Fucker of the Glen*.

The declining impact of fuck's north-of-the-border potency was legally recognised in 2001, during Kenneth Kinnaird's appeal against a breach of the peace conviction. Kinnaird, a forty-three-year-old Glaswegian, had been arrested and charged in Edinburgh after telling a traffic policeman to fuck off. His defence counsel enlisted a professor of English, who told the court, 'Fuck seems to me hardly countable as an expletive. Rather it is used as a reinforcing adverb: it's fucking cold, hot, terrible, whatever.' Kinnaird, of course, wasn't using the word in anything like this context; he was instead telling a policeman to fuck off. Nevertheless, the presiding judge sustained the appeal, excusing Kinnaird for doing no more than 'using the language of his generation'. As a member of that generation, I was already picturing myself knocking on the window of a stationary patrol car and clearing my throat.

I set off up Lochgelly's dark and deserted Main Street gasping breath in through clenched teeth and shuddering like a Maestro at tick-over – why, it's almost as if it was December, and I was in Scotland. Cars droned by. I pushed at the unyielding door of a pub before noting the boarded-up windows and a hopeful appeal for new ownership. Many other enterprises had been cleared away, leaving the straggly commercial survivors bordered with unsettling swathes of open land. A trio of hoodies mooched silently about the Christmas tree by the miners' memorial. Lochgelly seemed determined not to defy its local critics, though in fairness I uncovered little definite evidence of Syrian-backed guerrilla activity.

I can reserve particular praise for the native commentator who encapsulated his hometown as 'an S-bend with chip shops'. Lochgelly is home to six thousand souls, enough to sustain one each of the usual high-street enterprises: an undertaker, a Spar, a baker, a bookie's and so on. Above that it's a select group. I passed two tanning salons. I passed three pubs. And I passed four chip shops – make that five, because the China Chef prominently advertised its battered sideline. Even if you're having aromatic crispy duck, eating out in Lochgelly means stuffing in those deep-fried yellow sticks that up here they call Glasgow salad.

I went into the last, the Golden Fry, a swish and busy enterprise with half a dozen uniformed staff behind the counter and a parade of saturated fats advertised above it. Though not quite the full parade. I'd read that a quarter of Scottish chip shops offered the notorious catering cataclysm that is the battered, deep-fried Mars Bar, but it didn't feature on the Golden Fry. In fact, I never found the food world's unholy grail on offer anywhere in the land. Nor was I ever able to treat myself to the national drunkard's delight that is the 'munchy box': a foot-square pizza carton crammed with onion rings, doner meat shavings, hunks of nan bread and nuggets of assorted bhaji, all served on a bed of Glasgow salad. After some deliberation, having learnt somewhere that Scottish establishments generally gave it the dip-and-sizzle treatment, I plumped for a 'pizza supper'. The last word added a veneer of nutritional respectability to my order, suggesting a balanced meal with representation from across the food groups. But in Scotland it simply means 'and chips'.

There'd been a spot of linguistic awkwardness on the bus, when securing a ticket from the driver meant three attempts at the single word 'Lochgelly', the first two eliciting looks of embarrassed amusement, as if I'd just impersonated an animal. With this in mind, and perhaps eighteen local ears cocked in close attendance, when I reached the head of the Golden Fry queue I heard myself round off the word 'supper' in a ridiculous thrumming roll. The woman at the counter nodded blandly and started piling the right things into a big Styrofoam box.

Relief was swiftly subsumed by the realisation that this was how I'd have to talk until the end of my days, or until I left Scotland. On these rations it was going to be a close call.

My wife's youngest brother and his wife work as doctors in Scotland, and have both served time at a Fife-based coronary-care unit. This is handily located right opposite a chip shop, and it's apparently easier to count the outpatients who don't cross the road and walk straight into it upon leaving the clinic. Two-thirds of Scotsmen are overweight. Scottish women are the fattest in Europe. A fancy-that fact-box in a world atlas of human geography says of the nation: 'Scotland has the worst diet of any developed country in the western world, and the highest incidence of heart disease.'

With none of this in mind I prised open my Styrofoam casket on a bench up the road, and forced myself to register dismay that the pizza thus revealed was in no way battered or deep-fried. It just wasn't very nice, a ketchup-topped sponge soggy with the vinegar substitute that had been showered upon my supper as a non-optional extra. I tore off and ingested a ragged chunk before accepting that even with a lapful of hot food, it was much too cold to stay still. So off I stamped around the back streets of Lochgelly, wreathed in coal smoke and fumbling at super-heated chips with deep-frozen fingers. The roads were lined with cramped little semis and 1960s bungalows: Britain's cheapest houses, in their flimsy, pebble-dashed glory. All had the kind of scuffed and anonymous front door you could imagine a TV interviewer knocking upon at the end of a quest to track down some forgotten star of yesteryear: an aged footballing legend living alone in straitened circumstances, maybe, or a Bay City Roller back home with his mum. The curtained downstairs windows glowed with light and warmth: everyone was sensibly inside, perhaps watching Sky by two-bar electric fires, though definitely not drinking Kestrel – which, speaking as a major player in the crap-arse 3 per cent lager scene, I can confirm has not been brewed since around 2003.

After a premature mouthful of yellow embers I let my supper cool for a while. Once it had done so, and my blistered tastebuds were pulsing less furiously, I was able to establish that these were chips from the loftiest zenith of British high-street catering, made as only we can make them, and loved as only we would dare to love them: fat, soft and slippery with oil and non-brewed condiment. Just what the doctor ordered (everyone in Scotland to stop eating).

Replete and greasy, I headed back to Main Street, and its lonely pools of sodium light. I had three hours to kill before the last bus to Cowdenbeath, and put them slowly to death in Lochgelly's very strange pubs. The first was called the Silver Tassie, an entirely purple establishment I shared with an unhappy young barmaid, a sprightly old lady and an enormous industrial fan heater. Brilliantly effective in the production of throbbing decibels, this machine performed less ably in its primary role. When I successfully ordered a half-pint of Tarrrrrtan and raised it to my lips, breath steamed out across its brown surface, followed by the sound of teeth chattering against glass.

'Grey Oscar phone!' came a cheery bellow above the rotary roar. I looked up from my bar stool and saw the old lady, sat two tables away right in front of the heater, addressing somebody. Hopes that it might not have been me ebbed away when I noted the barmaid had sloped off. The old lady cupped her hands and tried again. 'Gayer star fun!' There was nothing for it: I stood up and walked across with benevolence and fore-boding battling it out on my features. The latter rallied strongly when I spotted the chaser hiding behind her half pint. 'It's perishing in here!' she shouted, white hair being whipped across her spectacles by the tepid and deafening gale. 'I was just saying to get your scarf on!'

I nodded and smiled, and so did she. In the circumstances it seemed unthinkably rude to walk away, so I sat down. We smiled, we nodded, we took small sips from our small glasses. Occasionally the companionable silence was punctured with a strident cry, and its yet more strident echo. 'Wee bit o' heat coming off that now!' she'd yell, hoicking a thumb at the wind machine. Then: 'I was just saying there's a WEE BIT O' HEAT COMING OFF THAT NOW!'

There wasn't – I'd just had to put my gloves back on – but of course I smiled and nodded anyway. Presently I cocked a hand to my mouth, bent towards her ear and yelled, 'So you're a regular here, then?' A very unhappy moment now passed, during which I pondered that of the two gambits implied by this approach, the least awful involved me accusing an eighty-year-old woman of being an alcoholic. But strangely, and wonderfully, she just looked out into the purple gloom, smiling, nodding, deaf as a post. I drained my half with a much larger sip, raised a gloved hand, then stepped outside and jogged up the road.

My second pub of the night offered a further bracing reminder that the rigid design diktats of chain ownership have no power in Lochgelly. With their chalkboard specials, artfully distressed wooden flooring and gas-fired fake coals, British pubs are starting to look more and more like each other. But Shardy's, a tough little cream-coloured cube with bars on the windows, looked more like a cowboy prison. Inside was a single room whose decor defied categorisation: a chestnut-roaster nailed obliquely to an orange wall, an overpowered spotlight slung from a yellow ceiling, dun-coloured carpet tiles, chrome chairs with brown Dralon cushions. The place had the ramshackle, thrown-together look of off-campus student accommodation. So too, in a mature, university-of-life kind of way, did the four-strong clientele.

'Heavy' looked promisingly weird when I spotted it on the front of a pump, and certainly sounded odd as I ordered a half of it. When the landlady flipped the tap I expected to watch alcoholic treacle coil forth into my glass, topped off with a sprinkle of crushed downers. In fact, in colour, consistency, taste and potency, it proved stupendously normal: mild bitter beer. I nursed it in an orange corner, accepted and benignly ignored by my fellow drinkers just as I had been in Gateshead.

It was warm and quiet; to keep the horror of public somnolence at bay I eavesdropped on my neighbours, two men in their fifties discussing the local unemployment situation. Their conversation could be described as faltering. Both were enthusiastic smokers, but for whatever reason – perhaps they thought

I might flob in their chasers – instead of going outside together for cigarette breaks, they took it in turns. 'You've got to have a car to get a job these days,' one would say, and then he'd get up and walk out the door, leaving his friend to sip beer and whisky and scratch his chin. Four minutes later the door would heave open, letting in a frozen waft of fags, and the pair were reunited just long enough for someone to say something like 'Aye, that's half the battle' – once it was just 'Aye' – before the chin-scratcher picked up his Regals and clomped out in turn. And so let us move on from the munchy box and the tanning booth to the final two fronts in Scotland's determined one-nation assault on global trends in human life expectancy.

It's taken a concerted effort by Scotland's drinkers and smokers – one imagines a generous overlap in the relevant Venn diagram – to keep their nation atop the European cancer and cirrhosis charts. A third of Fife's adult population smokes, and Scottish women lead their class as Europe's doughtiest puffers. The habit actually enjoyed a resurgence in the early part of this century, when the number of Scottish smokers rose for three consecutive years. The booze statistics are no less eye-reddening – some 40 per cent of Scotsmen are classified as binge drinkers – but I think you'll find these contributions to Fife Alcohol Support Service's online noticeboard rather more evocative.

'I don't drink during the day, but usually stop off on my way home after work and have about six pints. Can you give me some advice?'

'I drink in moderation but have recently begun to binge at the weekend. Now I've started to feel dizzy on Monday mornings, and wonder if the medication I'm taking for high blood pressure could be responsible.'

This entire nation is busily gorging, sizzling, smoking, idling and drinking itself to an early grave: the 2003 Scottish Health Survey declared that 97.5 per cent of Scots were 'living dangerously'. But here's the thing. In Lochgelly at least – where all those bad buttons are pushed hard and often – you'd be pressed to tell. Everyone I'd seen drinking had been doing so in profound earnest – the smoking tag-team dispatched three pints and three doubles in ninety minutes – yet there was none of the Hogarthian raucousness and dishevelment their intake merited. Just like the dapper old soaks in Cowdenbeath, they were indulging to dangerous, wanton excess with quiet decorum. It might not be what any prematurely bereaved relatives would choose as a tombstone epitaph, but these people can really take their drink.

'Goan watch fucken TV now or what?'

The Christmas tree hoodies tramped disconsolately by as I waited at the bus stop. It was only as I watched them slink away up Main Street that I wondered if the town's restrained behaviour might be related to its most famous export: the tawse, a three-tailed, two-foot leather strap first issued to Scottish teachers in 1886, and still being wielded by them over a hundred years later. Offered in four weights – from naughty-toddler Light to Begbie-grade Extra Heavy – the tawse was manufactured exclusively by Lochgelly-based saddler John Dick. So synonymous did the town become with flesh-striping retribution that the tawse was often referred to as a lochgelly.

Having attended a school that stoutly bucked trends in humanitarian decency by actually reintroducing corporal punishment in the late 1970s, I probably have a sharper axe to grind – ouch, sir! – than most. But at my school, as at most English schools, beatings were rare, carried out behind closed doors with the grim and exceptional ceremony of a prison hanging. In Scotland, being lashed with a big leather strap was simply an integral part of everyday school life. A 1980 study by Edinburgh University's Centre for Educational Sociology, conducted among forty thousand school leavers, found that only one in twenty Scottish boys went through secondary school without getting the tawse. Its functionality went way beyond the enforcement of discipline. Teachers across Scotland, and particularly in primary schools, raised weals on youthful skin as an incentive to learning: one Glaswegian girl remembers being tawsed nine times in a single lesson for stumbling over the words to a prayer the class had been told to learn by heart. This was in the 1960s: the girl was six years old at the time.

For the craftsmen at John Dick, tawse-making was consequently much more than a cottage-industry sideline. Demand for tawses actually boomed during the early Sixties, when the firm was selling over four thousand a year. By then, Scottish teachers had shifted their aim from bottom to palm. Most of them, at least: some schools held regular bareback public floggings until well into the 1970s. One pupil recalls the routine: 'If a boy had done something considered serious, such as stealing a pair of plimsolls, he'd be beaten in front of the whole school. Held across a school desk by two teachers and beaten on the bare backside by the headmaster. Female teachers would be excused, so they wouldn't have to see any buttocks.' John Dick suffered an unfortunate dip in business when primary schools started to phase out the whole infant-lashing thing in the early Seventies; the firm's Light model was discontinued in 1975. There was another downturn after 1982, when the European Court ruled that a Cowdenbeath schoolboy suspended after refusing a dose of the tawse had been denied the right to education. But Lochgelly straps were still shifting – at £5.90 a time with a new metric-standard strap length of 580mm – right up until the autumn of 1987, when corporal punishment was abolished in Scottish local-authority schools. John Dick closed down soon after, though the last proprietor's granddaughter still sells Lochgelly straps for what I'll just call a specialist market.

A year before the ban was announced, the schoolchildren of Lochgelly and Cowdenbeath were invited to celebrate the centenary of the local tawse-manufacturing industry. The consequence was a spontaneous rampage: baying pupils raided punishment cabinets and herded terrified teachers into the miners' institute gymnasium, where they were forced to perform humiliating naked jigs at tawse-point. At least that's how it should have been. In fact – and I still can't quite believe this – the children dutifully collected money and with it commissioned a 5-foot replica of a three-tail Heavy-grade Lochgelly tawse, which was then put on proud display in a local museum. That's just so toweringly wrong. These are damaged people. The kind of people, I couldn't help conclude, who overdose on unhealthy solace in later life. Too many lashes of Heavy means too many pints of it.

Having done my own drinking early and in moderation, I was rather looking forward to a night above a pub. As background lullabies go, there are none more soothing than the sounds of muffled debauchery: how fondly I recall nodding off as my parents and their cheeseclothed chums partied the night away with Lambrusco and *Goodbye Yellow Brick Road*, except for the time I nipped out of bed for a pee, and a woman I'd never seen before barged in and threw up in the bidet.

Anticipation waned when I came to terms with my room's fearsome lullaby-resistant properties. The bed was a little too small for Wee Jimmy Krankie, and much too creaky for Vincent Price. Applying Hans Christian Andersen's mattress-comfort index, we're talking 'The Princess and the Angle Grinder'. The companionable clinks and laughs from below were rudely overpowered every fifteen minutes or so when a fellow overnight resident entered the toilet, which was separated from my right ear by 10 inches and two layers of plasterboard. Some of these visits were inevitably more trying than others, but all ended with a tremendous crashing cascade that suggested sluices being voided at the Three Gorges Dam. I woke in the kind of position favoured during Pompeii's final moments, wearing an expression made famous by Edvard Munch.

Chapter Eight

It was a crisp and rosy dawn, one that cast a flattering blush upon Fife. Lochgelly's porridge-plastered, bargain-bin housing stock looked a lot better with a hint of pink on it, and so did the rank of chimneys lined up atop a neighbouring bluff: the massive petrochemical plant of Mossmorran, staffed by Lochgelly's former miners and tawse-testers. I yawned my way north-east on an empty road, the rising sun strobing painfully through the roadside oak trees. Past the brief shimmer that was Loch Gelly, past Kirkcaldy, Gordon Brown's constituency and at this stage of political history perhaps the only place in Britain where his name was more than a punchline. Music, Maestro: Babylon Zoo's 'Spaceman', the Gordon Brown of one-hit wonders, a track that promised much but delivered only failure and embarrassment.

Recorded in 1995, 'Spaceman' had been hanging around unnoticed for a year when an ad agency knob-twiddler chanced upon it, or rather one very, very small part of it. And so in 1996 Levi's released a TV commercial that incorporated a massively speeded-up sample of its stunted chorus, which severally employed the title in a manner I am not permitted to replicate. A swiftly released remix incorporating multiple repetitions of this sample sold 418,000 copies in Britain in its first week, and very quickly went on to top the singles charts in twenty-three countries. To the astonishment of those unlucky few familiar with the rambling, dirge-like original, Babylon Zoo were eagerly tipped for enduring global stardom – most energetically by Jas Mann, the band's Wolverhampton-born frontman and sole songwriter. As the persistently tuneless, repetitive and garbled album I now endured made plain, this could never and did not happen. Almost every track exceeded six minutes. One went on for precisely eleven months. Babylon Zoo's free-fall from grace swiftly achieved terminal velocity. Like many, I last saw Jas Mann making a ten-ton twat of himself on satire juggernaut *Brass Eye*, sombrely agreeing with the suggestion that he 'might have a few more genes than normal people'.

The approach to most of my bad places meant an air of ratcheting dread: the grotty ring road, the squat housing blocks, the brownfield wasteland. Not so Methil. One minute it was all heathery brae and crofters' cottages and villages called Milton of Balgonie. The next . . . well, here's how Wikipedia's overview of the town begins: 'Immediately adjacent to the mouth of the river is Methil power station, which is now unused and awaiting deconstruction.' A few months before I'd found some 1960s home movies on YouTube, showing Methil's heaving prime in jerky, luridly coloured silence. A logjam of railway trucks massed by a dockside full of smoke and funnels, a sea of sensibly trimmed heads packed into a football stand, bunting strung across a crowded, sunny street. I thought of them now as Craig bumped through the puddles in the car park outside East Fife FC, and came to a halt between two upside-down sofas.

Never before had the chasm between vibrant past and bleak present yawned more hugely. To one side stood the abandoned power station, its soaring concrete chimney an attempt to disperse the noxious aftermath of the slurried waste-coal burnt there. To the other a sprawl of rubbled nothing, the docklands that had once been home to the busiest coal port in Scotland and an oil-rig yard where the men of Methil had hammered together some of the world's largest steel structures. And in front of me a mouldering breezeblock football-stadium wall topped with a billboard reminding spectators of the twenty-four-hour emotional support available from the Samaritans (national rates apply).

Methil and its resident football team have never been short of critics. The club fondly recalled as one half of the most feted scoreline in football history (Scottish Second Division, 22 April 1964: Forfar 5 East Fife 4) achieved a grimmer notoriety when featured in Sky 3's *Football's Hardest Away Days*. The same online sources that had directed me to Hawick and Forth proposed twinning Methil with Kosovo, Beirut and Uranus. But by some distance the town's most prominent detractor – and it was only a matter of time before he made an appearance – was HRH Prince Philip, Duke of Edinburgh. Having spent much of his wartime naval service escorting convoys in and out of Methil docks, the Duke felt qualified to call it 'a dump', thus launching his more durable career in offensive indiscretion. 'He is highly unpopular here, to say the least,' said one local historian, asked to comment on the town's fifty-year grudge against the gaffemeister. Exceptionally, this inspired the Duke to issue a belated apology, or at least a denial. Writing to the Lower Methil Heritage Centre in 1995, he claimed never to have gone ashore there during the war, and concluded, 'I remember passing through Methil some years ago with the Queen, but am quite sure I never described it as "a dump".' One pictures him passing the envelope across a footman's proffered tongue, then turning to address his wife: '"A steaming cack-heap", wasn't it, dear?'

I fired Craig up and trundled off through cheerless residential terraces faced with crumbling flapjacks. An adulterated sign welcomed me to LOWER METHIL POOFS. I stopped by a corner shop and came out with breakfast: a mince and onion bridie, which sounded like something Hannibal Lecter might cook up on honeymoon, but was actually just a rather dull pasty. Contains gluten, ready to eat, delicious hot or cold, at least once you've nipped back in and bought that big jar of mustard.

Waiting at the till a second time I spotted a notice on the counter, apologising to patrons that in accordance with new laws passed by the Scottish parliament, they were unable to sell alcohol before 10 a.m. I wasn't sure what seemed more extraordinary: having to clamp down on people buying booze at dawn, or saying sorry to them for doing so.

'We do have our problems,' wrote one local in response to the Duke of Edinburgh's non-apology. 'As a teenager I was too embarrassed to admit I came from Methil. Twenty-five years ago we had a certain reputation because of ladies of the night. Now it's unemployment and alcohol.' Dunking the last flakes of bridie into my pot of yellow fire I wondered if a self-fulfilling prophecy was at work. Methil certainly sounded less convincing as a town than as the street name of some life-blighting home-made intoxicant. And when it comes to exploring novel and dangerous means of inebriation, no one puts in the R&D hours like a Scotsman. Let us take a moment to honour the Glaswegians who laid down their lives in perfecting the formula for a 'corporation cocktail': domestic coal gas bubbled through a carton of milk (I'm afraid I'm not making this up). And what of the doughty 'lacquer lads', whose tireless empirical zeal introduced a whole generation of Scottish tipplers to the refreshing tang of lemonade infused with hairspray? Metal polish, cleaning fluid, shoe dye – you name it, some curious Scot has drained it in one, whooped with exhilaration, and dropped down dead. In fact, it occurs to me that the morning booze ban is in fact a dangerously retrograde public-health measure: all across Scotland, people are now tiding themselves over until 10 a.m. with Hammerite and coke.

'Left at the rowundabowed, f-f-f-first exit.' Obeying Ozzy at the bypass intersection I realised I was turning back for home. Geographically at least, Methil stood top of the crap-heap: north of this point, and with apologies to the Aberdeen publican feted as Britain's rudest man, Scotland was simply too nice.

The hours ahead were spent on persistently tedious dual carriageways, the flat and featureless landscape swept away behind embankments whenever it threatened to undulate in a diverting manner. My foot eased down further on the accelerator, drowning out the sitar solo that was there to drown out

Naomi Campbell's voice. I settled into a dangerous trance-like state, and when Ozzy shook me from it – F-f-fookin left turn ahead! – I noted the speedo juddering around 85mph, and Craig's shrill related displeasure. I checked the oil in a Lidl car park: down once more to the blackened dregs of his sump.

I'd enjoyed many a happy surprise on my journey, but hardly expected Scotland's ugliest beach to provide another. I won't deny that the small curve of harbour-walled foreshore at North Queensferry East Sands was lavishly bestrewn with manmade detritus: in place of sand, the Firth of Forth appeared to have been edged with the disgorged stomach contents of a blue whale fed on landfill. But I couldn't have cared less. The watery world to my south was framed on either side by thrilling, mighty Forth-spanners: the Humber-esque, concrete-towered 1964 road crossing, and – towering right above my unworthy head – the iconic 1890 rail bridge, a cantilevered triple-jump across one and a half miles of deep, cold water. Snippet for those whose loins remain stubbornly undampened by really enormous bridges (what's *wrong* with you?): the perpetual-painting thing is a myth. Snippet for those who just changed their trousers: in Network Rail's considerable inventory, which refers to every building and structure as an index number, the Forth rail crossing is listed simply as 'The Bridge'.

The sun was gently sinking behind the becoming cluster of old roofs that was North Queensferry. Theatrically side-lit, the heroic steel-girdered backdrop haughtily overpowered the micro-horridness below my feet. Our shores would of course be far lovelier places if sailors stopped kicking oily flip-flops overboard, or dolphins were taught to eat aluminium. All I know is that with the sun setting on a view like that, I would happily have put a deckchair down on Scotland's ugliest beach and not even noticed the Strongbow bottles and lengths of mossy plastic rope heaped around my knees.

'It is different, and because it is different, it is controversial.' If you didn't know what the 'it' was, these words, and their narrator's severe and sombre delivery, might steer you towards something like the compulsory irradiation of school milk, or national socialism. In fact, they're the introduction to a 1970 promotional film entitled *Cumbernauld: Town for Tomorrow*, voiced by Magnus Magnusson and thus rich with such phrases as 'integrated uffisses' and 'cellular housing unerts with every ammennertee'.

The camera is slung from a helicopter, showing a lone Transit van negotiating the first in an Olympic logo of broad, landscaped roundabouts. 'In Cumbernauld there are no streets in the *old* sense,' Magnus intones, throttling back a sneer. 'Access to all parts of the town is via a complex road system designed exclusively for motor cars.' Then we're panning slowly along a terrace of wedge-roofed concrete homes with small, irregularly positioned windows: 'Not just a new town, but a new concept in community living.' We cut to a beehived waitress carrying a tray of dimpled pint pots across an enormous orange lounge, then zoom through the wall of angled glazing behind her to a young roller skater traversing a deserted plaza and disappearing into a pedestrian underpass. 'Farewell, little fool, trundling off into the void. Sorry – did I say that out loud?'

In early-evening darkness I muscled Craig through Cumbernauld's roundabout belt, and towards the stilt-propped flanks of its centrepiece 'megastructure'. Just as Brutalism's given name was enough to have had the movement stifled at birth, so Cumbernauld town centre's chief architect should have been dispatched straight back to the drawing board after selecting this word to describe his vision. But when Geoffrey Copcutt's enclosed conglomeration was opened in 1967, everyone loved it. Prospective residents and architecture students from around the world came to gawp in wonder. How their cries of praise and amazement must have gladdened Geoff's heart as he led them through the pedestrian walkways: 'Is this the fullest realisation of megastructure as an avant-garde urbanist conception, or what?' Because his creation was so much more than Britain's first indoor shopping mall – eight storeys high and half a mile long, Cumbernauld town centre was a one-stop shop satisfying every municipal, retail and leisure need of a town of seventy thousand, built around its own ensuite dual carriageway. Bonus!

A drive-through KFC flashed by on one side of Central Way, a McDonald's on the other. Then it was into The Megastructure: an eerie and unpeopled concrete corridor, vaulted by the occasional walkway, broadening on occasion to accommodate a taxi rank or a line of glass doors. Ramps, stairwells, underpass, overpass, then back out into the sculpted grass embankments and roundabouts. It was a sprawling, utterly anonymous environment that at the same time seemed strangely familiar. A couple of f-f-fooking second exits later it struck me: this was exactly like one of those curious, lonely journeys from the long-stay car park in an airport courtesy bus, with The Megastructure standing in as international departures.

In defiance of the empty car park before her, the receptionist at Cumbernauld's Premier Inn insisted she had no rooms to offer: I was beginning to wonder if I'd found my way on to some budget-executive-chain database of undesirables. And so it was out through the final roundabouts to an upscale motel called the Red Deer Inn, where I paid £52 – a new record – for artfully arranged bed pillows and a view of the many surrounding relief roads and bypasses.

'You rilly dinnae want to do tha.'

The youth at reception had looked flummoxed by my enquiry about bus services into Cumbernauld, and followed up with genuine concern when I proceeded to ask him the best way to get there on foot. I took his point. I knew it couldn't be more than a couple of miles, but I also knew – Magnus had told me – that Cumbernauld's 'complex road system' was no place for pedestrians. The entire town had been laid out on the understanding that every single household would own a car and would use it for every single journey. There wasn't a zebra crossing or even a set of traffic lights anywhere in Cumbernauld until 2004, when one of each accessorised the car park at the town centre's new Tesco Extra.

As a rule I find it very easy to resist any defiance-based

challenge, but watching the receptionist puff out his cheeks as he grappled with the unthinkable intention I had outlined, I felt a twinge in my underworked tenacity gland. Buying an Austin Maestro, eating a chicken parmo, failing to dash a booted heel into the stereo as soon as Orville the Duck's voice came out of it – this entire journey was predicated on doing things that people had told me I really didn't want to do. And so with a jut of the chin I strode outside and made off towards The Megastructure, in a direction that Google Maps has just informed me added almost a mile to my journey.

I hit a dark main road and found it edged with a comfortable swathe of pavement. Just as I was beginning to wonder what all the fuss was about, this degenerated into a gravelly border, deeply scored with the wayward skidmarks that betrayed it as a run-off area for drunk drivers. After jogging over a couple of roundabouts I found myself descending the slipway to a much busier and much larger road: in fact, as I noticed when it was just too late to consider turning back, a dual carriageway. Armco and steep embankments now distilled the pedestrian options to a central reservation laid with green-painted railway ballast. Progress was awkward and unsettling. The few motorists going slowly enough to notice me honked their disapproval. Naturally it began to rain, impairing my vision and adding a vicious swoosh to every elbow-brushing neeeeeeeEEEE-OWWW. Half a mile on another roundabout took fuzzy shape before me, and over-excited by a rare gap in the traffic I pelted across it. This manoeuvre propelled me on to a four-lane bridge slung across a four-lane underpass. So popular was this route, and so narrow its kerb, that after a nerve-shredding close encounter with a van's wing mirror I turned myself sideways, inching across crab-fashion like a novice cat burglar on a high-rise window ledge. Rain from without soon met sweat from within: I stumbled into the boggy verge at the other side sodden through and shivering. Through slitted eyes I saw the carriageway ahead fanning out into some complex multi-looped junction. One of the signs hung above it directed traffic to a suburb called Carbrain; under the roaring swish I could hear Magnus baiting me triumphantly. I stood there for a while, strobed by speeding headlights, feeling wet and helpless. Then I squinted at the grass embankment alongside and noticed a muddy upwards track, worn into it by two generations of lost and desperate feet. A drawn-out tug of war with gravity and traction brought me to the summit, and a footpath that wound dimly off towards the shadow of a cellular housing unit.

Cumbernauld was first designated in 1955, largest of four new towns intended to rehouse the occupants of Glasgow's abysmal tenements, 15-odd miles to the west. Seventy thousand of them were to start new lives in what the tirelessly hubristic press coverage dubbed 'Scotland's modernist utopia'. The mood of heady portent was captured by the New Towns Committee in their initial report to the Government: 'It is not enough in our handiwork to avoid the mistakes and omissions of the past. Our responsibility, as we see it, is rather to conduct an essay on civilisation, by seizing an opportunity to design, evolve and carry into execution for the benefit of coming generations the means for a happy and gracious way of life.' As the first clutch of four-storey blocks took shape in the gloomy drizzle, it was clear that someone had got hold of that essay on civilisation, and blown their nose in it.

'Small sturdy cottage homes that set their shoulders to the wind, houses that grow out of the ground itself.' Thus had Magnus described Cumbernauld's housing stock, in terms at variance with the endless residential slabs I recalled from *Gregory's Girl*, the coming-of-age romantic comedy filmed in Cumbernauld in 1980. Though only a few years old at the time, the geometric terraces were made to seem outmoded and rather silly, dream-homes for a flared, Formica future that even in Scotland had already been fast-tracked into the embarrassing past. (Gregory's dad, of course, was a driving instructor.)

I walked past the housing units quietly agog at their subsequent decay. Gregory's home was full of shoddy and risible electronic gadgets, like Soviet ripostes to Japanese technology – wobbly, shrieking tin openers, a massive toothbrush with a fat-coiled cord left buzzing about on a countertop like a fly in its death throes. Now I saw that his house had been built to the same specifications. These buildings were younger than Naomi Campbell, but looked older than Glen.

When Magnus spoke of 'a deliberate adherence to the traditions of Scottish building', what of course he meant was: We're going to pebble-dash the living shit out of this place, and we're going to do it really badly. Every knobbled wall facing me was stained and flaky. If these houses had grown out of the ground itself, then the ground itself was a giant mouldy flapjack. Even the bare flanks of the pedestrian underpass I now entered were riddled with structural ailments more complex than concrete cancer: the coarse rash of concrete scabies, the blot of concrete impetigo, the jagged voids of concrete leprosy. When and why did we forget how to make things properly? The rot had literally set in by 1977, when bits of Middlesbrough's Transporter Bridge that had held firm for seventy years were replaced with sections that would then rust away to nothing in under two decades. We can go back earlier to the Trinity Square car park, semi-condemned by structural decay before it was even finished. Perhaps the most pertinent examples are the two Forth bridges: recent inspections concluded that while the 1890 rail crossing still has a good hundred years in it, cables supporting the 1964 road bridge are corroding at a rate that will render the structure unsafe by 2020. It'll apparently be cheaper to build a new bridge than attempt the repairs. The sad conclusion is that by 1964 Britain had already lost its self-confidence, the pride and determination to build for a long-term future. As the New Town Committee's mission statement proves, the heroic vision was still there – tragically, the financial, spiritual and technical wherewithal to realise it were not. The Victorians compulsively over-engineered: they were putting their stamp on the world, and making damn sure that stamp was deep and true and permanent. From the Albert Hall to Cumbernauld.

Even before the whole place started to disintegrate Cumbernauld was struggling to win over potential Glaswegian relocators. In the early 1980s the town's authorities spread the net wider, launching a national TV campaign catchlined, *What's it called? Cumbernauld!* It didn't work. Cumbernauld is currently home to a busload shy of fifty thousand people, over a third below expectations.

Unburdened with the data, and discounting the several thousand motorists who had come out to spatter my flanks brown, I might have hazarded a significantly lower estimate of the resident population. Three digits would have been pushing it. It had stopped raining, but at 7.30 p.m. on what I realised with a start was a Friday night, I had every underpass and footpath to myself. When at last I did encounter some people, they were all teenagers participating in some miserablist reenactment of *Gregory's Girl*: a couple having a huge, sweary row at a bus shelter, another squatting side by side on the wet concrete slabs, both weeping helplessly, a huddled half-dozen grimly sharing a huge bottle of cider in an underpass.

As a hide-and-seek challenge it should have been more haystack than needle, but my quarry proved more cannily elusive than your typical half-mile block of concrete. Only by following the buzz of unseen traffic roaring through its innards did I eventually track it down, through a mid-urban swathe of landscaped greenery that since Gregory's time had matured into a forest – a dark and lonely forest, full of distant rustling and the dull gleams that helped the town top a nationwide count of dumped shopping trolleys. This was the Cumbernauld that Irvine Welsh – Irvine Welsh! – called 'scary'. When at last a massive, shadowy flank of grey took shape through a mantle of trees, it felt like stumbling upon some forgotten citadel of the damned. Here it was: The Megastructure.

'It's a little further than we want to go for the programme,' said presenter Kevin McCloud, at a press conference to introduce that aforementioned C4 series, *Demolition*. When the producers asked the public to nominate a place they'd like to see given the TNT and JCB treatment, they quickly found their switchboard jammed and inboxes clogged by residents of Scotland's modernist utopia. 'We're asking for individual buildings,' McCloud told the gathered journalists, 'but it seems people in Cumbernauld want their entire town to be razed.'

When the poll closed there was a runaway winner, but McCloud and his team felt obliged to distil the Cumbernauld voters' ground-zero suggestion to a single representative structure. Cumbernauld Town Centre, as The Megastructure is correctly and beguilingly named, was the obvious choice: architectural magazine *Urban Realm* had just awarded it their annual Carbuncle accolade for 'Scotland's Most Dismal Place', and a year later would do so again. After *Demolition* was broadcast, many Cumbernauldians stood up for their town with spirited online exonerations, but conspicuously, none could bring themselves to defend the building McCloud had slapped with a virtual anti-preservation order. That task was left to a man called Thomas, who commented: 'We must keep this 70s masterpiece; we need it to remember *Gregory's Girl*!' Thomas lives in Stockholm.

I gained access to The Megastructure through what must have been a back exit, though in Cumbernauld I imagine it's often hard to tell. At any rate, a large square hole in the concrete wall brought me into a lofty hangar, harshly illuminated by fluorescent tubes as long as flagpoles, stuck to a ceiling that resembled a gigantic ice-cube tray. The cheerfully hideous orange and brown decor I remembered from *Gregory's Girl* was no more – sorry, Thomas – hidden beneath white tiling tagged here and there with a desultory wodge of tinsel, giving the cavernous, unpeopled space the feel of a municipal swimming pool drained for Christmas. It was the least seductive retail environment I had ever entered – no idle claim given the amount of time I'd recently been spending in pound shops. I'd read that generous swathes of the centre were untenanted, foresworn by retailers, leisure service operators and all those employers who were expected to cram its half-mile storeys with their offices. One news report had called the place 'largely abandoned', which seemed a horribly bleak assessment of such a dominant edifice – the heart and soul of a town that still ranked as the eighth largest in Scotland. But apart from a chip shop by the concrete mouth I'd walked in through ('Last pickled eggs before Hades'), everything was closed, and there was no way to know which shutters had clanked down at 5.30 p.m., and which in 1983. Even in *Gregory's Girl* the place had looked sorry for itself, a forsaken, strip-lit facility with all the vibrant glamour of a factory-sized Wimpy Bar in 1970s Bratislava. The locals didn't like it then, and with every year that passed they liked it even less. For three decades Cumbernauld's authorities tinkered with its ambience, forever picking the wrong wrongs to right, and then not righting them anyway. 'Is it the soul-crushing expanses of bare concrete? I bet it is. There you go – we've painted some of them beige. No? Right, how about the whole dour and alien-ating wind-tunnel rabbit-warren thing with all the pedestrian walkways? I mean, we can't actually do anything about that, but I was thinking it might help if we named them after Scottish rivers. Spey Walk, Tweed Way – see, it feels more homely already! What's that? OK, though I have to say I'm unfamiliar with the River Ballbag. Is it that one in Methil?'

To appreciate the full might of the Babylon Zoo-scale delusion that has clouded the judgement of Cumbernauld's administrators over the years, let us consider just two things. A: the full-length storey of deluxe accommodation laid atop The Megastructure, in the sincere expectation that high-flying executives, Formula 1 racing drivers, Simon Bates and the like would be fighting over the keys to a penthouse apart-ment on the eighth floor of a North Lanarkshire shopping centre straddling a dual carriageway. B: the new branch of Woolworths that opened there in 2007.

Feeling rather uncomfortable I pressed on into the clinically illuminated emptiness, accompanied only by the distant clatter of security gates being wound down, and a ratcheting fear that I might somehow find myself being pulled into The Megastructure's death spiral. The white tiles began to close in around me: the bunkers became hallways, then corridors. An approaching echo built into the sound of hard, confident foot-steps, and by the time they were upon me I was preparing to explain myself to a man in a lab coat with an ID pass round his neck, holding a tray of glowing petri dishes or a beagle with three heads. In fact it was a security guard, who politely made me aware that the centre was now closed, and that the only exit still open was the one up by the chip shop. It took me twenty minutes to find my way back.

I tramped round The Megastructure's outdoor perimeter, on what soon became a very keen quest for somewhere to sit down and eat. Clinging to my journey's defining principles I nobly ignored the huge and radiant signs erected by Messrs McDonald, King, Sanders and Hut, beckoning through a gap between stairwells, or across a dark copse of upturned shopping trolleys. I only stopped ignoring them having tracked down and ruled out every other option: namely, a takeaway-only Chinese restaurant atop The Megastructure's car park. That really was it. In half an hour I didn't even walk past a single pub, which in the centre of Scotland's eighth largest town seemed an outrage against logic. Globalised dunce-fuel it would have to be.

But it's one thing to sight a golden arch, or a pizza wearing a red hat, or Rolf Harris in a bootlace tie – quite another, on foot and in Cumbernauld, to make your way to the establishment beneath it. I followed a walkway that pointed directly at the good Colonel's goatee, only to find it suddenly veering away and depositing me back at The Megastructure. A duplicitous little stub of pavement promised pedestrian access to a drive-through McDonald's, then abruptly opened into a wall of speeding traffic: Ronald sat impregnable inside his dual-carriageway moat. At one point I got to within two lanes of a Burger King, but the roadside vegetation was spiny, dense and flush up to the kerb, demanding a combination of talents I wasn't sure I could currently muster: strength, speed, precision and a readiness to order fast food in shredded trousers. And so, hungry and defeated, I allowed Cumbernauld to take me where it would. With my dispirited gaze on the puddled ground I trudged up car-park ramps, over boggy landscaped hillocks, across footbridges bookended with spiralled walkways. At length, by the foot of a concrete flight of steps signposted 'Stairs to Phase 4', I stumbled out of the lonely gloom and found myself engulfed by noise and light and everyone in Cumbernauld. A while later, swaying slightly and with a plastic-bagged Scotch pie knocking against my knees, I emerged from the largest Tesco in all Caledonia.

Chapter Nine

It was a greasy, grey morning and I greeted it with an expression to match. I'd taken a taxi back from Tesco, my dwindling mental and physical resources swiftly drained by the many repetitions of 'the Red Deer Inn' that had proved necessary to prevent the driver dropping me off at 'the railway station' (his first and third guesses) or 'the radio station' (his second and fourth). Enfeebled, ravenous and suddenly quite keen to make a terrible mess of his back seat, I'd unsheathed my pastry en route. My word, it was bad: a sawn-off suet drainpipe blocked with clumps of congealed haggis, smelling like it had been baked in an old lady's handbag. I had no condiments on hand with which to pimp my pie, but to forestall coma I forced half of it down.

The other half looked at me now from the bedside table, dented and sallow and leaching transfats into the wood-effect melamine veneer, a demi-pie reminder of the truly terrible crap I'd been running on for long days. I recalled that the Japanese, who eat very little in the way of dairy produce, find that Westerners reek of sour milk; it was only a matter of time, and probably not much of it, before my pores started to excrete some strange and ghastly new odour. Would my family disown the batter-sweating bridie-breath who was coming home for Christmas? After showering myself free of clinging bits of pastry and bypass I proceeded directly to the Red Deer Inn's breakfast buffet and ate five bananas.

Back in the room and packing up, it became apparent that reserves of usable clothing were running dangerously low. Almost automatically I threw a few socks and pants into the sink, cranked the taps on and with a seasoned king-of-the-road flourish squirted in a sachet of bath gel. When this failed to procure the requisite billows of froth, I retrieved the sachet from the bin and read its labelling with dismay: *Moisturising body lotion. Smoothes and nourishes skin; mires wet pants in slime.* My intention had been to quit Cumbernauld forthwith, but as I draped my viscous underwear across Craig's rear seat and parcel shelf, I sensed the imperative of a visit to a local launderette.

I drove off into the cellular housing units confident one would turn up, fairly certain a launderette had featured in *Gregory's Girl*, and adamantly unwilling to ask a local eight times and receive directions to Auchtermuchty badminton club. Even in grumbling drizzle it seemed inevitable that daylight would improve Cumbernauld. The landscaping certainly looked a lot better now that I wasn't having to conquer it on foot. All the smoothly sculpted vales and whalebacks I remembered from Magnus's film were now neatly embellished with forty-year-old trees and shrubs, no doubt each having matured exactly as their creators projected. I later read that students of landscape architecture are drawn to Cumbernauld from all over the world, to see how it should be done. And also that they're distantly outnumbered by their bricks-and-mortar counterparts, who come here to see how it shouldn't.

'Every four hundred homes are served by a corner shop,' Magnus had smoothly intoned, as birds twittered and pigtailed schoolgirls in Start-rites played hopscotch on newly laid cobbles. 'A little local store – in this case, a converted farmhouse.' With a few cellular housing units under my belt, it was clear that pledge had been lost somewhere along the way. Puttering around the cul-de-sacs of dank, dun-coloured terraces and apartment blocks, I had yet to encounter any sort of shop, let alone one that might have seen previous rural service.

Circling yet another roundabout I caught a smeary glimpse of The Megastructure, at this distance a dead ringer for the kilometre-long aluminium smelting plant that dominates the western approach to Reykjavik. Before it stood the glass-fronted rectangular solid that was the über-Tesco, and just up the road lay an only slightly smaller new Asda.

The brave-new-world Megastructure hadn't been rejected because the citizens of Cumbernauld found it hideous and soul-destroying, even though it most emphatically was. When it comes to shopping, I don't think people really care that much about environment or ambience. Let's face it, cultivating the seductive retail appeal of an automotive parts warehouse hasn't done places like Aldi and Lidl any harm. Hear my wife speak of John Lewis and you might picture a stately pleasure dome of ornamental cascades and hanging gardens, staffed by muscular centaurs who know all there is to know about kitchenware and soft furnishings. But really it's just a big hall full of wanky chrome fridges. No, The Megastructure failed because, ironically, it was too parochial – an enormous place filled with tiny retail units. At some point in my malnourished wanderings the previous night I'd found a store locator map, and noted that nearly all its surviving tenants were running the sort of businesses you'd expect to see on a small-town high street: T. McClean, chemists; Dunipace, Brown, solicitors; R. & J. McClachlan, optician's. Everything else had been swept away by what Cumbernauldians tended to describe online as 'the best news we've had in years' or even 'the only good things about Cumbernauld': that new Tesco and its neighbouring Asda.

It's tempting to conclude that Cumbernauld's planners were endeavouring to humanise the town's most brutal, crushing edifice by cramming it with homely little enterprises, local shops for local people. But actually that's just how shopping was back then: a chore made bearable by social interaction, a gossip over the corner-shop till, or a chat about bi-focals with nice Mr McClachlan at the optician's. Geoffrey Copcutt presciently anticipated a future in which shopping would take place in huge buildings accessed by motor car. His only failure, if you can call it that, was neglecting to predict the extraordinary march of mass consumerism that would elevate shopping to an end in itself, a leisure activity played out in ever more anonymous, ever huger retail theme parks like Tesco Extra. I had, with my own tired eyes, seen grown Cumbernauldian males taking turns to play Guitar Hero in the electrical aisle: glazed and slouchy, they had clearly been hanging around there for hours. The sad truth is that though we're forever bemoaning the decline of local retailers and the loss of Britain's high-street community spirit, that decline is nobody's fault but our own. However much we might like to picture ourselves wheeling tartan sholleys past bow-fronted shops and exchanging cheery waves with butchers and bakers and candlestick makers, the fact is that when offered a soulless, corporate, 40-billion-square-foot one-stop alternative, we grab it with both sweaty hands. And in doing so, we've effectively privatised town planning, shooing away the earnest if occasionally deluded public servants who once did the job, and allowing commercial developers to fashion our urban landscape to their cynical, self-serving whim. Superstores were once stuck out by the ring roads, but now we're letting them annex our town centres. I say 'we', but my wife – a diehard local shopper who gets Christmas cards from every candlestick maker in W4 – seems fairly certain it's all my fault.

Distantly wondering if Tesco Extra plumbed in any of its washing machines, I U-turned and dog-legged from one discouraging, shopless housing unit to the next. It was hardly hopscotch weather, but on a Saturday morning there wasn't a single kid out in the streets, and barely a parent either. Cumbernauld's domestic hibernation seemed almost heroic when you considered the horrid little houses its citizens had shut themselves up in, with their fungal blooms and mossy door frames, the poky windows that looked across ranks of lock-up garages made of soggy cardboard. It was another *Craigworld* centrespread: I nipped out with the camera and snapped a few moody portraits.

175

Though not in a way Magnus might have foreseen or desired, Cumbernauld was indeed a Town for Tomorrow. Completing the process that other towns had merely begun, it was now ahead of the sociological curve as a place that had completely and utterly eschewed any communal focus, whose insular downtime revolved around driving to the twenty-four-hour misanthro-mart or staying in to watch *Britain's Got Biscuits* and *Police, Camera, Nudism*.

Well, that was that. I flicked Ozzy to life and jabbed in the digits that would lead me to luncheon: G3 8RE, home to a Glasgow takeaway and its speciality, a saveloy swaddled in strips of kebab meat then deep-fried in batter. The 'stonner' – thus named in tribute to the local slang term for an erection – weighed in at 3lb and was considered so deleterious to health that its creator limited customers to one per week. 'Just Say No', as the cast of *Grange Hill* now warned me in song, and ad nauseam. I was rather glad to find my ponderings on a stonner's taste and appearance disrupted by the Vauxhall Corsa that now filled my rear-view mirror, flashing its headlights and moving about the carriageway in an excitable manner.

I smiled and hoisted a hand of acknowledgement, for it wasn't the first time that a citizen of Cumbernauld had transmitted their appreciation of Craig's rarity. Crossing the Red Deer Inn car park an hour or so before I'd noticed an executive in a snappy trenchcoat giving Craig a quizzical once over. 'First one of those I've seen on an R plate,' he announced when I came up and stuck a key in the boot.

'Well, there's actually quite a funny story attached to that,' I began, with an indulgent chuckle, and although at this point he was already walking smartly away across the tarmac, I felt myself warming to Cumbernauld as a place – so far the only place – where oddball native motoring tat was respected, or at least noticed. Why, this Corsa driver seemed exceptionally keen to satisfy his curiosity – so keen, in fact, that he now overtook and drove me right off the road. I bumped up on to the landscaped verge and slithered to a halt a foot from his rear bumper, in the process knocking my MP3 player out of its socket and cutting Zammo off in his quavery prime.

Who, or what, is a 'ned'? The *Concise Oxford Dictionary* speaks of 'a hooligan or petty criminal, a stupid or loutish boy or man (Scots, informal)'. Dr Rowland Atkinson, lecturer in the department of Urban Studies at Glasgow University, prefers a more informal definition: 'a young man in a baseball hat who hangs about the streets drinking Buckfast'. But to me, a ned is and shall always be the pinch-faced, tracksuited youth who now stood at Craig's door, working the handle vigorously and expressing in the most strident terms his desire that I grant him access, denied some micro-seconds earlier by a reflex clatter of elbow on locking knob.

'What are you doin' taken fucken pictures of my fucken flat?'

Those callow features seemed so distorted with rage that his own mother might not have recognised him, but his words were as clear as the raindrops beading the glass between us.

'What indeed, young ned, what indeed!' I replied, throwing open the door with a brilliant smile. 'Come take your ease beside me, and hear my curious tale. Scotch pie?'

Just one of the many gambits I now discarded in favour of lowering the window a quarter of an inch and aiming through it a bleat-like noise, part confused denial and part plea for mercy. Excluding those emitted in response to my children's appearance in school nativity plays, this might well have been the most pathetic sound I have ever made as an adult. It very shortly plunged down the rankings.

'We've got a wee boy in there, so how do I know you're not one of those fucken perverts?'

This last word came accessorised with a splendid pair of drawn-out thrumming r's, though I fear I may not have fully appreciated them at the time. Through a curious osmosis the blood drained from my face and reddened his with the righteous rage of an unhinged vigilante. Sounding like a livestock auctioneer with his pants full of scorpions, I launched into a jabbering saga, which began with my father's pivotal role in laying out Cumbernauld's cellular housing units, and didn't get much further.

'What the fuck are you on about?'

'I'm not sure,' I whimpered. 'I'm a travelling biscuit salesman with three children.' A tiny part of my brain registered that this pathetic deception had just enjoyed its final outing. The death of a salesman.

'You're a fucken pervert!' He dredged up a bolus of phlegm and noisily propelled it at the gap above the window; it struck the door frame and clung there, swinging its tail. 'Cumbernauld has no neds in the old sense,' breathed Magnus. 'Every four hundred homes are served by an integrated cellular ned, a ned that rises from the ground itself.'

He seemed to have said all he wanted to say, and I'd already said too much. Cautiously I moved an arthritic hand to the gearstick and engaged reverse, then looked over my shoulder to check the verge behind me for baying mobs, wee boys and the like. In doing so I confronted at close quarters two pairs of damp underpants smeared in hand cream, and I may not have been alone in doing so, because at this point the sole of a white training shoe was forcefully applied to Craig's driver's-side rear window.

This impact dislodged the relevant door's interior armrest, but before it hit upholstery I had dropped the clutch and was very nearly careering backwards through the grass and – ka-BOM, ka-DANG – down on to the road. Some brutal work on the wheel and the gears and Craig was lurching through an about turn. Its apex was a blur of yelling and sportswear: '. . . set fire to that fucken car WITH YOU INSIDE!'

I'll say this for Cumbernauld: when there's fucking-off to be done, you won't find a better place to do it. Two yanks of the wheel and a minute of unbroken acceleration saw me fairly barrelling out through The Megastructure, my peripheral vision a blur of concrete stilts and mildew. A series of roundabouts were dispatched in a fashion that would have upset Gregory's father no end, and then I was out of there and away, my heart and Craig's pumping hard and fast.

Off we fucked through the rain. Soon large buildings clustered the fuzzy horizon, and Ozzy was beseeching me to take the next left, then the next, then to turn around when possible. I ignored him. My after-lunch Glasgow schedule was to take in two fortified sectarian pubs, and a hotel variously reviewed as inferior to a shop doorway, a park and a bus station, overseen by a receptionist who swore at children and flaunted her amphetamine habit. In light of the morning's excitement, I found I had no stomach for any of this: the city of Glasgow in general, and its 3lb battered cocks in particular. Expressionlessly I registered that we'd hit the coast: a firth was broadening out to my right, its opposite bank patched with misty fields. Unhappy thoughts crowded my mind. What other words in common English usage incorporated the ae digraph and ended in o? I could summon but two: paedo and Maestro. Perhaps it was all Craig's fault. Or perhaps it was just time to accept, finally, that I had passed into a certain stage of life. It could have been that first grey hair, the first time I went to bed before my children, the moment I found myself typing 'what to do with leggy petunias' into the Google search box. But middle age only shut its doors behind me when I recognised that from now on, the threat of a good shoeing wouldn't be down to supporting the wrong team or getting on the wrong bus or dressing too damn sharp for my own good, but looking like a nonce.

Approaching the town of Port Glasgow I stopped for petrol – since leaving the filler cap in Forth I'd been too scared to drive about with more than a third of a tank full – and walking back across the forecourt I saw Craig through the eyes of an overwrought ned. A sorry old heap rendered weird by rarity, with a thousand miles of wintry road filth spattered up his black flanks: a seedy loner on wheels. When I placed my black-gloved hand on the grubby door handle it looked like a cutaway shot in some public information film about stranger danger. There was a carwash round the back and very soon Craig emerged through its furry rollers, steaming and glossy. Catching our reflection in a Port Glasgow shop window, I accepted the effect was wholly counterproductive, a frankly deviant exercise in turd-polishing. I remembered the sound of heels clicking nervously off into the dark as I crawled the kerbs of old Hull, and the question writ large on the young faces that ghosted into my rear-view mirror: what kind of sick creep cares so much about a car like that? At least I now had an answer: the kind that needs setting fire to.

Port Glasgow offered a complementary backdrop. Pebble-dashed housing blocks shared a cul-de-sac with British Polythene Industries. Ramshackle pubs opted for plywood as a glazing material. An enormous new Tesco sat in the wide open space that had once been docklands and shipbuilding yards. In its car park I squeezed in between a burnt-out van owned by some local tanning salon and a replica of 'Europe's first commercially successful steamboat'. Then I got out and found myself on wet pavements thronged with glowering descendants of the Dip the Dyer clan, most grotesque and sinister of all the Happy Families. PORT WOMAN 4 TIMES LIMIT, declared a local-rag newsboard, but the only paper still in stock at the shop behind it was the *Daily Mail*. I bought one and read it back in the paedowagon, slumped on the passenger seat with a battered black pudding in my lap. This tasted rather better than it looked, but then it looked like a forearm boiled in yogurt.

When you cross the Cheviot Hills you cross a great media divide. 'Except for viewers in Scotland' is the catchphrase that defines it, a motto bitterly parodied by satirist Armando Iannucci in a sketch mourning the televisual deprivations of his Scottish upbringing. Visiting TV heaven, Armando discovers that while he and his countrymen endured an animated series about Gaelic accidents, the rest of Britain was watching the first live interview with an alien, and being shown how to turn base metals into gold. The display of outraged violence aroused by this revelation sees him cast down to TV hell, where he is condemned for all eternity to watch a Grampian quiz show about hills.

I accept that the *Daily Mail* probably isn't ideal reading matter for anyone who fears they may be slipping into the clutches of paranoia. Its editorial policy is neatly summed up by a website entitled the Daily Mail Oncology Project, which details the publication's tireless efforts to classify all inanimate objects into two types: those that cause cancer and those that cure it. In fact, it occurred to me now that my battered black pudding came close to a *Mail* journalist's perfect storm: underclass ned-fodder, probably carcinogenic and definitely Scottish. Because even with Gordon Brown's career in its fading twilight, the paper was still running dire and almost daily warnings of the 'McMafia threat': a cabal of Scots that the paper's reporters had discovered nibbling away at the very fabric of England, infiltrating our politics and media, managing our football clubs, poisoning our swans with euros dipped in swine-flu. I candidly confess that at this stage of my relationship with the would-be me-burners of Scotland, I was looking forward to reading many such tales. After much jabbing at its tiny buttons I navigated my MP3 player to an anthology of appalling – but very English – football songs, and spread my appalling – but very English – newspaper across the dashboard.

I turned to the inside back page and felt a smile – accurately more of a sneer – annex my features: a column about the forthcoming World Cup, and Scotland's absence from it. A paragraph in and the expression was chased off my face by despair. Say it ain't so, jock-bothering journos of rant-land, say it ain't so! I had in my hands a very different *Daily Mail*, some 'except for readers in Scotland' edition that I couldn't believe the excitable Middle Englanders who wrote and read the paper had allowed to exist. This article was written by a Scottish columnist and from the usual Scottish perspective: to wit, the gleeful wishing of ill upon England and its footballing representatives. 'The target for our contempt is just so inviting,' he wrote, a quote deemed so toothsome that a sub-editor had stuck it in a box in bold.

The England 1970 World Cup squad launched into their anthem with wayward gusto, and I allowed myself to dwell upon its copyrighted lyrical sentiment. Presently I went outside and retrieved from the boot a tin of Quality Street the size of Lewis Hamilton's rear wheel, acquired some days before in another moment of homesick festive weakness. Eleven and a half hours later, knee-deep in harlequin foil wrappings, I eased Craig to a halt outside my house.

Chapter Ten

The festive season afforded Craig the opportunity to enjoy a well-earned service and a good hoovering, though in the event I chose not to grant him that opportunity. My innards reacquainted themselves with forgotten food groups, and my family at least considered forgiving me for having burst into their bedrooms at 3.40 a.m., wild of eye and brown of mouth. With the new year upon me I considered afresh the balance of my itinerary, with particular emphasis on the basic failures of intelligence that had left me rattling padlocked doors at wax museums and the like. In the end I targeted the February half-term sweet spot to head back north and pick up where I'd left off, a time when many of the seasonal attractions I wished to visit would be creaking open their gates, and in weather likely to make them regret it. So six weeks on there I was, back in the sticky saddle, Sellafield nuclear fuel reprocessing plant just a sleet-blurred chimney in Craig's rear-view mirror as we grumbled into Barrow-in-Furness past the toilet-paper factory.

'Hello, I'm conducting a survey on behalf of Cornhill Insurance.' Words that to most of us are an invitation to test out those click-brr reflexes, yet which evidently exert a come-hither appeal upon some – I'm seeing a person who lives alone, and has a hill of corn to insure. At any rate, the firm's relentless market-research drones apparently harvested at least one opinion, and published the result in a press release headed:

IDIOTICALLY SPURIOUS PHONE-POLL NAMES M6 AS BRITAIN'S
DULLEST ROAD.

As it was only weeks since the chocolate-powered all-nighter
that had taken in all 232.2 miles of the M6, reacquaintance
with 170.9 of them should have driven me to the edge of reason
and beyond. Four hundred miles of certified tarmac tedium!
Thankfully there's a simple remedy for motorway ennui, even
in its concentrated M6 form. As Dr Johnson so very nearly
said: 'Nothing more wonderfully concentrates a man's mind
than ragging the nuts off a 1.3 Maestro up the fast lane.'

Dull moments are rare behind a British Leyland steering
wheel. What's that flapping noise? Hang on, I think I can smell
burning plastic. Sorry – not sure what this bit is supposed to
do, but it just came off in my hands. All that before you've
even started moving. Attempt to drive almost the full length
of the M6 at speed, and you will find such fascinations magni-
fied many times. The passenger sun visor flopped off onto the
dashboard as we passed Crewe. A sixth sense and a faint whiff
of sooty despair drew me into a Welcome Break near Preston,
where Craig gulped down one of the bottles of Tesco Value
engine oil I'd given him for Christmas (along with a new petrol
cap, the spoilt bastard). To add to the fun, I started sticking up
for him whenever he was bullied, which was often. Right, I'd
think, clenching my jaw as yet another BMW dismissively cut
across Craig's bows at close range, bet you never thought a
Maestro could do THIS! Then, to his spiritual and mechanical
disadvantage, Craig would very noisily fail to do it. Despite
the view, the drizzle and *The Best of Robson & Jerome*, boring
it was not.

I turned off at junction 36 and headed west, leaving the
sketchy Lakeland peaks in the damp twilight behind. An excitable landscape of tilted pastures and wandering drystone walls
settled into somnabulent corrugations of cold mud. The bare
roadside trees were festooned with shreds of carrier bag, their
branches swept back into ragged quiffs by a lifetime of steady,
buffeting westerlies. Settlements were few and far between,
then fewer and further. I caught a whiff of coal smoke and a

lonely cry of, 'Fookinell!' A little orange light flashed up on the dashboard: acclimatisation process complete.

Great Yarmouth, Hull, Hartlepool, Middlesbrough: so many of the places I'd visited were dead ends, towns en route to nowhere and so deprived of passing trade and its life-giving succur. But Barrow-in-Furness was right out on a limb – so far out that the limb had been amputated and thrown off the Isle of Man ferry. Marooned at the end of Furness, a long and lonely peninsula halfway between Carlisle and Liverpool, Barrow is amongst the most isolated towns in Britain. The current population is seventy thousand: head out of Barrow in search of somewhere bigger and you're looking at a 70-mile drive in the direction of your choice (tip: unless you've got Jim Davidson trussed up in the boot, don't try west). In short, it's an excellent place for doing things you don't want to be seen doing, like tipping depleted uranium down the sink, making bog roll, or chasing an Austin Maestro hubcap along a dual carriageway.

Barrow didn't actually score too badly in any of the civic-performance charts. It was just one of those places, like Slough or Coventry, that everyone automatically assumed would feature on my itinerary, me included. But now, as the lights of Barrow beckoned me forth, I tried to think what it had done to deserve such reflex derision. As a boy, I knew it only as the team that always propped up Division 4: in 1972, Barrow AFC was booted out of the Football League on the rarely invoked grounds of perennial uselessness. Thereafter I lost contact with the town until 2002, when a faulty air-conditioning unit at Barrow's arts centre triggered the UK's worst outbreak of legionnaires' disease. Factory closures, a bit of radioactive contamination: this wasn't a town with a good-news vibe, but there still had to be more to it. Slowing to 30 and approaching its trading estates, I wondered if Barrow might be damned by no more than its own blunt, grim name. A town carting itself off to the dump. And that was before I'd heard a local unleash the blunter, grimmer, sawn-off 'Barra'.

The tyre-fitters and bus depots thinned out, and I passed into the familiar post-industrial urban landscape: retail sheds set in empty tarmac fields, the night lit up by totem poles clustered with gaudy logos. Carpet Right, Pizza Hut, PC World and – by now I could feel when one was coming upon me – a Tesco the size of Denmark. For once I'd found a Travelodge with spare overnight capacity, but suddenly felt certain that part of me would die if I even set foot in that overgrown bungalow opposite a twenty-four-hour Asda. Presently I spotted a parade of handsome old civic buildings, all towers and arched windows, and impulsively yanked the wheel. Almost straight away I was pulling up outside the River Kwai Guest House.

'This is supposed to be a hotel, not the Burma railway!' Basil Fawlty's reaction to the overnight death of a guest rang through my head as I stood at the porch. The breakfast menu almost wrote itself: no breakfast for you, foreign devil! I knocked again but no one came. Still, the broad pavements ahead were flanked with creaky old Edwardian piles that all looked like b.& b.s, and indeed largely proved to be. I walked under the first VACANCY sign and found myself at a porch flanked with red-lettered notices: DID YOU CLOSE THE GATE? on one side, NO MUDDY BOOTS on the other. A digital ding-dong ushered me into a hall edged with further printed exhortations, though my attention swiftly attached itself to the laminated card that read WE ARE NOT TOYS, affixed as this was to the trunk of one of the several hundred elephants with which I shared the room. From thumb-sized wooden miniatures to hefty renderings in garish ceramic, they stared in tight, silent ranks from every shelf and ledge and massed menacingly beneath every hallway chair and table. The largest, a pair of knee-high golden trunk-wavers, stood guard either side of the staircase, beneath the legend, THIS IS A RESPECTABLE HOTEL – KEEP IT THAT WAY.

One of the unsung joys of individual enterprise is the scope it offers for the indulging of personal eccentricities. My gaff, my rules, my whimsical derangement. For a long while it was just me, the pachyderms, and the diktats I now took the time to peruse in full. BREAKFAST IS SERVED FROM 7.00–8.30. DON'T BE LATE AS A "NO" CAN OFFEND; NO HOT FOOD OR UNPAID

GUESTS IN BEDROOMS; DON'T START WITH ME – YOU WILL NOT WIN. Presently a bespectacled boy of about twelve appeared, and processed my accommodation request in efficient silence. He led me up two dark flights of elephant-lined stairs, and along a wandering elephant-lined corridor, then held out a hand to indicate my allotted bathroom. I put my head round its door to be met with yet another printed order: PLEASE LEAVE THIS BATHROOM AS YOU WOULD LIKE TO FIND IT, which meant a delay while I took down several framed safari scenes and installed a sunken Jacuzzi. Then he opened a door opposite, gestured at the darkness within, and departed.

My appointed quarters were very small and unbelievably pink. The Dralon buttoned headboard, the sink, the bedspread, the curtains, the small bits of wall visible between no-smoking stickers: all was violently cerise. All except the inevitable grey mammal or three, and a mysterious rosewood and aluminium box that filled the bedside table. With its speaker grille and many knobs and rocker switches, it looked like something an early Miss Moneypenny might have employed to let M know that 007 was here to see him. None of the controls bore any identification, though a faded typewritten label above one read, PLEASE ENSURE THIS BUTTON IS DEPRESSED AT ALL TIMES. I smiled and nodded for a while, then quickly leant forward and clicked it out. Nothing happened, of course, though I did later learn that at precisely this moment Dumbo fell out of the sky in nearby Morecambe, damaging a bus shelter.

I walked back to town in a stiff wind that carried before it the sweet-and-sour dishwater whiff of Chinese takeaway. Little tornadoes of dust and litter rose up and stung my eyes; the wind turned and I was overtaken by skittering beer cans. Dalton Road, the desolate main drag, was full of pawnbrokers (one day I'm going to walk into a Money Shop and ask to buy a tenner) and soap-windowed errors of commercial judgement. ('You know what would do really well in Barrow? A casino. A casino called The High Street Casino.') I allowed myself to be blown past the grand but gloomy town hall and out to the waterfront, epicentre of the town's explosive awakening.

Barrow was a fishing village of thirty-two dwellings when the first Victorian industrialists arrived in 1840, attracted by its huge natural harbour, the legacy of a long, thin island that kept the ebullient Irish Sea at bay. Throw in the ample availability of local iron ore and a new railway, and you begin to understand how within fifty years Barrow-in-Furness found itself hosting England's busiest shipyards and the largest steelworks on earth. It was an extraordinary tale even by the standards of this golden age of industrial boom towns. You might, for instance, imagine that the *New York Times* would be busy reporting upon its own mercantile miracles, but in 1881 the paper felt compelled to report on the Barrow phenomenon, in an article dramatically headlined: AN IRON CITY BY THE SEA – THE GREAT SHIP-BUILDING YARDS AT BARROW-IN-FURNESS. FROM VILLAGE TO METROPOLIS – BUILDING OCEAN STEAMERS. It reads just like a story you might find today about some rampantly expanding industrial port in China, full of awed statistics and the same thinly veiled sense of economic dread and envy. At least it does for a thousand words or so, at which point the journalist abruptly runs out of portentous things to say about Barrow, and lets the reader know as much with this sentence: 'In the boiler shop a number of Mr Tweddell's hydraulic riveters are in use.'

Lights twinkled fetchingly along and across the harbour, and by narrowing my eyes slightly I managed to blur out the superstore car parks that the brighter ones shone down upon. There was a lively, fresh bite to the wind, and that stirring sense of quest and adventure that always hangs in the air by a large, dark sea. Somehow it seemed larger and darker on this side of the country: I had a palpable feeling that here stood a gateway to grander, more epic voyages – ocean voyages – than those suggested at previous docksides I'd bestridden. The *New York Times* reporter had sailed into Barrow aboard the town's weekly transltantic steamer service. At Great Yarmouth, or Hull, or Methil, a salty old pipe-puffing cove might fix his flinty gaze at the grey horizon and murmur, 'Out there lies a land that some call Belgium.'

The gale died away, replaced by a thin drizzle that hung in fuzzy orange halos around the streetlamps. I quickened my step across the quayside retail compounds, mixing regret and relief for all the stevedores and ironworkers who had once earnt their grubby crust here. But Barrow is still doing something it's always done, and it's doing it in the enormous beige shoebox – the tallest building in Cumbria, no less – that now reared up behind the Tesco Extra and across a stretch of black water. Over 120 years since the world's first torpedo-firing submarine rolled down a Barrow slipway, almost three thousand locals clock in at the BAE submarine yard, producing nuclear-powered jobbies for the Royal Navy. If I was going to see another Maestro it would be here: as a town with three thousand welders and easy access to rust-resistant submarine paint, Barrow is renowned as a Shangri-La for shitheaps.

There was certainly a *Life on Mars* timewarp feel to the balance of the evening, though no Craig-alike asserted his boxy features amongst all the eerily preserved Capris and Cortinas. I tramped down street after wet and empty street of cramped little Victorian terraces and – once it became plain there was nothing else to do of a night – in and out of a succession of timeless and exclusively male pubs. I'd recently read that the average British man spends over £65,000 and an entire year of his life down the pub. This man lives in Barrow.

It's a long time since I'd heard anyone order a pint of black and tan, or hum along to 'Forever in Blue Jeans'. My world was suddenly full of tubby blokes in under-sized knitwear, sipping brown froth, reading the sports pages of crumpled tabloids, stooping to release a clatter of pool balls with two fifties and a ratchety yank. And, as I noted after a while, doing it all in silence. There were nods, raised eyebrows and the odd phlegmy chuckle: every one of the principal communicative tools of restrained male companionship, but no words beyond those required to procure a fresh draught of ale or conduct a game of eight-ball pool (to wit: 'spots', 'stripes', 'two shots').

189

Some website recently declared Barrow 'the most working-class town in Britain', on the grounds that it was home to more chip shops, bookies, working men's clubs and trade union offices per capita than any other. However fatuous all that might sound, Barrow was plainly a town clinging tenaciously to its roots. I could just tell by looking at my hefty, oily-fingered fellow drinkers that they didn't work in retail security or customer care or anything else that might have been on offer at the Job Centre Plus in Middlesbrough – these were men who made stuff in factories, even if it was Andrex. As a British industrial town Barrow must have endured its fair share of economic kickings, but somehow the bottom had never fallen out of the place. In fact, the population has barely changed in the past hundred years, stuck at seventy thousand. Perhaps it was all down to the arse-end-of-beyond factor: the grass might well be greener, but when the fence is 70 miles wide who's going to cross it and find out?

ANYONE SEEN ON CAMERA DOING DAMAGE TO THIS HAND DRYER WILL BE BARRED. THE MANAGEMENT DO NOT CONDONE ILLEGAL DRUGS IN ANY FORM. ALL INCIDENTS WILL BE ENTERED IN OUR DRUGS REGISTER. Reading these and many similar notices in a succession of silent public houses, I began to see a civic trend developing. Was this how people communicated up here? Perhaps every Barrovian carried about a bundle of printed cards, to be displayed as appropriate in lieu of conversation: SEE YOU MONDAY, THEN, A CHOCOLATE DIGESTIVE, IF YOU'VE GOT ONE, WE'LL GET THAT PAEDO WHEN HE COMES BACK FROM THE BOGS.

I had a pint in a low-ceilinged Sixties blockhouse, where an old man alone at the next table drank three double whiskies in half an hour, then fell asleep, chin on chest. I had another in a bijou shrine to Manchester United, shared with the young David Beckham, seven Roy Keanes and the heady scent of marinading urinal cakes. My third and last was slowly sunk at a sepulchral old dockers' pub just back from the waterfront. I was draining it when an enormous young man walked in out of the rain, sat down at the bar and immediately let forth the most protracted, buttock-rippling guff it has ever been my misfortune to endure. 'Two-twenty for your Worthington,' said the barman, when at last he was done, 'and a tenner for a new seat cover.' It was the longest speech I heard all night.

Extremely fresh air and my curious failure to take onboard any solid calories since a Welcome Break near Preston made the walk back rather a light-headed adventure. Stepping carelessly off a kerb I was nearly mown down by a motability scooter: when the driver turned to berate me I recognised him as the old chap I'd seen an hour before, deep in blended-malt slumber. I rolled straight past my guest house, plunged in silent darkness as it was, then suffered a panicky pocket-patting key-hunt at its front door. By the time I found it my racing mind had imagined every fate that might befall those who committed this most deadly of guest house sins, all of them too complex and terrible to be encapsulated on a laminated card. And that was before I tripped over three trunks on the half-landing.

Chapter Eleven

'Another 'orrible day in Barra.' Thus did my landlady see me off into the grey morning, replete with fried bread and the blunt logistics of her pachydermal mania ('Got first twenty-nine years back. Stopped counting at three and half thousand. Clean buggers with hairdryer.'). But as I drove through the red-brick, rain-polished streets I realised that even in the cold light of a wet day, I rather liked this strange and remote old place.

Seagulls cawed from the town-hall clock tower. The flanks of venerable buildings were faintly emblazoned with hand-painted advertisements for furniture brokers and general dealers. I exchanged a flash of homofocals with an Austin Montego, the Maestro with a boot. I passed along a street lined with steamy-windowed launderettes and cosy little cafeterias, full of headscarved old dears having a natter and a break from the rain. There was a defiant, almost heroically traditional feel to the town, a sense that here at least the Tesco belt hadn't yet been pulled so tight that it stifled the life out of the place. The radio producer John Walters once declared that 'human society can be divided into two eras: pre-avocado and post-avocado'. Barrow, the town that time forgot, was stoutly pre-avocado and proud of it. And more than that, it had character, which as I was finding out is about as much as you can ask for from any British town these days. Everything seemed lightly dabbed with the brush of daftness: an ex-ferry party ship moored up by the Morrisons' car park, the existence of a street called Powerful Road. And a guest house breakfast room where the bland and age-old menu strictures of grapefruit segments OR orange juice OR cereals (porridge on request) were offset by a thousand watching elephants and a warning that smokers would be severely battered about the head and body.

The only way out of Barrow is the same way you came in, and I retraced the A590 at intemperate velocity. We sped across damp green undulations scarred by the occasional quarry, and through villages full of homely, good people – the sort of people who lived next to a big sign advertising The Walker's Hostel or Canal Adventures and never crept out at night with a pot of paint and a puerile snigger. Ozzy led the way as ever, and was presently accompanied by himself: Ozzy Osbourne's 2005 covers album, *Sing! These Days I Can Barely Talk!*, or something like that. This at least had the inestimable appeal of not being Paul McCartney's 'Frog Chorus', which had incited a small off-road adventure near the bog-roll factory. Plus it guaranteed plenty of gratifyingly surreal Ozzy-on-Ozzy action: 'I am the god of hell fire, and I bring you f-f-fookin left turn ahead!'

I hit the M6, headed a few junctions south, then turned off into the Lancastrian coastal flatlands. Above me the sky cast aside its cloud blanket and let forth the full force of a mid February frost: on went the gloves and scarf, and Ozzy was lost in the heater's tepid roar. The hedgerows holding the rippled potato plains at bay seemed to blacken and wither around me, as if some fairy-tale curse was passing across the kingdom. Then the heavens darkened anew, and grubby beige flecks began to spatter the screen at a jaunty angle. Three days at the seaside beckoned, and it was snowing.

Our True Intent Is All for Your Delight: it sounds like the sort of gibberish you might see printed on a Japanese T-shirt, but these words are actually the official motto of Butlin's. They wouldn't have made much sense to me as a child, and barely do now, but somewhere in that slogan lies the promise of carefree, communal holiday-camp fun that the pre-teen me pined for. For the thick end of a decade I fantasised about summer fortnights in a chalet at Minehead or Camber Sands, days of chips and splashing about and nights of noise and neon and – yes! – Crompton's Penny Falls. I lobbied hard for a couple of years, but always in vain. When it came to holidays my father was a rolling stone: to him I was just a loose pebble, the smallest of three sliding about on the hot back seat of a Peugeot estate. His was a summer wanderlust that could never be sated. When times were good, we drove all around Europe. When they weren't, we drove all around Wales. Our family never spent more than a single night at any hotel or campsite, having generally arrived well after dark. We weren't so much tourists as desperate fugitives.

A holiday camp offered the August inertia I craved, and also the raucous group larks that were always just starting up when we slammed the boot and drove away into the morning, or always just winding down when the Peugeot crunched to a halt on the moonlit reception gravel. The TV ads promised startling attractions – Billy Butlin had introduced the electric dodgem car to Britain, and his Skegness camp was home to the nation's first monorail – and a heady ambience of juvenile anarchy. I watched children being left alone to get on with it, children given the run of all-inclusive entertainment facilities, children wearing expressions they didn't wear whilst being dragged around an arboretum in Düsseldorf or Herefordshire's largest collection of Edwardian bottles. It all looked like a thrillingly unsupervised mass sleepover at a funfair, like *Pinocchio*'s Pleasure Island without the downsides (enforced cigar smoking, and being turned into a donkey). At some pertinent stage of early adolescence I was exposed to the film *That'll Be the Day*, which dramatically broadened the appeal of the British holiday camp by presenting it as a place where even Ringo Starr might open his chalet door to find a queue of young women demanding wanton satisfaction. But sadly, when at last I gained responsibility for planning my own holidays, I'd fallen under the influence of factors that hadn't hitherto seemed at all important, like hot weather and tremendously cheap booze. Off I went to the Mediterranean. And so did everyone else, which meant that before long there weren't any holiday camps left. Well, hardly any.

With six hundred chalets and uniformed entertainment officers, Butlin's Skegness – opened in 1936 – was the first proper British holiday camp. The idea for it came to Billy Butlin during a disastrous week with his family at the Welsh resort of Barry Island: in accordance with a practice then universal and which still lingers on in Barrow, the Butlins were ejected from their seaside guest house at 10.30 a.m., obliged to wander the seafront in teeming rain until the land-lady re-opened her doors in the late afternoon. Being British, his fellow holidaymakers thought they deserved no better and put up with it. Born in South Africa and raised in Canada, Billy felt something should be done, and did it. Three meals a day, organised in-house larks and the option of a roof over your head at all times: when the papers ran the first ad for Butlin's Skegness, under the winning catchline *A week's holiday for a week's pay*, ten thousand families placed book-ings overnight.

I'd always thought that Billy expanded his empire through the judicious post-war acquisition of decommissioned military camps, but in fact nearly every Butlin's was purpose-built. Most of that army-surplus rebadging was carried through by his arriviste competitor Fred Pontin, whose chain of smaller, cheaper, monorail-free holiday camps always seemed a poor relation: like Man City before the sheikhs turned up, right down to the whole bluecoat/redcoat rivalry. By the Sixties, Billy's nine super-camps were welcoming over a million British families a year, more than twice as many as Fred's bijou twenty-four. Holiday-camp bookings didn't actually peak until the 1980s, but by then Fred and Billy – sharp operators both – had seen the budget-flight future and sold up, bagging millions and a knighthood apiece. A succession of huge and stupid entertainment corporations oversaw the ensuing meltdown: today only three Butlin's camps survive, though the Pontin's empire, with its portfolio of more modest and economical sites, weathered the storm slightly better. Five remain, amongst them the razor-wired compound hunkered up before me in the twilight sleet.

Pontin's Southport was opened in 1970, the last old-school, pre-Center Parcs holiday camp ever built in Britain. By then, all the more obvious seasides – Somerset, Devon, Kent, Norfolk – were well covered, but with demand still burgeoning, the operators felt encouraged to tackle more challenging destinations. All the same, and even making due allowance for the time of year, Southport seemed a bridge too far. Driving up to the security gates I could imagine Fred's executives exchanging panicked glances as the old man pinned that final blue flag in the map on his office wall. Are you completely sure about this, boss? A holiday camp in *Merseyside*?

The guard slapped a huge and garish Pontin's sticker on Craig's filthy windscreen, and invited me to park up by reception. It was by now truly bitter – I had to gingerly half-skate my way from Craig to the check-in lobby. As I approached it, breath wisped forth from my gaping mouth: the place was loudly abustle. People, lots and lots and lots of people, had willingly chosen to go on holiday in Merseyside, in February, and – why else was I here? – in the most poorly regarded holiday camp in all of Britain.

Signs above the long check-in desk sorted arrivals into alphabetical groups; I took my place in the H–N queue. Everything was blue and yellow. A rank of posters advertised a forthcoming 1980s roadshow featuring Toyah Willcox, Paul Young and Brother Beyond, touring under a banner title I now forget – Tears of Shame, Dregs of Dignity or something like that. Most of my fellow arrivals were parents with many boisterous children in tow, but there were a few unburdened young couples – such as the one I now noticed at the adjacent customer services counter, on account of the noise they were making, and the 4-foot length of wood the husband held in his arm. 'This fell off the bed when I sat down on it,' he loudly declared, brandishing it like a one-man angry mob. 'The whole room's knackered!'

'And it stinks,' chimed in his wife. 'It's *rank*.'

It was a compelling encounter, yet as I craned and peered I realised that no one else was paying them any notice – least of all the blue-uniformed woman on the receiving end, who absorbed their outrage with a sort of dutiful, nodding boredom, like a desk sergeant being told about a stolen catflap or the loss of a favourite sock. Her heard-it-all-before demeanour was consistent with the research data. Of the many, many negative opinions I'd scrolled through over the past few months, none were more numerous, more heartfelt or more luridly improbable than those supplied by the erstwhile patrons of Pontin's Southport. I can't imagine the typical holiday-camp guest is especially hard to please, yet almost every single one of the 119 visitor reviews I'd read related an experience that had fallen distantly short of expectations. On the hi-de-hi scale, this place was the low-de-low.

I recalled some highlights as the H–N receptionist handed over my key and the sheaf of electricity-meter credit cards I had purchased to procure such holiday indulgences as heating, hot water and illumination.

'As I walked in, the smoke alarm fell on my head.'

'We went to search for somewhere else to stay and when we returned to the apartment our food and beer had been stolen.'

'Someone was thrown through a window, someone was thrown off a balcony . . . I had to repeatedly tell my wife that it was OK and we would survive.'

'Opened the bedroom window to let out the smell of damp and it completely fell out of the wall.'

'Unbelicvable filth – complained about the minging carpet and they gave us sheets to put down on it.'

'Hit on head by bottle thrown from upstairs balcony and taken to hospital in ambulance.'

'Opened a drawer and it was half full of water.'

New experiences are generally the sign of a good holiday, but at Pontin's Southport guests found themselves chalking up unwanted firsts: drinking Coke that smelt of lager, going to bed with their shoes on, scrubbing dried blood off a kettle. When praise was delivered, it came couched in the faintest terms: 'Little kids will enjoy it as they don't know any better.' I presumed this factor and the half-term break were one explanation for the healthy attendance. The other: for a three-night stay, I had paid £61.

I'd been required to enter my age when checking in, and understood why as I piloted Craig through the frozen puddles towards. my appointed dot on the camp map. The accommodation was laid out like a huge wheel, with spokes and rim formed of flat-roofed, two-storey blocks. Those closest to the main reception and its attached bars and entertainment facilities were allocated to youthful revellers; further around the perimeter I passed noisy families unloading people carriers. Finally I arrived at the camp's silent and lonely outer limits, the circle of Pontin's reserved for childless old men. Thus did the spirit of Cumbernauld Ned pursue me up a rusty staircase, along an undulating balcony walkway and – with the furious shriek of warped and swollen plywood parted against its will – into the gloom of apartment 556.

Finding the meter in the dark involved rearranging a lot of furniture with my shins and elbows, and a protracted end-game fumble with the stupid electrocard. In the harsh fluorescent light thus unleashed I saw straight away that I had drawn one of the longer straws: nothing was hanging off the wall or spattered with body fluids. A quick tour revealed no dramatic horrors. Someone had been plucking fretfully at the bedroom wallpaper, and the carpet looked as if it had been reclaimed from a Kwik-Fit customer waiting area. The dearth of kitchen linen and consumables was mildly disheartening: I'd remembered to bring my own towel, but hadn't expected it to stand in as oven glove and dishcloth, drying mugs washed-up with shampoo. My bath was one of those half-length jobs that downgrade a long relaxing soak to a shivery, knee-hugging squat, and the ashtray set into the wall by the lavatory conjured few appealing images. Much like the modest, blizzard-vision

TV, which proved both unwatchable and unlistenable: its volume knob offered a choice between silence and distorted cacophony.

But more significantly than any of that, apartment 556 was chest-huggingly, face-achingly frozen. That lone coat peg wouldn't be seeing much action. A technical glitch meant that each of my £1 electrocards notched up £10 of credit, but the surge of glee triggered by this discovery ebbed away as I pressed both hands and a cheek to one of the wall-mounted convection heaters and felt it very slowly attain the temperature of a day-old corpse. I set the oven to apocalypse and threw its door open, and cranked on all four of the hob rings; when I shuddered out into the blackness half an hour later ice was still rimed up the inside of the windows.

It had suddenly become a beautiful evening: a crisp, clear sky of deepest midnight blue inlaid with a Bethlehem crescent and stars. I cocked an ear and detected the gentle lapping of surf. Nature was doing its best, but it had been badly let down by man – 1960s British man. What would have been a moon-silvered ocean prospect was hidden by a floodlit tangle of rusty machinery and old tyres. My apartment block was one of four arranged around an exercise yard of sleet-sprinkled mud, edged with slivers of dislodged masonry. The mossy brick walls looked frail and wonky, the work of a Duplo-reared infant who had been moved on to Lego a couple of years too soon.

Pontin's Southport was conceived and constructed at the high-water mark of the British holiday camp, but also at the unfortunate zenith of a parallel national boom, in which we led the Western world in the construction of dehumanising edifices that looked shit and fell to bits. You don't even need to go there to see how bad it looks: as viewed on Google Earth, that weathered concrete wheel says correctional facility or abandoned military intelligence compound. It just doesn't make sense in any context related to leisure and entertainment, certainly not outside a country never ruled by a politburo. A holiday is supposed to feel like a reward; gripping the banister's frozen rust I had the sense of being punished for some fairly awful transgression.

The entertainment complex was a great big thronging barn of a place, fronted by a three-ride funfair where little girls in vest tops were whizzing around in the frozen night. I walked in through the fast-food area and into a hall full of men with assault rifles, most of them under seven. The air was filled with gunfire, rage and confusion: 'Billy! Where you gone, Billy? Take the head shot for me! Take the bastard out!' Blood coursed down screens all around; I hurried out of the arcade and into the neighbouring bar. In accordance with the generational apartheid that had always seemed to define the holiday-camp experience, all the parents were crowded in here, sat around four-pint jugs of lager. Husbands: very tight short-sleeved shirts, close-cropped heads. Wives: painfully scraped-back hair, meaty bare arms. I did a full 360-degree scan of my surroundings and established that I was at least slightly scared of everyone older than five.

Even the Bluecoat bingo caller up on the main hall's stage sounded hard, barking out numbers like Windsor Davies doing the national lottery. 'Four and seven, FORTY-SEVEN! One and oh, THE NUMBER TEN! On his own, Tim the Paedo, PAEDO TIM!' I thought about joining in – only some of the stout aunties hunched over their cards looked excessively dangerous – but this was not bingo as I knew it. The caller cranked up the speed and the volume; pens darted about number grids. Too fast, too furious. Instead I spent half an hour in the queue for bar meals, watching the small number of unoccupied dining tables dwindle steadily. The last was annexed just as the pimpled youth at the till aimed his next-please grunt at me.

That meant a frigid, rubbery burger from the fast-food zone, coaxed down with a pint at a rare free table near the back of the main hall. Bingo had given way to a Bluecoat formation-dance stage-show featuring heavy Black Lace content, compèred by a well-fed young man with access to no more than two words: 'lovely' and 'jubbly'. It didn't really matter, because no one was listening or watching. The audience seemed preoccupied with emptying or refilling their lager jugs, exchanging idle profanities ('Fucking must be minus fucking twelve out there, for fuck's sakes!') and plotting the theft of my table. So mine were the only ears to prick up when the announcer cast aside the previous limitations of his vocabulary and bellowed, 'LADIES AND GENTS, WOULD YOU PLEASE GIVE IT UP FOR THE LEGENDARY MR KEITH HARRIS!'

The house lights went down, James Brown's 'I Feel Good' burst forth, and with saucered eyes I watch a little man in a bright red suit dash out from the wings.

'How we doing? I said, how we doing?'

Keith's hairline had done a runner, and through a sea of uninterested heads, most of them facing away from the stage and with a tilted pint glass stuck in them, I could see the poor man's pride straining at the leash to follow it. 'It's brilliant to be here, ladies and gentlemen. You know, I haven't actually worked in this venue for about thirty-five years.'

He looked around the hall, and I fancied his showbiz life flashing before his eyes: from Pontin's to prime time and back. I thought: Please don't say 'but', Keith.

'But tonight we're going to have great fun. Boys and girls and mums – Orville's just having his nappy changed. Tough luck, dads – you're going to have to put up with that bloody duck after all!'

It is the ventriloquist's curse to play straight man to his own creation, and that curse doesn't come any cursier with a creation so punchably fatuous. When the gales of laughter swept across the 1980s clubs and theatres and TV studios, how did Keith never once crack? I know I would have. 'Right, ladies and gents, sorry to interrupt the old merriment, but just so as you know, the duck didn't say that. I did. It was me. To be honest, without me the duck isn't really up to much. Oops – there he goes, down on the floor in a heap. What's up, Orville? Come on, give us a funny. No? Looking a bit lifeless down there, mate. Bit fibreglass.'

But those gales of laughter blew themselves out some years back, and there wouldn't be much limelight for the pair to squabble over tonight. The audience was chuntering swearily on and milling about and necking Foster's; Keith kept having to beg for a bit of quiet. Self-deprecation didn't get anyone's attention, and nor did a desperate foray into potty-mouthed innuendo, the 'adult set' I imagine he keeps in reserve for student-union bookings. I couldn't quite deal with Orville the Duck's creator up there saying 'arse' and 'bugger', and going on about having something big in his pockets. Much of this material flowed from the rigid lips of Cuddles the Monkey, the first puppet out of the big box at Keith's feet. Cuddles was a bitter misanthropist, endowed with the catchphrase: 'I hate that duck.' By the time that duck came out of the box, I was beginning to wonder if Keith had put a lot of himself into Cuddles.

'I've had a hundred and seventy characters,' Keith recently told an interviewer from regtransfers.com, Britain's leading online personalised registration-plate broker. 'I had a snake called Sidney Ram Jam, which I'm not allowed to do any more – he spoke with an Indian accent and wore a little fez. I had a gay rabbit, too, and I'm going back a long time, he was called Percy Pickletooth.' Keith still couldn't understand why such inherently more entertaining creations had failed to grab the public's interest, and I sensed he resented his perpetual professional enslavement to the sickly, stupid bird they had inexplicably fallen for. Keith Harris was a hard-grafting variety entertainer, one of the last of the line, but in the end he'd hit the big time through dumb luck, with a dumb duck. Where was the variety now? Keith had so much more to offer, a multitude of talents honed in his early years on the club circuit: singing, magic tricks, all those Mike Yarwood 'And this is me!' moments. As his own website maintains, 'There is little doubt that Keith's genius has given him International Stardom for many years.'

Even from 50 yards I was taken aback by the creature Keith now bent down and surreptitiously stuck his right arm up.

Orville was much, much larger than I imagined, a big green unit with a head the size of Keith's and cheeks like polished elephant's knackers. Retrimming the body beneath must have involved shaving every My Little Pony in the land. Then Orville spoke, in the shuddersome ickle-girl Lancastrian croak with which Keith had blessed him. It was a voice I had heard in my head that very morning, as I read these words on a painted mirror while emptying my bladder in a Barrow cafeteria: IF YOU SPRINKLE WHEN YOU TINKLE, BE SWEET AND WIPE THE SEAT. All part of the baby-faced faux-cute 'Love Is' culture that held this country in its thrall throughout Orville's heyday, and which now incites a terrible urge to sprinkle with abandon, like a dog drying itself.

Orville's success was as much a mystery to me as it must still be to Keith, as his bird tellingly revealed in the torrent of self-loathing that is 'Orville's Song'. At a stretch I could imagine him appealing to those who found Little Jimmy Osmond adorable, and would have found even more adorable had he been an incontinent green animal with extensive learning difficulties. Personally speaking, Orville put the 'S' in my mothering instinct. Yet without this infantilised, bollock-cheeked freak-beak, Keith Harris was nothing. This, I decided, was the grotesque irony that still tortured his every waking hour. Perhaps the interviewer from regtransfers.com decided it too, even though he'd only popped by for a quick chat about ORV 1L, recently acquired by the ventriloquist at an auction of cherished registration plates.

The atmosphere was becoming slightly uncomfortable, with a new harshness to the profane badinage around me. People seemed distracted and on-edge, and I soon realised why: they were all really drunk. Was this the only way a British adult now knew how to entertain himself? A few weeks before I'd watched a rerun of an old *Morecambe and Wise* Christmas show, and had been surprised to find none of it even slightly funny. Yet this had been the pinnacle of comic entertainment, a moment when the nation, the young me included, tuned in and split their Seventies sides open. For all I know I might be repressing memories of sitting there in front of *The Keith Harris Show*, finding Orville both endearing and hilarious. Perhaps we were just more easily pleased back in the golden age of crap culture. Simple but happy, innocent and certainly more sober. Anyway, something's changed, and surveying the lairy jostlers around I concluded it probably wasn't for the best.

Orville simpered croakily on; I nipped out for a tinkle and returned to find my table fully occupied by three big women and a jug of lager. With dismay I saw that the proprietorial scarf I'd draped hopefully across a chair was now wrapped around a pair of heavily tattooed shoulders. I was settling into an awkward hover behind these when a familiar keyboard tootle drew my attention to the stage.

'We're going to sing you a song that went to the top of the charts twenty-eight years ago: an actual *Top of the Pops* number one!' Not quite, Keith: 'Orville's Song' peaked at number four. 'And also voted the worst song ever recorded!' Not quite, Keith: it came second to 'Agadoo' in the big *Q Magazine* shite-off, made number eleven in a Channel 4 'worst 100 singles' poll, and wasn't even mentioned in my third principal library of musical infelicity, a 2004 survey organised by confectionery giant Mars (why?). 'Still, I got a house in Portugal out of it, so what do I care?' And with that mutter hanging in the air, the backing track swelled hugely and Keith and Orville were off and away, giving it up club style.

What happened over the next four minutes was really rather lovely. For some time the children in the audience had been slowly gathering at the foot of the stage, magnetically drawn by the primitive, pre-modern appeal of a talking puppet. As Keith muscled Orville to the song's key-change climax, the young mob pressed forward and began waving their arms in unison, a good hundred of them by now. Keith saw what was happening and beamed his way through the sign-off chorus, all the bitterness washed away. Orville waved a stumpy green wing at the kids and the kids waved back, and Keith was seen off stage with a resounding falsetto cheer. Their parents might have forgotten how to have good old-fashioned family fun, but these happy young campers were just finding out what it meant. Emboldened with goodwill, I whisked my scarf from its new owner's colourful flesh and dashed smoothly outside, where a boy of ten was being sick into the fag bin.

Chapter Twelve

I awoke with a faceful of sun streaming down on me through the kitchen-paper curtains. A bright dawn was the successor to a clear and bitter night: I'd slept with hands wedged in armpits, and my nose felt like it belonged to someone else, someone who'd been dead for three days. All that £3.86 worth of overnight heating had achieved was to condense my breath over every window, a process which had resurrected ghostly finger art from holidays past, mostly unfinished renditions of the Cerne Abbas giant at play. Steaming hot ablutions were very much in order, and I left the half-bath's red tap running while shaving the heads off my facial goosebumps. My shuddering respirations brought to life a detailed finger-art tableau in the mirror, featuring Mr Happy being extremely unwell across the initials of many Premiership football clubs. Then I dipped an appraising digit into the bath and found it filled to the brim with glacial meltwater. By the time I located the switch for the water heater – next to the oven, obviously – I was in no mood for the forty-five-minute wait advised by an attached notice (along with a warning that water could not be heated while the cooker was on, an edict necessary to stamp out voltage-crazed holiday excesses such as washing up after a meal). Pontin's Southport, my base for a three-day regional craporama, was doing much too well at being awful.

Grimy and ill-tempered, I put on most of the clothing I'd

brought with me and heaved open the apartment door. Every other set of curtains was drawn and the exercise yard lay entombed in perma-frost; icicles hung becomingly from every gutter and overflow pipe. The sky was huge and blue and the sunlight pure, pouring gold across the sand-dune crests that rose up beyond the camp walls. Immediately I felt better: it was an absolutely glorious morning, and I had it all to myself.

I walked round the camp's deserted perimeter, then headed to the beach. Everything down here was vast: the yawning emptiness of the rippled sand, my thousand-foot shadow across it, the boarded-up Victorian hotel sat between the dunes. The sea looked a million miles away, just a fuzzy silver line out near the horizon. It was all so stirring and epic: a big place for big dreams. In days gone by that meant Red Rum thudding across these sands in pursuit of the speed and strength that would win him three Grand Nationals. Now it means that the dunes behind Ainsdale Beach are home to north-west England's most active dogging community.

I crunched back to the camp through crusted sand ridges and puddles of hard sea – when brine freezes over, hell can't be far behind. From bumper to bumper Craig was thickly dusted with ice, and I allowed myself a self-congratulatory smile: the night before, taking stock of the conditions and Craig's related medical history, I'd prudently removed the WD40 and de-icer from the boot and taken them up to my apartment. Feeling – and looking – very pleased with myself I now extracted both aerosols from my bag and lavishly unleashed them over glazed surfaces and into locks, as appropriate. Then I climbed inside, aimed another what-the-hell squirt of each behind the choke knob, and to my immense satisfaction coaxed Craig into a first-time start. A quick flick of the wipers, and off we . . . oh. I heard frail machinery endure immense strain and surrender with a reverberating twang; I saw the wipers flop limply down on to the bonnet, useless and dead.

And so West Lancashire passed by in a smeary blur, my nose pressed up to the screen and my eyes trying to distinguish oncoming traffic from less potent hazards such as roadside vegetation and livestock. As I weaved blindly about the tarmac, my respect for Craig and the men who brought him to life – nearly enormous following his non-stop transnational marathon – ebbed steadily away. The last dregs of it were drained by a very close shave with a stationary milk float. Soon afterwards, I pulled over in a village and made further efforts to wipe away the semi-de-iced chemical sludge, now topped with the spatterings of gritty slush thrown up by motorists who overtook at speed, honking their rage at my lethargic meandering. All around was flat and cold and lightly hazed in fog: I hadn't been missing much. Then I looked over the road and saw to my surprise and delight that I'd stopped right outside an automotive electrician's.

'First car I ever bought new!' declared a cheerful man in overalls after I'd nosed Craig gingerly into the yard round the back. 'Not many of those left now.' We exchanged manly wonder-why laughs: with his smeared glass frontage Craig was a soap-windowed shop at the end of a closing-down sale.

On his instruction I opened the bonnet and activated the wipers; he cocked a practised ear and immediately diagnosed a malfunction beyond his remit. 'It's not electrical, that. Whole linkage has gone. First you'll need to . . .' With much oily-fingered pointing he now embarked on a lengthy account of the remedial procedure. I lost track and all hope with the phrase 'once you've got the scuttle out', but somehow my head kept on nodding. When he was done ('And reassembly is the reverse of removal, as they say in the Haynes manuals') I offered thanks via my full repertoire of toe-curling blokeisms: cheers mate, nice one, howay the lads, look at the tits on that. And then I drove very slowly away into a world steadily Jackson Pollocked by accumulating splatter.

St Helens has been decreed 'the most traditionally British urban area', on the grounds that in our last national census its residents ticked the 'Christian' and 'White British' boxes in unrivalled droves. On a misty Saturday noon Westfield Street certainly had a flat-capped feel to it, a coal-smutted parade of run-down old shops encircled by the gleaming retail dreadnoughts of Asda, Comet and the rest. Its pavements were sparsely populated by aimless, blotchy-faced men sucking the life out of their fags, and its walls studded with shabby and deflating pronouncements: PART-WORN TYRES FOR SALE; NO FLY TIPPING; LEASE FOR ASSIGNMENT; TOILETS CLOSED DUE TO CONSTANT VANDALISM. Through a backdrop of lingering fog I could just make out the chimneys of Pilkington's, final survivor of the half-dozen glassmaking plants that once defined the local economy. In the 1970s, these pumped out such huge volumes of hot water that St Helens' canals supported several species of tropical fish and a healthy colony of terrapins. I suspected that today they'd be frozen over. Once again I looked around at the post-industrial superstore colonies and tried to understand how Britain sustained itself, when all the places where we used to make stuff were now devoted to buying stuff. I remembered the archive films I'd seen at Hull's Maritime Museum, and the fruity, cocksure newsreel voiceover as flat-capped dockers shovelled up wheat: 'England is the very model of an import–export economy. We buy our grain from abroad, and pay for it with manufactures.' That seemed to make sense. What I'd seen in modern Hull and almost every town since absolutely didn't. How could we keep on consuming more and more while producing less and less? I felt myself suddenly weighed down with impending doom: a man who fears for his children's future, and is about to have a really terrible haircut.

Pawnbrokers, tanning salons and grimy, garish takeaways: all the usual commercial suspects were present and correct. Sandwiched between examples of the last two sat a little brick edifice, its tatty gold awning slung over a sign that read: AVANTI HAIR TEAM. Beneath this and a phone number ran the legend, THE SALON WITH NATIONAL AWARDS IN HAIR FASHION. My eyebrows disappeared behind a fringe that would shortly be no more: it seemed a tremendously bold description of the proprietor's triumph in a Channel 5 quest entitled *Britain's Worst Hairdresser*. 'Appointments not always necessary,' said a note on the front door. I pushed it open and walked in.

As a man of middle years, I consider it my duty to regard

most developments in popular culture with alarm and bewilderment. It's not a big ask: I find myself at a moment in history where public display of lavish swathes of underpant and buttock flesh is a coveted young look, rather than a scene from some Freudian anxiety nightmare whose mere memory compels the victim to see out the balance of adolescence locked in their bedroom in a foetal clench of shame. But more inexplicable to me than this, more than even sports utility vehicles or the unstoppable rise of the tattoo, is the British public's ratcheting desperation to appear on television. We appear to have reached a stage where absolutely any humiliation, personal or professional, is worth enduring if the reward is a fleeting moment on one of the 19,400 channels currently available on Freeview alone. There is no pale left to go beyond; I honestly cannot think of a title that might deter either TV commissioning executives or the volunteering public. *Britain's Ugliest Dunce. Britain's Drunkest Dentist. Britain's Deadest Dog.*

I recently watched a programme on intimate surgery in which patients gladly disrobed for full-frontal before and after interviews: no pixellated faces, no distorted voices, no *PLEASE JUST KILL ME NOW* etched in blood across foreheads. One man seemed especially eager to show his relations, friends, work colleagues and fellow Britons what had previously been hidden, even from him, by a pendulous flap of 'pubic apron': a tiny button-mushroom nubbin of penile tissue.

Anyway, John Beirne was a hairdresser, an experienced professional hairdresser, who in 2005, without inducement, threat or deception, offered himself to a TV production team for inclusion in a Channel 5 show which – let us just remind ourselves – was entitled *Britain's Worst Hairdresser*. I have to report here that I missed the broadcast – it clashed with *Christ, I Stink* on Sky 11 – and failed to track down a recording. (The revelation that the show was hosted by Quentin Willson, who is a little irksome and almost entirely bald, may have sapped my investigative enthusiasm.) What I did gather, from generally sympathetic coverage in the local papers, was that John's success had been less to do with any technical shortcomings than his 'repertoire of withering put-downs and a tongue as sharp as his scissors'. At one point he told the show's judge that she looked good for her age, 'considering you've been dead for three weeks'.

The salon was the size of a small studio flat, made smaller by its border of chairs and basins. The chequered floor tiles were lightly bestrewn with hair; tinny hits of yesteryear issued forth from a radio on the reception desk. Two women were at work: a junior stylist stood twisting bits of foil into an old woman's scalp, while a more senior colleague snipped tenderly away at the gingery curls of a toddler, wide-eyed and rigid in his father's lap. I took a seat by the door and waited. On cue a middle-aged man with short, spiky and rather aubergine hair strode briskly in through a door at the back of the salon and installed himself at the reception desk in a proprietorial and excitingly ill-tempered manner. He flung open the appointments book and tutted all over it, then slammed it shut and huffed at the ceiling. I raised myself slightly off my chair and let out one of the vague preludial mumbles available from an extensive repertoire. The effect on Britain's worst hairdresser was immediate. He wheeled round, glowered imperiously down at me, then grabbed a coat from the peg by the door and with a whoosh and a slam disappeared into the misty street.

'That's him gone for the day,' murmured the junior stylist without looking up from her work. Here we go again, I thought. Eyes on the rusty prize, watching it once more snatched away at the last. Could I walk out now, without looking rude or weird? I was weighing it up when the ginger child, still stiff with terror, was carried out past me, tucked under his father's arm like a small surfboard. The oldest present member of the Avanti Hair Team turned to me and proffered an expectant hand at her now vacant chair. I'd come for a bad job; might as well make the best of it.

As someone who really hates having their hair cut – the stilted banter, the spiny offcuts down the back of the neck, the nagging conviction that with three mirrors and a slightly longer right arm I could be doing it myself for free – my tonsorial service regime is a strictly binary affair. Every eight months I go into the barber's looking like James May might if he brushed his hair with a balloon, and come out of it close-shorn in a style my wife has compared to a covered button.

Cut all of my hair off, please: it should be a straightforward process. But it never is, because although I've been to the same barber for almost ten years, he still plainly has no idea who I am, and greets my simple and unchanging request with considerably more bewilderment than it merits. It is one of my fondest wishes to patronise an establishment, any establishment, that I can go into and ask for the usual, but it's not going to happen there. Frankly, unless a shop selling nothing but big bags of cheap crap opens up down the road, it's not going to happen anywhere.

'Half an inch long all over,' I say every time, and every time he asks if I mean to take off half an inch, and I correct him, and then I look up at the mirror and see something close to panic pass across his face. Because my regular barber only really knows how to do one haircut, a style prevalent in the land of his birth in the troubled era that he departed it. His every reflex flick of comb and snip of scissor is made with but one archetype in mind, and which I've since seen immortalised on a great many black-and-white heads at the Museum of Occupation overlooking Famagusta: a 1970s Cypriot schoolboy.

Anyway, this time it was going to be different – and obviously better, with Britain's worst hairdresser now out of the picture. 'What's it to be then, love?' asked the stylist, draping a plastic shroud around me and fastening its Velcro strap behind my neck. Together we looked in the mirror at a head weighed down by eight – in fact nine – months' worth of grizzled haystack. I figured I might as well say what I'd intended to say to her absent boss. 'Up to you. Whatever you think will suit me.'

Liberated by these words, and soothed by the salon's cocooning warmth and the low monotone of my stylist's small talk, I eased back into the chair. The stylist's fingers fluffed and tugged my overgrown busby into some sort of order, then with practised ease she began to snip away at it. If I was ever going to enjoy an experience that involved bits of me being cut off, it would be now. 'Just taking some of the weight out and layering things in a bit at the back and sides,' she said, her hands almost a blur in the mirror as a cascade of shorn locks slid down my gown. 'So what you doing in Sinellens?'

I blew hair out of my eyes and looked in the mirror. Curious things were happening, and happening fast. A rogue shelf of hair leapt free from my left temple, and I could see a patch of scalp just above the opposite ear.

'I'm, er, just kind of looking around and doing things.'

'Oh, right.'

On she snipped, fashioning a wallpaper-brush fringe with a single drastic thwick, then busily eradicating any vestige of symmetry from the curtains that flanked it. I watched my reflection settle into the now familiar blend of horror and exhilaration – the face of a man who has gone in search of the truly dreadful, and found it. 'Of course, John's big into his competitions,' I heard her say at one point, which should have been my cue for some artful probing. If it had, I'd have discovered that John Beirne has in fact won over three hundred awards for being good at cutting hair, but by then I was transfixed into silence. What had until recently been a head of hair was now something else – a helmet made out of old cats. And very badly made. The whole of one ear stood out proud and free, while the other skulked unseen beneath a silver-tabby side-flap. Tufts and clumps erupted at will from the lopsided crown.

'There you go. How's that?'

I swivelled my head from side to side in the mirror, raising a hand to pull a slab of neighbouring hair over the lateral scalp-patch.

'What in the name of Mr Keith Harris have you done to me?' I wailed passionately, in my head. 'Absolutely perfect,' said my mouth.

'Want any product on it?'

She waved her scissors at the bottles and tubs of styling gels and unguents lined luridly up beneath the mirror. A hundred sticky ways of making everything much, much worse.

'Lots,' I said. Five minutes later I walked outside wearing a crested grebe plucked from an oil slick.

I followed a pylon-flanked dual carriageway towards Liverpool, the Irish Sea glinting behind its distant skyline as the sun dispersed the last wisps of fog. It's a city that boasts an impressive portfolio of urban tribulations, and I expected to find most of them showcased in the metropolitan borough of Knowsley, a feature of the *Location, Trumpet, Brantub* bottom ten. *The Future is KNOWsley!* shouted a huge hoarding by the road, which was a promising start. I'd come to understand that the most strident regeneration slogans took a city's true plight and turned it completely on its head, so that when Hull declared itself *Stepping Up*, you knew it was actually falling down, and instead of *Moving Forward*, Middlesbrough kept sliding back. 'The Past was *THEN*sley!' I cried, above the distressing sound of Joe Strummer finding out that he couldn't write songs without Mick Jones.

But the Knowsley Ozzy led me to was an entirely unobjectionable village set in greenery some way outside the city. No matter how hard I stared at the hefty Victorian church it doggedly refused to turn into a derelict factory, and the pensioners seated in neat rows at the bus shelters didn't look like they'd be resuming a brutal turf war as soon as I was round the corner. So I flicked Ozzy off and aimed Craig towards the largest concentration of close-packed roofs, which as later geographical enquiries revealed took me almost immediately out of the challenged borough.

Knowsley's evasion seemed somehow typical of Liverpool, a haughty and insular city that you sense would happily cut itself off entirely, reluctantly emerging every few years to show the outside world how to play football or popular music. Without wishing to come over all Boris Johnson – there's a phrase you don't want to get wrong – I find Liverpudlians rather a contrary bunch. The default civic mentality is a strange blend of chippiness and superiority: most Scousers feel desperately hard done by, even as they're belittling their own neighbours with casual disdain. Southport and St Helens might both lie within Merseyside, but by virtue of falling outside the tight and rigidly defined borders of Scouseland, the residents of each and all points between are sneeringly derided as 'woollybacks', a nickname that dates back to the days when Lancastrian shepherds arrived in Liverpool's markets toting fleeces on their shoulders. (Though I do accept that it is quite funny.)

In a civic delusion that today, with Beatlemania and Bill Shankly now distant memories, seems at best curious, Liverpudlians remain quite convinced that it is the secret and dearest wish of every world citizen to have been born a Scouser. To keep these wannabe billions at bay they've had to install a number of metaphorical barriers to entry. Some, viz the woollyback belt, are geographic: residents of the Wirral – an area comfortably within Liverpool's metropolitan area as it's demarcated on the maps – are dismissed as 'plastic Scousers', or just 'plazzies', for living on the wrong bank of the Mersey. It's a bit like the *appellation contrôlée* system, but with pot-smoking layabouts in grubby sportswear instead of fine French wines. And some are linguistic: when I stopped for petrol halfway from St Helens, with Liverpool already a blatant presence on the horizon, the till attendant and everyone in her queue spoke flat, straight Lancastrian – not even a hint of the mile-a-minute, phlegm-rattling singalong that would assail my ears just up the road. There's no dialectical overlap, no halfway Scouse. It's apartheid by tongue.

That afternoon, driven to despair by the synthesised brass blunderings of The Clash in their death throes, I listened to a lot of BBC Radio Merseyside, and discovered two things. Firstly, that in contravention of the BBC's much declaimed stance on deregionalised, equal-geographic-opportunity, no one without a very strong native accent is allowed behind a Radio Merseyside microphone. Secondly, despite the evident and clearly audible assumption amongst those blessed with this accent that simple possession of it imbues everything they say with a cheeky-chappy, streetwise wit, it really, really doesn't. This may partly explain the very poor opinion of the city and its residents I appear to be expressing here. The rest is down to a simple and unedifying desire to get some retaliation in first, for I now became gradually aware, via road signs, shop fronts and community halls, that I had strayed into the scally badlands.

Croxteth and Norris Green: two places nationally synonymous with deadly territorial feuding. Crocky and Nogzy: their local nicknames, two deeply guttural utterances guaranteed to have a Scouser hacking his tonsils right out onto the pavement. A good old grudge falls right in the sweet-spot of Liverpool's personality matrix, the one with sentimental, never-walk-alone tribalism up one axis and aggrieved, no-surrender stroppiness along the other. Ask a Scouser to bury the hatchet and he'll immediately oblige, deep into your radiator grille. So when these insatiable bearers of enmity reached vendetta saturation point – not a town, national newspaper or football club left in the land that they didn't already hate for ever – they had no choice but to turn on each other. Hence the ridiculous and tragic Nogzy/Crocky feud, a long running battle for 'respect' fought between neighbouring gangs of crop-haired junior Rooneys on stolen mountain bikes. Tragic because it culminated in a completely innocent small boy being shot dead in a pub car park, and ridiculous because – as I now discovered – these badlands weren't at all bad. No smouldering mattresses on the pavement, no wheelless wrecks on bricks, not even a single boarded-up house – just street after quiet and well-kept street of Forties and Fifties council terraces, each with a freshly washed car on the crazy paving. Every hedge was clipped square, and every wheelie bin – each household had three of each, in a range of exciting fashion colours – stood in geometric alignment. The lavish areas of parkland were trimmed and attractive, bearing no relation to the churned and needle-strewn joyriding arenas of my imagination.

Put together, Croxteth and Norris Green would form one of the world's largest council estates, but here there were none of the many environmental inducements to anti-social behaviour that characterised the likes of Bransholme in Hull, or in fact half the streets in half the towns I'd been through. There was deprivation, of course – the estates were built to house workers at a huge English Electric factory whose demolished remains I'd driven past on the way in – but really, for the gang-affiliated youth of these areas to carry on like nothing-to-live-for South Central desperadoes is frankly embarrassing. I might even have told them as much had they been about, but as luck would have it the entire neighbourhood was currently just up the road at Goodison Park – partly to support Everton FC, but mainly to heap abuse upon Manchester United in general and Crocky-reared traitor Wayne Rooney in particular.

Soothed by afternoon sun and a deep purging of pent-up Scousophobia, I drove under the Mersey with a smile and a whistle – an incompatible demeanour for an unwashed man with a terrible museum and a filthy beach to visit. But contrary to every indication on the Wirral Borough Council website, and indeed the stubborn insistence of the plazzie-Scouser desk sergeant on duty at a police station directly opposite, I found the Wirral Museum closed, and keeping its 'laughable mess of random artefacts' very much to itself. In fact I've just discovered – the Maestro-driving Angel of Death had struck once more – that its scattergun exhibits (think mayoral chains of office draped over Viking blankets) will never again see the light of day.

The museum was housed in Birkenhead Town Hall, a granite and sandstone edifice of a heft and grandeur tremendous even by Victorian standards, with half a Parthenon stuck on the front and a mighty 200-foot clock tower. I stepped over the chain strung across its leaf-scattered portico stairway, walked up and looked out across a gracious and expansive stretch of grass, statuary and noble old townhouses: Hamilton Square, home to more Grade 1 listed structures than any address in England but Trafalgar Square. A now familiar pathos took hold. Another symbol of a city's bustling prime reduced to an abandoned mausoleum, another painful contrast between mighty, munificent past and fumbling, impoverished present. The fate of Birkenhead Town Hall – an enormous structure that fills an entire block – now lies ominously in the hands of a Strategic Asset Review panel. As things stand, the only active part of the place appears to be the magistrates' court round the back.

The filthy beach proved a happier let-down. I parked Craig up on the promenade at Hoylake, by the tablecloth lawns of a crown-green bowls club, and saw at once that the rippled sands running off to the distant waters of Liverpool Bay had been ill served by whoever deemed this beach the second horridest in Britain. Little knots of weekend walkers were dotted across the enormous sunlit shore, Boden families in pink wellies, couples arm-in-arm behind hearty, panting dogs. The sky was big and the hilly fields to the west lay becomingly sprinkled with clean white snow. To cartographers, the Wirral Peninsula; to locals, the Scouse Riviera. Neither name did justice to this entirely wonderful prospect, and I couldn't wait to walk far out into it and take wanky album-cover self-portraits with the new camera I'd got for Christmas.

Down on the sand I wandered past shells and seagulls and puddles full of starfish, and generally failed to find myself clambering over bloated livestock carcasses or kicking a path through drifts of faecal coliform and rusty hospital sharps. I was a good 400 yards out before I confronted my first item of human detritus: a single grey sock. To give the survey compilers more leeway than they probably deserve, I concluded that filth was truly in the eye of the beholder. As I gaze out of my window now, I see a back garden that some would doubtless view with disdain. Yet others might nod approvingly, and think: Here lives a man who knows a thing or two about bicycle maintenance (thing one: how to take a bicycle to pieces; thing two: how to pile those pieces up under an enormous blue tarpaulin).

I looked up from the sand with a start: the sun was almost down and I was miles and miles out, nearer to the windfarms and container ships than Craig and the crown-green bowlers. The local paper headline tolled up before me: PLAZZIE COCKNEY WHO WENT TOO FAR, above one of my recovered self-portraits (*Woollyback haircut – the final straw?*). I briskly pursued my lengthening shadow back across the sand, stamped half the

Scouse Riviera into Craig's footwells and set off back for Southport, full of ozone and good cheer. Driving in through the Pontin's security gates felt like returning from day-release.

The heating had now been on for twenty-six hours straight, but my apartment was still no cosier than a branch-line waiting room. After a huddled half-bath I hurried away to the warmth and noise of the entertainment zone, where the previous night repeated itself in Orville-free form. Same failure to secure a dining table, same cheerless handheld roundel of flash-fried flesh, same pervasive air of beery unease. A dance troupe up on the stage stamped and smiled their way desperately through a medley of Barry Manilow hits, utterly ignored by an audience focused on texting and alcohol. Gum-chewing security operatives with headsets cast their dead-eyed gaze across the profane clamour. All the kids were either shooting zombies in the face or watching Ultimate Fight Championship in the bar. Those in the thinnest T-shirts were outside in the dark frost, amongst them a red-cheeked youngster of about seven or eight endeavouring to cajole some smoking teenage girls – I assume his big sister and a few friends – into a game of chase. 'Come on, come on, I bet you couldn't catch me even if I was just walking!' As he hopped expectantly about beside them one of the girls half-turned to him, her face screwed up in disdain, and said, 'You on the weed or something? Shut your bleeding head and piss off.'

I crawled into my tiny, tomb-cold bed feeling queasy and hollow, as if every scrap of those happy-camper fantasies had just been plucked from my childhood memory banks and nasally extracted. All through the night I imagined cheerful thoughts seeping out of my scalp, though the bathroom mirror at dawn explained this sensation in more prosaic terms: twelve hours after the stylist laid down her scissors, new things were still going wrong with my haircut. Even as I watched, two Yiddish ringlets bounced free from a craggy temple, like springs through an old sofa.

Light overnight snow had laid a patchy white veneer over

219

the exercise-yard mud. Every window looking down on it was steamed up and curtained. Standing there wrapped in my bedding, hair akimbo, I looked out and suddenly felt desperate and alone, as if I was on the run and holed up. 'Police traced Moore to a Pontin's holiday camp in Southport, Merseyside,' I said aloud, and in that instant resolved to leave this place at once and for good, even if it meant passing up a night's accommodation that I'd paid for in advance, and a thick wad of unused electrocards (they're still in my wallet: any offer over 25p per kwH considered). Five minutes later I was throwing my bags into Craig's boot. And half an hour after that, with the legacy of my frenzied efforts at manual frost dispersal smeared and streaked across the windscreen, I finally inched out of the compound. Matey nods were exchanged with the security guard, though I might as well have given him a great big slobbery kiss of death: within a year, Pontin's found itself in receivership.

Chapter Thirteen

It was another crisp and magnificent day – and this one came with scenery to match, though appreciating the majesty of North Wales without windscreen wipers necessitated several hard-shoulder stops, four litres of Tesco Value table water and an entire box of mansize tissues. Muscular, snow-capped foot-hills of Snowdonia to the left, sun-dappled Irish Sea to the right, and ahead long miles of empty tarmac and – whoa there, young Craig! – the odd slick of black ice.

Ozzy's announcement that we had reached our fucking destination took me rather by surprise. Lost in the landscapes, and the surprisingly extensive acoustic hinterland charted by the Wombles' second album, I'd forgotten that my 65-mile journey had a goal, and that this goal was Sw Môr Môn. An unusually economic use of the Welsh language – the nearest settlement had announced itself, mercifully not aloud, as Llanfairpwllgwynyll – this was the translation emblazoned beneath the cartoon prawn who welcomed me to Anglesey Sea Zoo. To some visitors 'shoddy', to others 'weird', but to all an unmissable opportunity to indulge the abysmal pun reflex that fish seem fated to trigger. From the zoo's website comments: 'It was eely good', 'we don't think it cod be batter', 'we had a whale of a time in a great plaice'. I pulled up in the empty carp-ark and thought: Fins can only get wetter.

'That'll be £7.25,' said the young man at the entrance desk, sounding a little apologetic, and then a little desperate: 'Though your ticket does entitle you to come back as often as you like for the next seven days.' Consultation of the opening hours posted beside him inspired a brief, wild fantasy in which I sought to extract forty-nine hours' worth of enjoyment from his establishment.

Anglesey Sea Zoo, I very quickly gathered, is a showcase of the underwater quotidian. Its first dim chamber was dominated by a shallow tank full of plaice doing what they do best, namely very little beyond blending in with the seabed. Those that followed allowed many further native marine creatures to demonstrate a similar appetite for humble inertia: mussels, starfish, anemones. In short, anyone who arrives at Sw Môr Môn hoping to ride a manatee or watch dolphins vault through laser hoops will leave underwhelmed. This is a place for those whose sober aquatic interests are not catered for by the more prevalent breed of glitzy aquaria: the kind of people who don't snigger when invited to adopt a grey mullet, or to press a button labelled, *Bellamy on flat fish* (sadly not on a snack vending machine).

For two hours I walked alone through the dark and dripping cold, pressing my numb nose up to laminated information sheets about the common prawn, gazing at bland and cod-like British sharks, and being severally reminded of the dangers posed to marine life by plastic waste. There was standing water, a pervasive smell of fuel oil, and much stooping through corroded bulkheads. A low-tech wave machine periodically dumped a rusty skipful of brine onto some mocked-up rock pools with a great booming crash. I began to feel like a captain going down with his stricken trawler. This strange and ominous vibe encapsulated the shoddy weirdness that previous visitors had referred to, and which was now keenly emoted by a very straight-faced middle-aged couple who passed me at the speed of a Benny Hill title sequence. But in my new capacity as a connoisseur of the odd and the awful, I liked it. It was so mundane, yet so mad. I found myself drawing especial vicarious pleasure from the Welsh translations, imagining the happy challenge presented by 'skates and rays can detect electrical pulses through tiny pores on their undersides' to a native linguist more commonly obliged to earn his or her crust from 'give way to sheep' or 'driver carries no cash, look you'.

As I walked on I came to appreciate and then internally applaud Anglesey Sea Zoo's dogged repudiation of the gloss and glamour that defines their better-known rivals. At Seaworld, a demonstration of marine biology in action would mean some perma-tanned high-fiver in a cutdown wetsuit counting clown fish aloud. Here, through streaky Perspex, I watched a silent Open University type in a crumpled lab coat do painstaking things with a pipette. A yellowy Sellotaped sheet laid out his scientific agenda: an incest-proof breeding programme for short-snouted seahorses. For whatever reason, this was not explained in Welsh.

Having failed to squeeze into my itinerary the roundly denounced National Lobster Hatchery in Cornwall – 'smaller than my bedroom, with some portholes through which you can see a lobster' – you may imagine how my already buoyant enjoyment levels now soared on finding that Anglesey Sea Zoo incorporated the National Lobster Hatchery of Wales. It wasn't a sprawling complex. A newspaper clipping stuck to the relevant viewing area recounted a 'scandal' in which hot lobster-on-lobster content filmed here had been passed off as natural-environment footage in the BBC series *Blue Planet*. The evidence of my eyes suggested this deception would have required some very lavish set-dressing. 'When a mummy lobster and a daddy lobster love each other very much,' an honest information panel might have read, 'they get it on in a big white bucket.'

At length I made it to the cafeteria, where I sat down with a cup of tea and a big bun and concluded that Anglesey Sea Zoo's perceived shortcomings were all of society's own making. On the face of it, beyond a little light seahorse-sexing, the place offered nothing a family couldn't experience for free on any of the long stretches of shoreline available close at hand. But then these days families can't seem to face combing beaches or poking about in rock pools, in fact can't seem to face anything that isn't a packaged and processed experience presented by some half-arsed cartoon mascot, and which doesn't offer en-suite refreshments and a hateful giftshop packed full of tenuously relevant rubbish (in ASZ's case, anything with a picture of Sponge Bob Square Pants on it was considered fair game). And though £7.25 did seem a bit much, I strongly suspected this barely covered the insurance premiums in an age where a splashed pair of shoes might spark off ruinous litigation. We sue sea zoos on the sea shore. With all that said, I drove out of Sw Môr Môn vowing to bring my children here should the family find itself in the Anglesey area. Apart from anything else, it would be worth it just to see their faces when we drew up in the car park for the seventh morning in a row.

A stiff wind blew me back over the Menai Straits, past fields of hunkered-down static caravans and into the doyenne of terrible North Welsh seaside resorts. Its introductory thorough-fare was impressively unwelcoming: scrubby dunes to one side, and to the other an endless blue hoarding that kept at bay a mountain range of demolished rubble. This, I knew, was all that remained of a once famous old funfair, home to a number of historic rides, amongst them the world's last surviving circular water chute. But the developers had just gone bust, leaving their vision for the site no more than faded words on a weatherbeaten 'coming soon' billboard: a 92,000-square-foot Asda, and the legend, RHYL – GOING FORWARD.

From residents to erstwhile holidaymakers, it's hard to find anyone with a good word to say about Rhyl. 'My aunt is the Mayor of Rhyl,' began my favourite onslaught, 'but family loyalty aside, it's the most awful place I know.' The town was 'an absolute scum-hole', a place where 'seagulls fly upside-down because there's nothing worth shitting on'. *The Times* called it 'Britain's first shanty town', and the Consumer Association took a break from testing dishwashers to slag off Rhyl as 'depressing and down at heel'. The last time the place made the news was when John Prescott punched a man in the face there, and with the waning of Carol Vorderman's celebrity the mantle of Rhyl's most famous daughter has passed back to Ruth Ellis, the last British woman to be hanged. Then there's the issue of nomenclature. Rhyl: it's another of those stark and plug-ugly town-names, hanging over the place like an albatross, with a beakful of your chips.

The dunes disappeared behind a flank of bare concrete desultorily topped with brown-leaved yucca plants, and the mothballed building site gave way to Homebase-sized amusement sheds – bleeping and open, as such places always seem to be whenever there are helpless fruit-machine addicts to amuse. Then it was into a long, ramshackle parade of towering Victorian boarding houses, some boarded up, some knocked down, and most of the rest – according to locals and the press – divided into bedsitting accommodation for the benefit of unemployed Liverpudlian opiate enthusiasts.

I pulled up in a pay-and-display bay and set off up the promenade with a whistle, the sound a budget-conscious motorist makes when it's Sunday. But jaunty tootling quickly proved ill-suited to my environment. A local website had informed me that 'Rhyl basks in a micro-climate said to match the temperatures in Torbay'. Said by who? The bitter Irish Sea wind forcing itself up my sleeves and trouser legs had the answer: said by liars. I think you'll find that at least 98 per cent of all 'micro-climates' are complete fabrications, made up by tourist boards or friends who have moved somewhere horrid but still want you to visit them.

The seafront parade, in sympathy with the conditions, proved comfortably more dreadful than any I had yet experienced. Some of it was shut down for the season, but most of it was shut down for ever. Rhyl had even managed to kill off its retailers of last resort, those elsewhere indestructible commercial cockroaches who moved in when all else failed: CHEAP STORE – MANY ITEMS £1 – EVERYTHING NOW 50P – WE HAVE CLOSED DOWN. Every frontage was peeling and scabbed. A lot of upper floors had been completely painted over with thick magnolia emulsion, windows and all. Day-glo starbursts blared shabby inducements like FREE LAGER WITH ROAST MEAL! and CHEAPEST

CHIPS IN RHYL. An invisible asterisk had hovered above most of the previous scenes of decay and decline I'd passed through, reminding me that whatever was no longer being done there, it probably hadn't been much fun to do in the first place, like mining coal or making sulphuric acid. But there was no asterisk here: just the betrayed and haunting air of a place that had been purpose-built for having a good time, and now wasn't.

In desperation I struck off down a side street. A mistake: it was worse. The pavement looked like it had been cluster bombed, and half the boarding-house hulks that lined it were shedding roof tiles and had their doors and windows sealed up behind drilled-metal shutters. Looping back round I passed an estate agent's window, and saw houses priced in four figures. I plunged my hands deep into my coat pockets, bowed my head to the incoming bluster and hurried back to the seafront.

The first bathing machines were wheeled out onto the Rhyl sands in the early years of Victoria's reign, but in accordance with the usual pattern, the place took off as a seaside destination when the railway came to town in 1848. At a stroke this opened up the resort to millions of city dwellers – most of them in the deeply land-locked West Midlands, who found that despite being 100 miles from Birmingham, Rhyl was nonetheless their nearest beach. For over a hundred years the Brummies came in happy droves. Rhyl was soon home to the largest fairground in Wales, a half-mile pier, and the splendidly ornate five-domed Pavilion Theatre, whose massive, illuminated central hemisphere was visible from way out to sea. A mechanical elephant carried children along the prom. So too did the oldest miniature railway in Britain.

Unusually for those in charge of a post-war British seaside town, Rhyl's elders saw the cheap-flight package-holiday crisis coming and took action – but because they did so in the early 1970s, all of it was horribly wrongheaded. The pier was pulled down in 1972, and the wondrous Pavilion Theatre a year later – reborn soon after as a corrugated oatmeal hangar with all the ritzy good-time appeal of a supermarket distribution centre. A number of shopping arcades were built in homage to the most dispiriting trends in period retail architecture, and the mechanical elephant was tarred and feathered and pushed down a well. In a few short years, every trace of the character that had made Rhyl seem glamorous and exuberant was brutally stripped away. People go on holiday to find something different, even if that difference is only the weather. But by the end of the 1970s, Rhyl was beginning to look and feel like every other slightly downbeat, grey-skied town in Britain – a process completed once the funfair went and the beach was shielded from sight by that big concrete wall. Holidaymakers from Wolverhampton got off the train or out of their cars and found themselves in Wolverhampton-by-Sea – in fact, Wolverhampton-by-Wall. Llandudno, just up the coast from Rhyl and for a century its poor and backward relation, was run by clueless Luddites who wouldn't knock down their pier and other outdated embarrassments. As a result, the town has cleaned up from the current boom in genteel and nostalgic mini-breaks, and now counts itself the largest seaside resort in Wales.

Rhyl's fall from grace was swift and dramatic. Between 1979 and 1988, the number of visitor nights fell by over a quarter, and then by another third in the seven years that followed. Of the eighteen separate seafront properties that offered tourist accommodation in the 1977 season, just three were still doing so by 2000. And so Rhyl skulked away into the shadowy overlap that exists between the melancholy of a faded seaside resort and the heavier shit of hardcore urban degeneration. Attracted by the ample availability of cheap accommodation, jobless drifters gravitated towards the town. By the mid 1980s, the tabloids had dubbed it the 'Costa del Dole', and today a quarter of Rhyl's 26,000 population lives in long-term b. & b. accommodation. The West End ward – which takes in the seafront – rates as the most deprived area in Wales, and the town as a whole is burdened with the highest unemployment rate in Britain: 48.9 per cent of the adult population is classified as economically inactive. A third of all Denbighshire crimes are committed in Rhyl. The Scousers-and-smack reputation seems to date back to 1996, when local police discovered that most of Rhyl's heroin addicts were being supplied by a fourteen-year-old boy from Liverpool. (He kept his stash in those plastic capsules out of Kinder Eggs, and was driven around in a big car by two heavies: the whole operation seems like some *Young Apprentice* for class-A drug dealers.)

Back on West Parade even the seagulls sounded mournful. Rhyl's Victorian visitors had gazed up at the town's snowed-on Snowdonian backdrop with hearty relish, but today the mountains looked less of an inspiration than a reproach, there to emphasise the frail impermanence of the dying town laid out at their feet, in fact the futility of all human endeavour. Everything kept going wrong for Rhyl, yet still they kept trying to put it right. To atone for the misguided demolition of their pier and that splendid theatre, Rhyl's authorities had erected some faux Victorian booths with roof finials and Gothic arches, housing the tourist office and the snack bars and coin-slot attractions of a 'children's village'. But it all looked so half-baked and shoddy: sagging fibreglass, stained concrete and business-park brickwork, a bad copy of a fake, like Main Street USA in Disneyland recommissioned by Leonid Brezhnev. His input would certainly explain the starkly incompatible 250-foot glory-to-the-people observation tower that speared into the cold, dead sky.

Further up, the seafront pleasure gardens that had been one of Rhyl's many pride and joys were now a skatepark, an abstract landscape of ramps and half-pipes. While appreciating the value of such a facility in a town where needle-sharing is only a bored afternoon away, I couldn't understand why it had to be put here. Rhyl is hardly short of vacant land, yet the town had opted to hand over its showpiece public space – the promenade's focal point, backdrop to a million sepia postcards – to hooded teenage miserablists.

I peered over the sea wall and beheld Rhyl's fabled miles of golden sand, shrunk by high tide to a muddy ribbon of shingle. By this stage it hardly seemed to matter: I fancied that even in high season, the British bucket-and-spade holiday demanded a degree of goose-pimpled hardiness that today's centrally heated, double-glazed native namby-pambies no longer possessed. Lay out a towel on just one Mediterranean beach, and there's no going back to windbreaks.

Hence the Sun Centre, Rhyl's attempt to 'bring the seaside inside', opened to great hurrahs in 1980. Permanent summer! Tropical storm effects! Europe's first indoor surfing pool! But even from the outside I could sense the excitement hadn't been sustained. A massive plastic barn, weathered and anonymous, the Sun Centre looked less like a climate-controlled aquatic paradise than the sort of place where you might find yourself losing an argument with customer services about a faulty leaf blower.

I knew it wouldn't be open again for two months, but I was keen to see what had inspired contributors at reviewcentre. com to rate the place as the worst tourist attraction in all of Wales. Happily, it shared a lobby with the New Pavilion Theatre, which was preparing for a matinée performance of *Noddy in Toyland* (forthcoming highlights: *Roger Dee Sings the Johnny Cash Story* and *Go West – the 25th Anniversary Tour*). I walked in and pressed my face up to the Sun Centre's locked glass doors, catching a thin waft of chlorine, mouldy towels and last season's chip fat. Drained and stained, the irregular-shaped pools seemed sad and creepy; the primary-hued plastic employed for everything from water slides to snack huts had dulled and roughened like an old toothbrush. The whole Chernobyl fairground look.

Poor Rhyl. They'd drained the civic coffers building this place, only to see its attractions swiftly matched, then trumped, by every other suburban leisure centre in Britain. Beyond the odd mouthful of Elastoplast, most of the online gripes focused on the Sun Centre's failure to improve or update, to offer jaded regulars something more, something different for their £7.95. Today, Europe's first indoor surfing pool isn't even the best in Wales.

I tramped across the gum-blotted carpet tiles and pushed my way out into the wind. Opposite stood a pair of large Victorian hotels in the mock-Tudor style: one was for sale, the other long-since burnt-out. 'Rhyl just needs to stop pretending it's a tourist town,' said one local commentator. 'There's nothing for tourists here, so why keep hoping they'll come back?' Walking back towards Craig, I wondered what choice the place had. Perhaps in America, or somewhere else more ruthlessly commercial, the local authorities would have bowed to market forces, accepted their town had outlived its usefulness and abandoned it. I fired Craig up, stuck the heater on max and puttered off towards Rhyl's caravan belt. 'The best thing about Rhyl is the A548 out of it,' wrote one local, introducing a new spin on an old joke. 'The worst thing is that this takes you straight to Prestatyn.'

Craig built up a decent head of steam as darkness fell and we reeled our way back north-west on England's motorway network. I drove much too fast to Castleford, which offered no room at any of its shittier inns, and even faster to Doncaster, which did.

Doncaster ranked fifteenth on the *Location* list, and was my wife's personal nomination – courtesy of many bleak and hypothermic evenings spent changing trains there en route to York University, whose memory even twenty years on brings out her thousand-yard stare. An Ozzy-resistant roundabout network and the MP3 player's decision to engage 'repeat' mode during Kevin Rowland's cover version of 'The Greatest Love of All' meant I arrived in central Doncaster ready to hate everything about the place, but it just didn't happen. My downtown hotel had been damned in the harshest terms by reviews that ranked it worse than 597 Yorkshire rivals, and better than only eight, but had naturally just emerged from a comprehensive makeover. So too, as I discovered during a brisk walk through Doncaster's silent night, had the railway station, restored to the airy, bright, monochrome grandeur of its 1938 refit – the very year that the Doncaster-built *Mallard* set a record it still holds as the fastest steam locomotive on earth. I found it hard to imagine such an inspiringly historic building playing host to the worst nights of my wife's life, though she may be pleased to hear that the forebearance displayed during her many ordeals is commemorated by a discreet plaque near the platform 3 waiting room.

Doncaster's shopping malls seemed no worse than averagely bland and ill-considered, and its streets displayed no signs of rampant civic despair beyond a few too many Cash Converters and the odd 99p-all-night booze promotion. And the flag-stoned market square was a proper delight, congregated with venerable coaching inns and the fancy old façades of Doncaster's corn and wool exchanges. I'd forgotten that places like this ever survived in British town centres, and felt something akin to relief when I walked round the back and saw St George's Minster, a jewel of Victorian Gothic and the town's loveliest edifice, cowering in the middle of a gyratory system.

What's bright yellow and contains 1,872 calories? That's right: deep-fried Scotsman's liver on a bed of Quavers. But lagging just one calorie behind is Chinese lemon chicken, a dish that had been on my to-eat list as the unhealthiest available on British high streets, and which fate now chose to offer up in a menu affixed to a restaurant window directly opposite my hotel.

'Is sweet, yeh?' said the terrifically enthusiastic waitress when I placed my order. 'You like sweet?'

'I absolutely love it,' I lied, for my place on the Chinese takeaway taste spectrum lies at the distant other extreme: sour-and-sourer.

'Oh, I tell husband in kitchen! He make special for you, extra sweet!'

The restaurant was the usual study in red, gold and heavily lacquered imperial black. On my table a plastic sprig of pink blossom sat in a vase full of coloured glass gravel; it was promptly joined by a basket of prawn crackers and a pint of lager – not my last of the evening, if the waitress's terrible parting words lived up to their tongue-varnishing promise. I didn't quite have the place to myself. A few tables back a young executive was trying to impress two female colleagues – and doing an excellent job of it, if one assumed they were interviewing him for a position as South Yorkshire's most insufferable

231

arse. At one point I heard him say, 'Let me offer you ladies a king prawn – I'm in chill-out project-handover mode.' At no point did I hear his companions say anything that wasn't a request for more wine.

My yellow peril arrived during a monologue on the interpersonal shortcomings of Carl in the finance department over at Derby HQ. 'You lucky!' said the waitress, laying down a steaming plate and a bowl neatly filled with a little sphere of boiled rice. 'I go in kitchen and husband has coat on, want to go home!' My face did its best to register curious concern through a mist of challenging odours. 'Today, whole day, we have seven customer – you eight! Yesterday five!'

The rise and fall of the high-street Chinese restaurant, as I later established, is directly and curiously connected to the similar parabola traced by another British institution. In 1958, London-based restaurateur John Koon met Billy Butlin, a regular customer at the Chinese takeaway – Britain's first – that Koon had recently opened on Queensway. As his dabbling with monorails made clear, Billy had a weakness for exotic novelty, and eagerly struck up an agreement with Koon to open a 'Chinese kitchen' in every one of his holiday camps (signature dish: chicken chop suey and chips). The popularity of this strange new food was instant and enormous, and when the Butlin's millions went back home they wanted more of it. Within a decade, Britain was home to over a thousand Chinese restaurants.

After the waitress had gone, I took a steadying draught of Carlsberg, then assessed the task at hand. My plate was a stack of battered meat wedges doused in amber gel: it looked like the result of some ill-fated experiment by the young Colonel Sanders. 'To my great consternation,' I imagined him writing in his journal, 'it appears that Kentucky folk have no taste for roosters boiled in marmalade.'

I speared a wedge with a chopstick and crammed the whole thing into my mouth. Extraordinary sensations were unleashed at once, all of them strange and wrong, as if my palate had been shortcircuited. It was like one of those salt/sugar cereal mishaps we've all endured, except without the end bit where you spit Brine Flakes out all over the table then tip the balance down the sink, spluttering imprecations.

Chinese Lemon Chicken has been described in print as 'the most offensive gastronomic insult to any indigenous culinary tradition', and it's a truism that oriental food as served on British high streets bears little relation to the genuine article, heavily corrupted as it has been to suit native tastes. That much was evident in the terrible things being done inside my mouth by the flagrant chief ingredient: lemon curd is a comestible I don't imagine you'd find on many a Beijing shelf. Nor indeed, I thought during another Carlsberg rinse-out, on many a Doncastrian shelf, not these days. There seemed something stubbornly unreconstructed about this dish, something very 1958: a post-rationing splurge of sugar and spice and all things nice (more sugar). Lemon chicken packs the gut-wobbling punch of three Big Macs and a packet of crisps – 94 per cent of a woman's recommended daily calorie intake on a single plate, and as much as 112 per cent of a man's, should he find himself obliged to sluice it down with three pints of lager. But in 1958, post-war and pre-car, too many calories was a good thing.

Anyway, just as Butlin's found itself superseded by more glamorous, more authentic and less stodgy alternatives, so did Chinese restaurants. They've been a declining high-street presence since the 1990s, some rebranded as Thai or Malaysian, many more just throwing in the soy-stained towel: by 2009, fifteen Chinese restaurants or takeaways were closing every week. A recent catering-industry survey identified 'a reputation for being fatty and laden with additives' as the key factor. I've just looked up a recipe for 'takeaway style lemon chicken': amongst the more troubling ingredients is something called 'chicken powder'.

But after everything the waitress had said to me I knew I would have to clean my plate, even as I watched its contents congeal beneath a wrinkled, iridescent crust, like radioactive rice pudding. The final mouthful was dispatched in the manner of Cool Hand Luke tackling that fiftieth boiled egg. Twelve hours later its legacy was still taking the edge off my appetite, though that might have had something to do with my curious decision to eat jelly babies for lunch.

Prepare yourself for the future – tomorrow will become the future. Thus read the legend inside the uneaten fortune cookie I'd lethargically thumped asunder, and which – in a *Mordor – Going Forward* kind of way – proved a decent encapsulation of the day.

Chapter Fourteen

The three years I spent at Sheffield University bequeathed me such a strong and lasting affection for the town that in the decades since I must have been back there – ooooh, let's think – once. In the mid 1980s Sheffield was a tragic mess, shell shocked by the sudden and complete collapse of its industrial heritage, from be-all to end-all in ten years flat. I used to walk into lectures across the derelict factories and foundries that filled huge swathes of the urban landscape, even right near the centre. If walls could talk, Sheffield's were mumbling, 'Well, that's great. Now what?' All except for the massive concrete brow of Park Hill flats, staring me out from the hilltop behind the station, then letting rip with a ragged yell: 'Fuck off, student TWAT!'

Most university cities have a bit of a town-v-gown situation, and in Sheffield's, Park Hill doubled as Berlin Wall and killing fields. The estate's menacing, fortified enormity was complemented by a terrifying reputation for lawless violence. Large and heavy objects – sideboards, domestic appliances, crates full of milk bottles – were heaved off the thirteenth-floor roof so regularly that the council had been obliged to paint a yellow 'safety line' on the footpaths beneath, six feet out from the walls. Cab drivers talked in hushed tones of stairwells blocked with drifts of rusty needles and dead dogs. Whenever the local TV news crew was sent in to cover some sordid atrocity, the reporter's reedy gabblings were all but drowned out by the cameraman gunning their van's engine. In three years I only twice crossed into the badlands behind Park Hill, once to get a tyre for my Morris Minor van, and once to buy some garden gnomes to decorate an ironic rockery (fuck off, student TWAT!). On both occasions I afforded the glowering fortress of doom a generously wide berth.

So I was laying a few ghosts to rest as Craig eased to a halt in one of Britain's largest shadows. I cranked up the handbrake, bit off another soft sugared head, then walked out to discover what I'd been missing all those years ago – and what side of the Park Hill fence I now sat on. Because on one hand, it's the biggest listed building in Europe, awarded Grade II status by English Heritage in 1997. On the other, Park Hill was the only residential structure that the British public hated badly enough to vote onto that *Demolition* shortlist.

Consult the original planning documentation or hear the testimonies of the first tenants, and you'll wonder how on earth anyone could even think of tearing down this landmark icon, this giant stride in forward-thinking public housing. But stand in the gale of cold piss that howls beneath those dour concrete cliffs, as I did now, and you'll be shaking your head for a very different reason. It's perhaps appropriate that I saw Park Hill in a netherworld between life and death: bereft of residents, and stripped to the bare skeleton whose influential design and construction earnt it that listing.

Sketched out in the mid 1950s and completed in 1960, Park Hill was acclaimed as the world's most ambitious inner-city development: an attempt to transplant an entire slum-zone community of 3,500 people into a single enormous building. What could possibly go wrong? Yet impressively, indeed incredibly, the planners did everything right. 'The problem facing anyone designing a high-density project such as Park Hill,' they wrote, 'is to avoid creating a vast inhuman block.' Problem? Avoid? You can almost hear the incredulous disdain of those who went on to give us Cumbernauld's Megastructure, the Trinity Square car park and other spirit-crushing memorials to the unknown citizen. But Sheffield's planning department somehow managed to avoid mistakes that hadn't even been made yet: it was as if they'd been visited in their dreams by some council-block resident from the future, offering detailed and articulate insights into his plight.

Most fundamentally, they took great pains to preserve the transplanted community, and maintain an environment where its spirit could flourish. Neighbouring families were moved together into blocks named after their old roads. Every flat was spread over two floors, at least a bit like a house. Every front door opened onto a wide landing, at least a bit like a street – broad enough to play games, ride bikes, and famously broad enough for the cheery local milkman to do his rounds in a float (ingenious exploitation of the site's steep gradients afforded him – and offered the residents – direct and more or less level access from the ground to every floor but the thirteenth). The same careful micro-management endowed continuity upon all the new services and facilities housed in the Park Hill complex. Brand-new school but same classmates and teachers; brand-new pubs but same regulars and landlords; brand-new shops but same butchers and bakers. Bingo at the social club, wide green spaces round the back and a bird's-eye view of the *Flying Scotsman* pulling out of the station far below. Then of course there were the obvious lifestyle enhancements: indoor sanitation, fitted kitchens, central heating. Silent footage of early residents – plentifully available on the Yorkshire Film Archive's splendid website – shows faces a-glow with promised-land rapture, families who still can't believe their luck. A complementary set of clips depicts the mouldering, sub-Dickensian slumlands that in 1961 they had just vacated.

Park Hill's front line, the hefty battlement that looks down at the city, was now a stripped-down, fenced-off building site, but I found I could freely roam the blocks and spurs behind, connected at irregular angles like a buckled swastika. Vacant council estates are not famously easy on the eye, but behind all the spot-welded shutters and spray paint, Park Hill's original merits were plain. Those milkfloat-friendly landings really were capacious, a good 10 feet wide: proper 'streets in the sky', albeit now pressed into service as 'toilets in the night'. A discreet chimney sprang from the onsite incinerator that heated every flat in Park Hill, fuelled by the estate's own rubbish – how's that for 1959? The grassy communal areas were expansive and bright, and in the sharp winter sun the view was sensational – especially now that the sad gaps in the skyline as I remembered it were now decorously plugged with shiny new hotels and offices, even an observation wheel. And though the whole place was as grubby as you might reasonably expect of a structure that went up when the *Flying Scotsman* was still chuffing out smuts, nothing had cracked or fallen off or gone mouldy. From first sketch to last brick, Park Hill was a proper job.

Throughout the 1960s, life at the estate carried on in line with the happiest expectations, all for one and one for all, homely and houseproud: online reminiscences are particularly emphatic on the regularity with which every housewife mopped her doorstep and its adjacent area of landing. And then, in just a few short years, everything went Bransholme. Men of working age had been conspicuous by their absence in those archive films, all of them away doing a shift down the spoon factory. But in the mid Seventies, Sheffield's age-old industries tipped into the aforementioned decline, and by the time I pitched up in my Swarovski-encrusted mortarboard and ermine-trimmed gown there were no spoon factories left. The hard-working, threshold-polishing families moved away in search of jobs, or fragmented into unemployed disaffection. We'll build you a shiny model community, and you keep it that way: this was the unwritten Park Hill contract, but it went unread and unsigned by the new tenants, largely plucked from the council's growing list of 'problem families'. Out with the doorstep-moppers, in with the lift-pissers. In just a few years, the estate degenerated from a one-owner, lovingly maintained pride and joy to an abandoned joyrider's cast-off.

I'd grown accustomed to coming away from failed residential schemes feeling unalloyed pity for the residents, and the soulless, decaying chicken-coops they had been forced to call home.

But the second-generation of Park Hill tenants had inherited a rather wonderful model coop, then crapped all over it and rolled eggs off the roof. I suppose these things happen when you've got too much time on your talons.

Stretching a hand towards Craig's door I finally saw someone: a youngish community support officer, doing his beat. I buttonholed him and he cheerfully responded, supplying a wry rundown of the scheduled refurbishments – 'funny-coloured' cladding, 'some sort of flowery meadow' and (a dangerous flirtation with student-twat irony) a crown-green bowls club. The scheme involved passing one of Britain's largest and most heroic public projects into private hands, which didn't seem right, and had indeed already gone wrong: with property prices in freefall, the redevelopment was being mothballed. 'A thousand flats at £130,000 each?' he declared, a little wildly. 'I don't think so. Everyone up here still thinks of Park Hill as the Alamo.' And with that he recalled some of the professional challenges he had faced as a semi-policeman on the estate, confirming my memories of the 'safety line' and describing at colourful length the fight at an estate pub that had ended with two severed ears on the floor. 'Always been a hot-spot for us, this place, even now it's empty,' he said. 'You know the kind of illegal activities people like to do when they think they can't be seen.' That'll be everything but streaking, I thought, but I smiled and nodded manfully all the same. Then, in fading light, I drove away through a very different Sheffield, all swish Continental trams and Waitroses, one of which I soon found myself walking out of with two bags of winegums and a Crunchie. I was unwrapping a tube of fruit pastilles in a Nottingham petrol station when I realised what was happening to me: one heavy fix of lemon chicken, and I'd become a hopeless slave to glucose.

There was one standout reason to visit Nottingham, but I found myself reluctant to investigate the city's long-standing record as Britain's gunshot-wound capital. Instead I came to experience Maid Marian Way: a suitably awful name for a thoroughfare variously denounced as the fourth worst in England (by an urban-design quango), the ugliest in Britain (by listeners to BBC Radio 4's *Today* programme) and no less than the most appalling in all of Europe (by a professor of architecture at the city's own university). By way of a preparatory bonus, as the evening rush hour droned by I found myself in the antechamber of hell itself, chewing down the last of the green ones.

Railway hotels are generally a bit horrid, and their guests generally don't care. They arrive ground down by the dispiriting rigours of long-distance rail travel, exhausted and abused, unworthy of all that is clean or warm or comfy. And why should the proprietors make the effort? It's not as if they're going to get any repeat business from patrons cast into their reception area by a one-off roll of the traveller's dice. So what if the odd especially dissatisfied customer storms out, making everyone loudly aware of his intention never to return? He wouldn't have returned anyway, even if you'd bestrewn his pillow with complimentary sovereigns and laid on a naked string quartet to welcome him into breakfast.

The Gresham Hotel, a four-square Gothic hulk squeezed between Nottingham station and a stub of industrial canal, had evidently been in the grim and grimy game for long decades. I parked in a cobbled yard round the back, all oily puddles and steepling old warehouses, like the scene of Bill Sikes's last stand. Opening the Gresham's streaky glass door released that come-hither institutional scent of stale cabbage and dribble, which intensified as I walked up the two flights of stairs to reception. This revealed itself, just about, as a fortified minicab-office hunkered away in the corner of a gloomy, panelled cavern, hot as an engine room and twice as smelly.

The receptionist was a timid young African woman who apologetically asked for payment in advance (£24 plus a very ambitious £6 charge for parking), then handed over my key with a flinching don't-blame-me quarter-smile. 'How long has this place been a hotel?' I asked, in genuine curiosity. It was far more convincing as an oppressive and seedily dingy snooker club.

'Long time,' she whispered, shaking her head slowly. 'Long, long time.'

The journey to my room took in some very broad staircases and a succession of claustrophobic corridors, lined with bare wooden doors and laid with carpeting designed by some Victorian on a bad opium trip. Decoration was restricted to images of green stick men proceeding towards open thresholds with more than their usual urgency. Throughout this trek the ambient temperature fell steadily, and when I heaved open my door I was met by a morgue-strength chill. I gazed in wonder at the compact, ancient miseries thus revealed. 'Just try to imagine you're in a Bogart movie,' read a review which uniquely tried to extract positives from the Gresham experience, though I've since studied Humph's filmography and can find no mention of *The Suicidal Vagrant*.

The corridors had smelt like the inside of a very old wardrobe; this room smelt like the outside of a very old dog. I threw the light switch and beheld its cramped and spartan squalor: not enough room to swing a cat, though the dented, blotted woodchip walls suggested someone had given it a good go. A blue-veined sink sagged forward on its brackets, forever home to half an inch of cold Bovril. The old fireplace had been kind of blocked up with a kind of square bit of cardboard, and every pipe and wire was crudely clamped on to the wandering contours of the walls. The bedclothes – benchclothes – looked, and felt, as if they'd been stitched together from old tights. I could have made a snowman from the drifts of hairy lint piled up beneath the furniture, and someone had recently borrowed the net curtains to wipe down a locomotive. On the scarred table beneath them lay a 'hospitality tray' that made a mockery of a term which admittedly demands it: a single tea bag, a single sachet of coffee and of whitener, and – knock yourself out, Bogey! – two of granulated sugar. The stale-crust carpet tiles didn't look like they'd been laid so much as pasted on both sides and tossed in from the doorway. I opened the mean little hardboard wardrobe and saw two M&S hangers swinging back at me; I plucked out one of the many angrily crumpled paper balls in the bin and found myself reading a one-night bill dated seven months previously. If my stay at Pontin's Southport had seemed like a punishment for doing something bad, then this time I'd done something much worse, and I'd done it in 1952.

'I stayed at this hotel on a stag do, so really there wasn't any standards we required,' read the Gresham's most recent review on TripAdvisor. 'Nevertheless this place was absolutely terrible. DO NOT STAY here unless you are going on the beer.' The dedication with which I now heeded this gentleman's thoughtful advice made for a rather wayward appreciation of Europe's ugliest street. Maid Marian Way was an awful smear of shame, a stinking skidmark right across the proud face of a great city. But it was also home to some pubs, only one of which was boarded up.

Inner ring-road dual carriageway, pedestrian underpass interchange with sunken plaza, integrated multi-level parking: Maid Marian Way boasted the full set of dread phrases from the 1960s book of *Great Big Urban Fuck-Ups*. It announced itself, just up the road from my hotel, with a six-lane arc of traffic that snarled out from beneath four storeys of NCP's finest. I negotiated this and found myself faced with a sweeping incline of motorway, flanked with painstakingly undistinguished concrete boxes. Nearly all bore tribute to the period rule that no structure could not be enhanced by sticking a multi-storey car park on top of it. So far, so predictably awful. I only grasped what set Maid Marian Way apart from its umpteen bumfaced brethren when I glanced down the first street that led off it. This truncated throughfare was home to a modest parade of handsome Georgian townhouses, and identified itself as Castle Gate – which I employed my Scandi-by-marriage super-powers to date to Viking times (*gata* being Norse for street). A floodlit section of old wall at the road's nearby fundament indeed proved to be the outer defences of Nottingham Castle, and with a nauseous lurch of innards I suddenly grasped the enormity of what had happened here – Maid Marian Way had been driven right through the very heart of old Nottingham, with all the tender grace of Monty Python's foot. Medieval inns and merchants' homes, a row of Pevsner-feted almshouses, street after elegant street of eighteenth-century residences: my later research detailed the toll. A half-mile swathe of the city's most treasured and historically significant buildings wilfully dashed away at a stroke, a go-faster stripe for a streamlined, speeding future that never came to pass.

You only had to look at what survived to realise how much history had been lost. One of the few remaining houses on Castle Gate bore a plaque in honour of Marshal Tallard, commander of the French forces defeated at Blenheim in 1704. How so? Well, the captured marshal spent six years living there under house arrest, during which time he won round the citizenry by teaching them how to bake white bread and cultivate celery, a vegetable that Britons had never previously considered edible. A thousand such wonderful tales bulldozed away. How apt it seemed that having laid waste to so much of Nottingham's genuine heritage, the civic authorities named the ghastly ring road thus accommodated after a fairy-tale fiction: a made-up maid who the storytellers didn't even associate with a made-up merry man until the late sixteenth century, three hundred years after neither of them were born.

The first pub I grumbled moodily into was another plucky survivor, spared from the Python foot by half a toenail, evening traffic flashing past its gabled frontage. I went down to the vaulted cellar bar and found it well populated with besuited office workers, all gamely endeavouring to enjoy a restrained after-work drink above the shrieking incoherence of the very heaviest of metal. It seemed too safe to connect this soundtrack to the buckle-belted, eyelinered barman, not that it had brought much joy into his life. His entirely blank expression didn't even twitch when I bellowed my order for a Kola Kube vodka shot. Somewhere under that wailing wall of distortion I could just make out the squelchy chomp of a man being eaten alive by his own sweet tooth.

It wasn't a place to linger, but for two shots and a half of cider I did anyway, suspecting that on Europe's ugliest street this might be as good as it got. Then I went out and rather unsteadily pondered my next move. While doing so I came to note something curious: one section of Maid Marian Way was not as the others were, edged by newer glass-faced structures and conspicuously home to its only pedestrian crossing. The 1960s cement shoeboxes were set back, facing the street at oblique angles. I went out to the middle of the crossing and realised I was standing on what had been the famously horrible sunken plaza. At some point in the recent past – in 2004, as I later established – the council had filled in this blighting entity and refashioned the gigantic roundabout that girthed it as an inestimably more humane junction. How heartening, I thought. But then I gazed at the onrushing corridors of speeding metal and the great dumb blocks that hemmed them in and thought: But how futile.

When the war ended, liberated coastal cities from Bergen to Bordeaux eagerly set about demolishing the coastal defences, U-boat bunkers and other hated legacies of Nazi occupation. But very often, they found they simply couldn't – the structures were too enormous and too heavily reinforced. They just had to learn to live with them. Without wishing to upset too many urban planners of the period, it's the same with every British town centre redeveloped in the 1960s and early Seventies, which is to say almost all of them. The scale is just so huge. Putting these things up demanded brutal self-confidence and loads of money – and so will pulling them down, which is a shame, as these days we don't have either.

At the time I fancied this a considered observation, but you will be glad to hear that it was my last of the evening. Thereafter my discipline, geographical and otherwise, faltered badly. First I went into a pub that was just off Maid Marian Way, and then another that wasn't, and thus by short, sharp boozy stages proceeded to Old Market Square, an infinitely more handsome and inviting urban expanse – one whose attractions had more than once lured me down from Sheffield for a properly cosmopolitan day out. On a Monday night the in-pub vibe was inevitably muted even here: stony-faced middle-aged couples playing the slots, young men watching Sky Sports over their girlfriends' shoulders. But with a view of grand old civic buildings and a bellyful of the sweetest happy-juice, I really didn't mind at all. Though I started to a bit during my fifth packet of crisps, and an awful lot more when I found myself stumbling down a rain-lashed street, just me and the bellowing nutters and the world's worst room at the end of it.

Chapter Fifteen

It was never going to be a throw-back-the-covers-and-burst-into-song kind of a morning, and a bad start to the day got worse when the Gresham's kitchen chose to serve my full-English pick-me-up on a bed of partially defrosted potato waffles. The rain was still at it, which obliged me to tackle Craig's wiper situation with a pair of pliers in one hand and a pound-shop umbrella in the other. With a small inward cheer, I identified and removed the scuttle, a 4-foot length of plastic covering; with a large outward groan I beheld the mechanism thus revealed. The wiper linkage was a tribute to 1980s British engineering – to wit, a feeble, rickety shambles fashioned largely from coat hangers. A few days later, I experienced a powerful sense of mechanical déjà vu when a gust of wind turned that pound-shop umbrella inside out. Anyway, one bit of coat hanger had fallen out of some pipe thing, so I stuck it back in and applied my signature squirt of WD40. This proved a curate's egg of a repair – the wipers now did a splendid job of dispersing water from a generous arc of bonnet, but their upward sweep took them no more than 7 inches into the more vital windscreen zone. So it was that I headed on to a very wet A42 with the driver's seat almost fully reclined and my head on my left shoulder, monitoring the back end of a lorry through a wedge-shaped porthole.

Tribulation was steadily heaped upon tribulation. The pain

in my neck already had a pain in my head for company, and every glimpsed sliver of my surroundings brought some new heartache: another distribution centre, another motorway junction, another monumental cluster of hour-glass cooling towers. A fistful of wine gums confirmed that my passion for glucose was now a thing of the past, at the expense of brimming Craig's ashtray with chewed slurry. My ears weren't on holiday, either: aware that he was directing me towards his homeland, Ozzy seemed unusually excitable. He swore at me, I swore at him, and then – for a numbing hour – Mr Royston Vasey swore at the pair of us.

Roy 'Chubby' Brown, as he is better known, had earnt his place on my playlist by virtue of a collaboration with the band Smokie. This was a 1995 cover of their 1976 hit 'Living Next Door to Alice', which customised a story of unrequited neighbourly love with a discourteous rhetorical phrase that I have chosen to spare you. Comfortably outselling the original, this peaked at number three and remained in the UK charts for nineteen weeks, shifting half a million copies along the way. Eight years later it made the top twenty in Channel 4's worst-singles poll.

The Roy 'Chubby' Brown I knew was a stand-up comedian who had fashioned a career from the humorous potential of relentless profanity and being fat, and doing both of these while wearing a multi-coloured patchwork suit and an old flying helmet. I have to confess an unfamiliarity with his musical output as it existed beyond that aforementioned family singalong standard, and was surprised, when I located a copy of it, to find an associated greatest-hits album. Its track titles alone demanded that this entire work be drafted into my anthology forthwith.

I could perhaps have mentioned Roy 'Chubby' Brown earlier as a feted son of Middlesbrough, or as a regular performer on the seaside stages of Great Yarmouth and Skegness. But as things stand he's being introduced here as the lyricist and performer of the movingly confessional composition, 'I'm a Cunt'. So Roy severally insisted above the jaunty tinkling of a pub piano, as the rain intensified and a small quadrant of Spaghetti Junction loomed up sideways before me. His self-denigration built to the bluntest imaginable climax: naturally I'm not inclined to share this with you.

As Mr Brown's Wikipedia entry emphasises, 'Roy's shows are very rarely seen on television, as nearly all of his material contains a lot of strong language, especially the word "cunt".' The man's own website proudly, if a little coyly, boasts of his claim to fame as 'the first person ever to say the C word on stage in the UK'. On this basis, the ditty that now faded away seemed an unimprovable encapsulation of both his talent and his appeal. But Roy was not done yet. As Ozzy saw us past his birthplace, Aston, with a 21-fuck salute, so Chubby embarked on a retrospective tour of festive fellatio. At inevitable length this segued into 'Toss Me Off', 'I'd Use Your Shit for Toothpaste' and other such considered appraisals of the human condition.

Battered by coprophilic single entendres and the bluntest, least imaginative expletives, I tried to understand how such material could ever be deemed entertaining. A review I'd read of a recent Chubby gig described an audience that didn't laugh but cheered: it wasn't a comedy show so much as a joyous rally, a mutual celebration of secret universal truths about asylum seekers, single-sex relationships and, above all, the curiously magnetic repulsiveness of the female pudenda. It was all very strange, and I wondered if this helped explain why *The League of Gentlemen* had chosen to endow their very strange fictional village with Chubby's real name. But what's truly arresting about the whole phenomenon is its inexhaustible popularity. Roy Chubby Brown performs across the country to 350,000 people every year, and has to date sold more than 4.5 million DVDs. To get an idea of what these figures actually mean, carve them into a table while shrieking at the very top of your lungs.

As I swung off the M6, the rain died away and my neck slowly ratcheted back to its usual position. Chubby chose this moment to check out, and did so in some style. 'Hello, my name's Awful the Duck,' he talk-sang, in ickle-girl Lancastrian, 'and I know a man called Teeth Harris.' Here an 'Our Tune'-style instrumental backdrop swelled poignantly. 'Sometimes Teeth sticks his dick in me, and gets all my feathers sticky with his bellend.' Then it was on to Terry Wogan's 'Floral Dance' and the worst road in Britain.

In line with Johnny Nash's musical farewell to precipitation, I could see clearly now the rain had gone. I could see – whoa! – all obstacles in my way. Above all I could see the sign advertising 'MHS Horse Disposal' that welcomed me onto the 8.1 -mile stretch of the A34 Ringway from Cannock to Walsall – declared Britain's fourth worst 'driving road' (by sports-car enthusiasts), its ninth most tedious stretch of tarmac (in that Cornhill survey) and runner-up to the nation's most poorly laid-out mixed-use urban boulevard (as declared by some West Midlands-based regeneration committee who chose not to reveal their sources, or indeed the winner). No other thoroughfare came close to matching this all-round performance, and I was keen to see what made the A34 Ringway so multivariously awful.

Pebble-dashed, chimney-potted terraces hard up by the kerb, units to let on a brown-glass trading estate, a high street where you'd struggle to spend over a pound unless you fancied a second Greggs Steakbake or a tattoo: the initial stretches seemed no more than a drive-through compendium of twenty-first-century Britain as I'd been experiencing it. Following a short blurt of countryside after Cannock, we broached the fringes of Britain's second largest conurbation, and thereafter all was single-carriageway, mixed-use, mid-urban non-controversy. I eventually came to realise that the A34 Ringway bore but one distinctive feature, and that this alone explained why so many motorists had singled it out for castigation. I might have noticed it sooner in my previous life as the owner-driver of a vehicle capable of rapid progress, though just in case I now activated the relevant sat-nav option. And so for the balance of those 8.1 miles, my highly strung navigator, Mr J. M. Osbourne, was accompanied by his carer: a calm and assured woman who kept him in check with almost unbroken repetitions of her soothing mantra, 'Warning, Gatso ahead, speed limit 30 miles per hour.'

Home to twelve yellow boxes on poles in its first 3 miles, and another thirty-three between then and Birmingham, the A34 Ringway is the most densely camera-policed road in Britain – in fact anywhere in the world. It has thus found itself routinely vilified in the press, and targeted by motoring-rights extremists: in 2007, fifteen of its cameras were sabotaged by fire or the judicious application of aerosol paint, with a sixteenth 'pulled over by unknown means'. Like *Gladiators* and horseradish sauce straight from the jar, driving too fast is something I have been known to enjoy but cannot defend. Even blessed with the right machinery I don't think I'd have been tempted on the A34 Ringway, wending its way through heavily built-up areas in a manner that said, 'You know what, chaps, even thirty is probably pushing it.' Unless you're the *Daily Mail* you can't argue with figures: since the West Midlands police and local authorities went snap-happy, the annual toll of serious injuries on the region's roads has very nearly halved.

The A34 Ringway did at least have one trick up its tarmac-adam sleeve. I spotted it on the forecourt of a 'Funeral Centre' in Bloxwich, lantern-jawed but demure, staring blank-eyed at the traffic from under a granite fringe: the notorious 'Black Diana'. Commissioned at the height of national mourning by Andrew Walsh, grief-stricken MD of Walsh Memorials, this ill-starred statue of the late Princess of Wales was intended for display in Walsall's new bus centre, then under construction. However, Walsh's choice of raw material and the free-spirited artistry of the Indian masons he contracted drew the wrong sort of gasps at the unveiling ceremony. 'Demonic,' whispered one local dignitary; 'creepy and offensive,' shuddered another. Eleven years on, their choice of words seemed more a reflection of the febrile hysteria of the hour. 'Totally' and 'hilarious' would have been my own selections: it was as if along with his cheque for £16,000, Walsh had handed the craftsmen a negative print of the bloke from Dollar wearing a ballgown. As I watched, two passing housewives stopped before it and shook their heads in amused wonder, still in thrall to the statue's glorious wrongness.

But back then it was far from a laughing matter. To keep pace with the press-fuelled national outrage, Buckingham Palace issued a cold statement forbidding the statue to be labelled or identified as an image of Diana. Her family even threatened to 'look further into the matter', presumably hoping for a conviction under the Rubbish Sculpture Act, with Andrew Walsh put in the stocks on Bloxwich Green, or ideally turned to stone. Asked to defend himself, the confused and bereft businessman could only mumble: 'It's a finely carved life-size tribute which weighs 1.5 tons.' And so it still stands there, nameless and unloved, facial extremities fading to light grey, just next to the granite kitchen-worktop showroom that Walsh Memorials now runs as a sideline.

A couple of miles and six cameras up the A34 I turned off Gatsowoman and recalibrated my crapometer, keen to know precisely when the seamless mixed-use sprawl around started to call itself Walsall. Sightings of the word on a carpet warehouse and a shed offering to buy scrap copper for cash placed me on full alert: I was nudging into a town that has been decreed the most hideous on earth. 'Nowhere in the world is it possible to travel such long distances without seeing anything grateful to the eye,' wrote Theodore Dalrymple in 2000, describing a visit to Walsall for the benefit of subscribers to the US arts review *New Criterion*. 'It is possible that there are uglier towns than Walsall, but if so I do not know them,' he continued, before encapsulating the place as 'Ceauşescu's Romania with fast food outlets'. If Theo was even half right, little wonder that the place had been outed as 'Britain's unhappiest town', albeit in some asinine poll commissioned, with the usual cavalier disregard for commercial relevance, by an internet banking venture. Just 49 per cent of Wallsalludlianerists professed themselves satisfied with their lot, and did so in a regional accent that – as I had been stutteringly, swearily reminded several hundred times a day – is well established as the nation's least sonorous. It all sounded too bad to be true.

Named after the outcroppings of surface coal that streaked its hillsides, the Black Country welcomed the Industrial Revolution pre-smutted. By the time Queen Victoria was travelling her realm by royal train, Walsall and its neighbouring towns were so unregally slathered in sooty filth that she routinely ordered the blinds to be lowered when passing through the region. By the 1850s, multi-industrial Walsall styled itself 'the town of a hundred trades', dominant amongst them that honoured by the museum I now espied, parked outside and entered.

As I've discovered at the stockport Hat Museum, Kendal's Pencil Museum and the British Lawnmower Museum in Southport, museums that sound boring never are. The Walsall Leather Museum dutifully revealed itself as a repository of fascinating insights – no mean feat, given that most were delivered in a particularly nasal variant of the regional drone, by an elderly guide in a shopcoat. In my habitual capacity as solitary visitor I was easy meat: he pounced as I walked away from a display headed, GLOVES – WALSALL'S FORGOTTEN INDUSTRY.

'In noinedeenundred, alboast every logal fably would have employed at least wun saddler or arness-baker,' he began, sounding like Mr Woolley off *The Archers* talking in his sleep. 'Walzle was the sender of the leather-bacon universe, and that was all down to the roise of the orse.' It's easy to forget, unless you're in the company of an old bloke in a shopcoat, that the railway age was no death knell for Dobbin. Quite the reverse: as I now learnt, the number of horses on London's streets actually trebled during Victoria's reign, peaking at 300,000 in 1900. Horses demanded all sorts of leathery accessories, and Walsall – as a longstanding manufacturer of the metal bits that held these together – profitably diversified. The local leathermakers were at their busiest in the early years of the First World War, equipping the million British horses requisitioned for service: one Walsall firm alone turned out 100,000 military saddles from 1914 to 1916. Production rather fell away after that. Over seven thousand horses were killed in a single day at the Battle of Verdun, and by 1918 half a million British horses had perished from disease, exhaustion and injury – almost a third of the pre-war national total. This dreadful cull coincided with the mass production of petrol-engined vehicles, and that was pretty much it for the British working horse in general and Walsall's leathermakers in particular.

'Walzle bade fudballs for the FA Cup foinal for a woile,' droned my guide, 'and the building we're in banufactured handbags for Barks and Spencer until the Fifties. And so, well, there we are. Then.' He seemed rather taken aback to have got through to the end of his spiel; I wondered if it was the first time he'd been allowed to. Aware that I still had at least ten minutes of pay-and-display time on the clock, I took the opportunity to coax him out of his leathery cocoon. As a man who had seen seventy Walsall summers or more, he was surely well-placed to put the town's recent travails – wholesale civic depression, internationally acclaimed hideousness – into some kind of context.

'Seen any changes? I boast surdandly av.' A rueful smile. 'It's just the odd workshop bacon wallets and fancy goods now.'

'Right, but what about in general?'

'General leather goods?'

'No, just sort of general life. Changes in the general life of Walsall.'

'My woife gets her gloves down the barket. Bachine-stitched Choinese rubbish.'

And so I went outside and conducted my own nine-minute overview, scoping out downtown Walsall from the museum's hilltop car park. It was all distribution barns and rubbled wasteland: not much to force Theodore Dalrymple's head down to a steaming bowlful of his own words. In fact, the Leather Museum itself was about as becoming as Walsall got: a red-brick, iron-windowed workshop buffed up to its Victorian prime.

When British journalists got wind of Theo's published opinion, they rushed to Walsall to chronicle the partisan outrage thus unleashed. Yet all they encountered were shrugs, hollow laughter and just the odd nomination for somewhere slightly more horrid (usually Coventry). As a nation we've made an art out of doing ourselves down, and the people of Walsall have simply perfected that art. The most-depressed-town survey was a masterclass in asking a silly question, and as confirmed by the psycho-physical assessment I now carried out upon passers-by, Walsall had answered in kind. I scanned features and demeanour for tell-tale signs of dejection: the sagging shoulders of mirthless drudgery, the neck-twitch of murderous despair. But give or take a few lugubrious emos, the pedestrians seemed significantly more lively and upbeat than the ground-down miserablists I see trudging down my London street – some of whom aren't even en route to my front door.

Yes, Walsall was ugly – but it wasn't *that* ugly, not Forth ugly, not Hartlepool ugly. And more than that, it was doing a lot better for itself than almost anywhere else I'd visited. There was much reconstruction to be done, but as the skyline presence of cranes proved, at least it was *being* done (I hesitate to reveal the fate of downtown Walsall's most enormous rubble-heap, though as you ask – yes, it's another über-Tesco, hard up by the UK's largest town-centre Asda). None of the dead-duck, now-what hopelessness that had infused so many of my destinations.

Walsall's old trades now lived on only as local shopping malls (whoever decided on the Tanners' Centre can't have been familiar with the uniquely repulsive process of curing animal hides) and Walsall FC's nickname, 'The Handbags' (no, hang on: 'The Saddlers'). But new trades had arrived to take up the slack: local unemployment stood at 6 per cent, and falling. How genuinely depressed can you be when you've got a job, and it doesn't involve hosing down flayed cows with dog piss? When at last I did spot a wince of world-weary dismay it was in Craig's mirror: I'd just seen the sign announcing the current suspension of pay-and-display parking charges.

Waiting at a red in the dimming light I spotted a hoarding that identified an adjacent swathe of semi-regenerated brown-field as Longbridge, the former Austin Rover factory. To think that this had once been the largest manufacturing plant not just in Britain but anywhere in the world, employing 30,000 workers and producing over 200,000 cars a year. Five million

Minis alone rolled off the Longbridge lines. All that, and now nothing. In fact worse than nothing, as the Chinese motor corporation who acquired the pathetic remains of British Leyland – by then not much more than the MG Rover brand and the Longbridge leasehold – is now producing an insultingly tiny number of awful, cheap sports cars in some distant corner of the site, having flogged the rest off for housing, a further education college and a big trading estate. I'm sure I felt Craig skip a beat as we pulled away. Even though he actually came into the world 50 miles down the M40 at Cowley, in bits that some Bulgarians would later ineffectually push together.

In any event, the Black Country was a literal shadow of its former self. No belching, noxious heavy-metal smuts to stain the walls or taint the air. These days – and certainly that day, under a gloomy late-afternoon sky – it's more of the Beigey-Grey Country, the Taupe Country, the colour of the Bloxwich Diana's washed-out nose.

I had a horrible-sounding motel lined up in Birmingham, but somehow forgot all about it. The outward-bound commuters were heading home and I just seemed to get caught up in the flow: lights, roundabout, dual carriageway, lights, roundabout. It probably didn't help that having snapped during Big Country's unbearably sincere cover of 'Don't Fear The Reaper', I'd been listening to BBC Radio West Midlands. Well, I say listening, but it was less active than that: more like being hooked up to some kind of sedative audio drip. The drive-time presenter spoke in an unplaceable monotone cobbled together from the world's dreariest vowel sounds – one or two of them local, others from as far away as Australia. Everything he said seemed perfectly adapted to this way of speaking.

'What I love about camping is you just *never* know who you might meet.'

'Hello, Jackie, so what's *your* problem with foxes?'

I felt my jaw slacken and begin to fill with drool. Drawled snatches of hypnotic inanity swam around Craig's dark and fuggy interior; it was genuinely impossible to maintain concentration.

'Now, I've got a leather sofa but I have to admit it's about *four years* since I last moisturised it . . . Jeggings: a cross between "jeans" and "leggings", would you believe? . . . And this is a great story, by the way . . . Well, not any more, according to a recent survey conducted by Farnston Drells of MHS Horse Disposal, who joins me now.' It was as if a malevolent broadcast engineer had found some way of transmitting a parallel silent signal on the frequency – a bit like that traffic-report thing, but with the effect of covertly depressing higher brain function.

After a long and vacant round of follow-the-brake-lights I found myself in total darkness, bypassing Kidderminster. This rang a bell in my cloudy mind, but too quietly; I dully proceeded south-west, leaving a nationally reviled 1960s town centre unexplored. Only when BBC Radio West Midlands fuzzed and crackled its last, somewhere in the Worcestershire night, did I pull up into a lay-by and take stock. A riffle through the itinerary, a few bleepy jabs on Ozzy's screen. Window down, volume up: a bracing twin blast of cold wind and *The Essential Wally Party Medley*. I was going where the pubs were hard, and the miners ex. I was going to Merthyr Tydfil.

The final approach to most settlements in distress, as I had established, was invariably a broad stretch of under-trafficked carriageway, the legacy of better and busier times. For long black miles Craig and I had the generously proportioned A465 to ourselves; for good measure, at the last moment it swept down from the Brecon Beacons and into a bowl full of cold, wet fog. Streetlights cast a muted glow across fuzzy, winding ranks of tiny terraced homes, dating to a mid-Victorian, heavy-industrial prime. It sounded all wrong when I researched the town's history, and still seemed slightly ridiculous now that I saw the humble place with my own eyes, but the facts are these: Merthyr Tydfil was for many decades the world's dominant producer of iron, and comfortably the largest town in all of Wales.

I'd phoned ahead to book a room at the Castle, the only surviving hotel of any sort in Merthyr but an establishment with quite a heritage. On 3 June 1831, ten thousand local ironworkers massed around the Castle Inn, seeking to impress a committee of local employers gathered therein with their low opinion of the 'truck system': the payment of wages as vouchers that could only be redeemed at company stores, which offered a modest range of staple comestibles at outrageous prices. What followed was a bloody four-day siege that came to be known as the Merthyr Rising, feted by trade unionists both as a pivotal moment in their development and as the first outing of the red flag as a rallying symbol of the working class. The scale and fury of the protest petrified the authorities: concerned that the army's massacre of twenty-four protestors might prove an insufficient deterrent, prime minister Lord Melbourne covertly demanded the execution of at least one rioter; in the end, contrived evidence bagged him two.

But one glance at its Formica-faced, five-floor frontage suggested the Castle Hotel I now approached had witnessed little in the way of revolutionary martyrdom. My room duly harboured all the humdrum trappings of a hugely lapelled executive's life on the road: rosewood trouser press, buttoned Dralon headboard, swagged pelmet concealing view of pebble-dashed tax office. Anyone looking for evidence of native radicalism would have had to content themselves with the sachets of *gel baddon* and *siampw* in the en suite.

Named in honour of a fifth-century martyr, Merthyr Tydfil has spent much of its recent history striving towards a sympathetic end. The town's vast ironworks began downsizing in the 1860s, undone by their logistically unhelpful inland location. Coal mining picked up the economic slack, but as at Easington, the local collieries fell into decline after the Royal Navy switched to oil just before the Great War. Huge numbers of migrants from all across Europe had swelled Merthyr's population in the boom years – a synagogue was consecrated in 1875 – but their grandchildren now moved out in droves. The town shed a third of its citizenry in the Twenties, and by 1932 local unemployment stood at 80 per cent.

Even in its prosperous heyday, Merthyr had been a challenging place to live and work: after a visit in 1850, Thomas Carlyle described the town as 'a vision of Hell, filled with such unguided, hard-worked, fierce and miserable-looking sons of Adam as I never saw before'. Almost ninety years later, readers of *The Times* were appalled by the fate of those who had chosen to remain in the jobless town: 'Men and women are starving: not starving outright, but gradually wasting away through lack of nourishment.' The government decided the only anwer to Merthyr's irredeemably dreadful plight was to evacuate and demolish the town and start again from scratch: a well-developed plan to relocate Merthyr Tydfil to a site 30 miles away in the Usk Valley was only interrupted by the outbreak of war in 1939.

A handful of local collieries struggled on in peacetime, but were employing no more than a couple of thousand men of Merthyr by 1966. That was the year of the terrible Aberfan disaster, when a rain-loosened flank of the Merthyr Vale pit's slag heap thundered into a village school up the valley, killing 121 children. This tragedy rather drained Merthyr's enthusiasm for the business of coal mining, and Margaret Thatcher did the rest. Merthyr Vale closed in 1989, and the area's final survivor followed it a couple of years later. That should have been Merthyr's one-way ticket to Easington – but it wasn't, not quite. Back in 1948, the many Welshmen prominent in Clement Attlee's post-war government had helped put together a package of inducements that persuaded the American-owned Hoover company to open a washing-machine plant in Merthyr Tydfil. It sounds like the sort of ill-considered venture that would end with two-thousand half-made Maestros sitting in a weed-pierced Bulgarian car lot, but the Hoover factory proved a runaway success, a beacon of hope for all those British towns then sliding into the bottomless abyss set aside for former mining communities. The light after the darkness: from filthy-faced past to white-coated, technocratic future. By 1973 the plant employed five thousand workers, already well established as one of Europe's largest white-goods factories; when the Queen visited that year, she was shown plans for an expansion that would create a further three thousand jobs. The Castle Hotel,

I now realised, had been built to accommodate executives on Hoover-centric visits.

The first suggestion that Hoover's management might be losing their touch came in 1985, when they proudly announced that the Merthyr plant would be producing Clive Sinclair's extravagantly ill-fated C5 'twat chariot'. The second, and effectively last, followed in 1992 – the very year that Merthyr's final colliery closed, leaving Hoover as the area's only significant employer. Tasked with clearing a glut of unsold vacuum cleaners, that summer Hoover's marketing team contrived a promotion which offered two free return flights – to any European or American destination – for all British customers who spent £100 on any Hoover product. It is now universally acknowledged as the stupidest thing any company has ever done.

Accustomed to dealing with malleable and witless American consumers, the marketing executives calculated that those drawn in by the offer could initially be cajoled into spending much more than £100 on Hoover goods, and afterwards confused into defeat by the convoluted redemption conditions. In doing so they failed to account for the gimlet-eyed tenacity of the British bargain hunter: a failure that would cost the firm £48 million, and – as a final and very British humiliation – its royal warrant. 'Fair enough, but we certainly shifted a few vacuum cleaners,' said one executive, as three large Welshmen wordlessly crammed him into a front-loader.

This trumpeting fiasco was enough to bring Hoover to its knees, and Merthyr with it. Acquired by an Italian white-goods firm shortly after, the factory was steadily downsized; by the time it closed for good in 2009, just 337 workers were made redundant. In desperation, Merthyr now volunteers for even the most demeaning, disfiguring and unsavoury work. The town is home to one of the UK's biggest abattoirs, and its three landfill sites accommodate most of South Wales's rubbish. Inaugurated in 2008, Britain's largest opencast coal mine now scars a whole hillside on the outskirts, feeding one of the dirtiest power stations in Europe. A new prison, a massive incinerator – if it means jobs, the people of Merthyr will welcome it with open arms. I'm reminded of the heartbreakingly work-eager Bulgarian who stayed with my wife and me one summer, and the advertisement we dissuaded him from displaying in our local newsagent's window: *Healthy young man will do anything for £10.*

Yet despite all this, the town's unemployment rate remains entrenched at 28 per cent, meaning that a huge number of the 38,600 people who still call Merthyr Tydfil home have nothing to do but find new ways to express their idle hopelessness. A dumbfounding ten thousand of them claim incapacity benefit, by some margin the highest proportion in the land. Some 58 per cent of residents are overweight or obese. The town's GPs prescribe anti-depressants to one in ten patients – the second-highest proportion in Britain. Two thirds of children leave Merthyr's schools with fewer than five A*–C GCSEs, half of those without a single academic qualification of any sort to their name. It might only have made fifth place in the *Location* survey, but Merthyr Tydfil stands alone as Britain's capital of blank-faced, empty-headed, chip-fed loitering.

I put on an extra layer and hit the streets. They didn't hit back: misty drizzle, empty pavements, the look of a town that had faked its own death. Fronds of thick vegetation cascaded down the front of an old cinema. The narrow, wandering high road was home to the usual Chicken Lands, Cash Generators and soaped windows, along with an unusual preponderance of adult education and training centres. EMPLOYMENT MATTERS! insisted the sign above one. A tackle shop reminded me of a report in *The Times* that declared Merthyr 'the unlikely host of an international angling contest'. Not unlikely at all, I thought, given the presence of a river and an embarrassment of free time. What do you give to the man who has nothing? A fishing rod and a stool.

I'd walked halfway round town and ingested a cone full of vinegared potato mush before finding the place I'd been looking for – had I turned left outside the hotel instead of right I'd have been there in a skip and a jump. Because I hadn't come to see

Merthyr's sad and sickly youth, born into a town with no future and vacantly tagging along as it shuffled off its mortal coil. My quarry was the leathery reveller who had known Merthyr in its black-faced, white-goods pomp, and now raged against the dying of the light.

'What type of hard bastard drinks in the Wyndham Arms?' enquired the rhetorical voiceover, introducing the stand-out segment in *Britain's Toughest Pubs*. A pause, and a shot of a grizzled cackler baring all three of his teeth right into the lens. 'Old hard bastards.'

There it stood, opposite a double-fronted Money Shop, its aged frontage painted cerise since Sky 3's visit in 2003. I pushed open the dark little door wondering if this bold redecoration was an experiment in the psychology of colour, a cunning ruse to soothe incoming regulars bent on reproducing the alcoholic turbulence so fulsomely portrayed on television.

'Get your fucking facts right – you think you're an attractive man, but you fucking are not!'

Not words I expected to hear bellowed at 8 p.m. on a Tuesday, or indeed at any time from the wrinkled lips of a sixty-five-year-old man, into the hairy ear of another. All the same, I should have savoured this rare encounter with a communication that was soon extinct: the intelligible sentence.

Ignoring a long, tapering annexe at the rear, the Wyndham Arms was a snug, dim, beam-ceilinged affair with all the usual trappings: framed old photos of colliery sporting teams and Brylcreemed boxers on the battle-scarred wainscoting, bare wooden floors, a NO BLOODY SWEARING brass plaque by the bar. Above the filled-in fireplace hung a TV, broadcasting *World's Rudest Adverts* at low volume. My entrance had raised the total of incumbent drinkers by 10 per cent, but the rest were all squashed up in the darkest corner, too busy belittling each other's physical appeal to notice me. I gave them a discreet once-over as the young barman poured my pint. All were cut from the same beer towel: the bridge of every nose deeply crevassed by decades of clumsy or violent mishap, the surrounding flesh ruddy and porous. But one or two looked extremely familiar, even allowing for the seven years of ravaging Wyndhamian excess that had elapsed since the harrowed Sky 3 crew beat a hasty retreat. In particular, the one with the hairy ears, who bore a striking resemblance to the sausage-fingered former bare-knuckle fighter – not the Wyndham's oldest bastard, but certainly its hardest. I remembered him now, fixing the interviewer with a rheumy stare and rasping, 'We get the odd stranger in here, but they don't stop long. Put it that way. They don't stop long.'

I'd just sat down at a table by the door when it opened and another familiar figure walked in. I say walked, but it was more of a rotary collapse, effected in such faltering instalments that I had long since raised my glass safely away from the table before the new arrival upended it and himself via heavy lateral contact. For a good half-minute thereafter man and table wrestled it out lethargically on the floor, a fitful thrashing of trousered and wooden legs. I raised my own clear of the mêlée and looked up to see that not even the barman deemed this noisy enmeshment worthy of attention. Presently the man kicked himself free and tottered stagily to his feet, wearing a prank-victim's expression of bemused innocence, as if he'd just opened a wardrobe full of Space Hoppers. As I righted the table our eyes met, after a fashion: only then did I recognise him as one of the chest-prodding protagonists in a televised dispute about who had acquitted themselves best on the night the Wyndham took on a platoon of gurkhas.

And so it continued. I nursed that single pint all night, reluctant to compromise my defensive reflexes, and powerfully deterred by scenes that came to suggest a cautionary tableau put on by the Temperance Society. Every jelly-brained, jelly-limbed trans-pub journey – stool to bar, bar to bog, bog to stool – was undertaken via all points of the compass, with my table as magnetic north. Twice more I had to snatch my pint aloft as its supporting surface was dashed to the floor – the second time by a seated man being carried outside to have a fag. I was intrigued to behold so many different ways of not being able to walk: the arms-out Karloff blunder, the Pingu-on-ice quickstep, the clenched determination of a naval night-watchman crossing his deck in high seas.

Between wary sips, I watched the Wyndham slowly fill. The most conspicuous arrival was a fearsomely dishevelled man who pushed the door open with a stick and shuffled across to a table in front of the telly, where he sat down and began cramming haphazard chunks of a Subway sandwich through the hole in his beard. He was a good 10 feet from me but I very swiftly became aware of a quite extraordinarily pungent odour. His coat, a padded high-visibility number of the type favoured by binmen, had been freshly tarred and feathered, and the trouser bottoms beneath looked waxy and rigid; it had clearly been some considerable time since any of this clothing had been removed, or – how can I say this? – in any way lowered, loosened or otherwise adjusted. The barman walked across to him with a pint of Guinness in one hand and an aerosol in the other. The first he laid on the table, in exchange for a phlegmy grunt. He aimed the second at the ceiling directly above the man's head, and in an air of weary ritual shared by both parties hissed out a huge, choking cloud of floral air-freshener. 'Sorry about this, but what can I do?' he said to me as he walked past. 'He spends thirty quid a day in here.' When the air cleared, the Guinness had been drained.

By now even the briefest exhortations were demanding an oral dexterity that proved beyond most, though not through want of trying. 'F-F-FAH-G-G-A-GAH-F-F . . . FUGOFF!' Then ragged jeers and harsh laughter. It wasn't yet half nine and we were pretty much down at the level of tramps hanging out under a canal bridge, with all the confused volatility that defines such gatherings, the sense that at any moment someone might get bottled for saying something that someone else hadn't even said. Amongst its many ailments and disabilities, Merthyr ranks as the deafest town in Britain: 19 per cent of the population find it either difficult or impossible to hear a voice in a conversation.

It was like *Last of the Summer Wine* scripted by Irvine

Welsh, or *Under Milk Wood* gone *Shameless*. Every so often Pig-Pen's granddad would abruptly emit a farmyard snort or honk, or embark on a horrible, hacking, everything-must-go mucus clear-out. When he shot out a wild arm and whelped I had a flash of déjà vu: the most voluble, and drunkest, of the Wyndham regulars depicted in *Britain's Toughest Pubs* had punctuated his most spirited utterances in precisely this manner. 'Fuck the English, fuck everybody!' – out went the arm. 'This is the best bastard pub in fucking Wales!' – out went the arm. It jerked around like a man fighting off a swarm of bees during the account of how he'd seen off a party of French tourists by sitting at their table and setting fire to his hair. Could it really be him? Both had beards and very few teeth, but beyond that it was very hard to tell. Seven unshaven years on a £30-a-day pub habit must exert a potent levelling effect on the appearance of the senior male.

It was my good fortune, I suppose, to return from the Gents and find that I would henceforth be sharing my table with the least incapable Welshman this side of the bar. He was a pudgy chap with the benign, rumpled look of a hungover Ken Barlow, though his opening gambit revealed a rather more vigorous way with words.

'What do you think of the fucking pub we run here, then?'

The humming nod I essayed in response would soon be seeing a lot of action. For an hour or more my companion kept me supplied with highlights from his inner monologue, and the occasional pundit's take on the eight-way shouting match that slurred endlessly on in the corner. The mellifluous Welsh emphasis he lavished upon each syllable ensured I plainly understood every individual word he said, which only served to highlight the impenetrable mysteries of their sense and context.

'Quite a girl, is that Naa-taa-lee!'

'Fucking funny that, though, wasn't it? Bought his Vi-aa-ga-raa on a Barr-clee-card! Fucking Bar-clee-card!'

'You know, it didn't really work out for me that year, Madge-orrr-ca.'

'Fucking Barr-clee-card! Funny that, wasn't it?'

Though this question hardly demanded an answer, after a third repetition I felt constrained to provide one: I agreed that it was. At once his face lit up. 'That's it – that's *exactly* it!' He turned to the pub at large and raised his voice.

'English fellow here says . . . what was it again?'

My buttocks consumed my underwear; something close to silence fell across the Wyndham. I frowned into the remains of my pint, and thought there would never be a better time to set fire to my hair. Then I looked up, met a dozen unsteady gazes and said, 'Well, Barclaycard – it's funny. Barclaycard?'

I could see the bare-knuckle boxer looking at me as if I'd said something else, something to do with his private parts. Then Pig-Pen threw out an arm and barked, and whatever passed for normal service in this madhouse was resumed. As soon as it was polite to do so, in fact a little before that, I tipped back the last half-inch of my pint, knotted my scarf and stood up. My companion abruptly extracted himself from a prolonged sigh of private amusement and jabbed a discreet elbow into my thigh. I bent down to him and he addressed me in a new way: whispered, brisk, direct. 'Listen, if you need any diazepam, I can do you strips of two migs or five.'

The Castle's reception was empty but for two sacks of potato peelings. I bid them goodnight and retired to my room, where a mood of troubled restlessness promptly asserted itself. It was not dispersed in the half-hour I spent with my face pressed to the window, watching pairs of men stumble home in misty drizzle, spilling chips and pissing up against the tax office. A town down on its uppers and up on its downers, off its face in a rolling civic wake. Suddenly I was gripped with a need to discover something uplifting about Merthyr Tydfil, and after twenty expensive minutes of squinty faffing with my telephone's rarely employed internet function, I succeeded in the most literal manner imaginable. Back in 1992, a Merthyr GP trialling a proposed angina treatment upon local male volunteers informed the drug company of a conspicuous and unexpected side effect. Thus did Merthyr Tydfil endow the world with a medication that has since brought smiles to sixty million faces – and not just because of the comic possibilities apparently inherent in purchasing it on a Barclaycard.

Chapter Sixteen

The Taff Valley fog lifted just past Merthyr's last roundabout, and I glanced in the mirror at a town left to stew in its own foggy juices. As the sun burst through and gilded the tree-less, brown-bracken hillsides, I couldn't help feeling that I'd now seen the very worst my nation had to throw at me, that there were no fresher hells to experience, that from here on things could only get better. Right on cue, the gruesome, flatu-lent anthem of Britain's cultural nadir – think spotted, pink and *Noel's House Party* if you must, though be warned that you'll bitterly regret doing so – gave way to a profound, post-apocalyptic silence. I jiggled the MP3 player to no effect, and cranked up the volume to max. This lent an exceptionally portentous quality to the words that now boomed forth from somewhere deep within Craig's very soul:

'Yoko?'

'John?'

Reacquaintance with the St Winifred's School Choir had washed over me, but there was no avoiding these words and their significance. I'd gone round the horn: back to the start of my 358 audio excursions to hell and back. My musical journey, at least, was at an end. I joyfully yanked the player out of the fag-lighter socket and flung it into the nest of oiled chip paper and bridie shavings that brimmed the door pocket. With its hijacked frequency thus liberated, the radio burst into

267

deafening life: 'ENJOY ROSS-ON-WYE'S FINEST INDIAN CUISINE – IN ATTRACTIVE AND CONTEMPORARY SURROUNDINGS!'

Suspicions that my quest might have bottomed out began to harden in Barry Island. The south Welsh seaside town had earnt a pin on my map as the resort whose damp and tedious misery had compelled Billy Butlin to invent holiday camps, but it had always seemed no worse than faded and genially naff in *Gavin and Stacey*, and on a bright and breezy February morning Barry Island looked rather better than that. The seafront amusement arcades and cafés were protected by a pretty wrought-iron Victorian canopy, and the cars I parked between were both polished Rovers, each home to a snug elderly couple sharing a tartan thermos. Slipping on my sunglasses for the first time in many months, I walked down on to the beach: a deserted eternity of smooth gold, looking out at a sparkling sea and the shadowy superstructures of Lundy and Cornwall. I'm fairly certain the tourist board won't thank me for revealing that Fred West's ashes are scattered on Barry Island's sands.

Just up the promenade I found myself outside Barry Island Pleasure Park, whose unsparing shonkiness had seen it singled out for online opprobrium. Through the padlocked gates I spotted what must surely be the only pound shop resident in such an establishment, yet the overall ambience seemed cheerfully, deliberately ridiculous: silver Assyrian cavalrymen stood guard over the handful of tarpaulin-shrouded rides, and the log flume's mossy frontage was crowned with a colossal fibreglass goose. As a comic shambles I had to conclude that it fell comfortably the right side of the with/at laughter divide.

I followed my towering shadow back to Craig and glanced around at the sunlit sand, the bleeping, empty arcades, the peeling enormity of the interwar bunker labelled, PUBLIC CONVENIENCES, LAVATORIES & CLOAKROOMS. There were shades of Leysdown-on-Sea, echoes of Great Yarmouth, the frailest suggestion of Skegness. But not even a tiny pinch of Rhyl. I'd already scraped the bottom of the seaside bucket.

And so my slow but unstoppable rise continued, onwards

and upwards. I proceeded at leisurely pace through countryside that wasn't Lincolnshire, past villages that weren't New Holland or Forth, into and out of towns that didn't smell or croak for mercy. The sagging pastry satchel I ate for lunch was ferociously dull but no Scotch pie; the Balti-burger dispatched that evening proved many dry-retches shy of a parmo. The Midlands' most poorly rated greyhound racing stadium failed to serve up the topless vomiting reported by more than one reviewer, delivering instead a night of chilly excitement, crowned by a win on 7/2 shot Vatican Seamus. This financed nine-elevenths of a celebratory pint of cider at a purportedly horrendous pub in the shadow of Spaghetti Junction, where everyone – almost everyone – proved a model of restrained good cheer. I then made away for a night's sleep that was no better or worse than might reasonably be expected at a motel alongside a busy Birmingham roundabout, run by young men in bare feet. Silverfish frolicked in the shower tray and I found a bra under the bedside table, but as an overnight experience it ranked at least seventeen times less dreadful than the Gresham Hotel in Nottingham, and cost a quid less. I seemed to have developed an immunity to ramshackle tedium, and couldn't decide whether that was heartening or deeply worrisome. On one hand I now lived at beatific peace with my nation, warts and all, but on the other I'd become institutionalised to discomfort and unloveliness, a man who didn't appreciate or in fact deserve clean sheets or salad or power steering.

The next morning even Coventry let me down. Coventry – the granddaddy of God-awful city-centre redevelopments, the default response volunteered by the residents of Middlesbrough, Hull, Hartlepool and Many Many More, asked to name somewhere more terrible than the terrible place they called home. I could hardly fault the town for effort. I arrived to find Coventry sulking in thick fog, and my downtown multi-storey was so fulsomely streaked with mossy slime it might have just been raised from the seabed. Mist coiled forth from bleak pedestrian underpasses, and breakfast came in the form of an advertised question: *Is THIS the best jumbo sausage roll in Coventry?*

(Answer: I really hope not.) Every thoroughfare was a windswept retail plaza, and every flanking structure resembled a North Korean technical college. All the familiar half-arsed makeovers were on show: a weathered Perspex canopy here, a scattering of timeshare terrazzo tiles there. In short, a dutiful ticking of the usual boxes, along with a couple of new ones: I wandered into one of the many pound shops and found it staffed by people in pyjamas and dressing gowns.

But it wasn't just that I'd seen it all before, and then some. At the head of an especially dispiriting vista, I chanced upon a plaque that detailed the achievements of Sir Donald Gibson, Coventry's city architect in the late 1940s and early 1950s. *The first pedestrian precinct, the first rooftop parking . . .* My reflex chortle soon died away, because of course Coventry's redevelopment wasn't the product of self-indulgent, wankily bowtied architectural whimsy, but a stark necessity enforced by the catastrophic destruction of 14 November 1940. And though Gibson and his team made some enormous mistakes, as pioneers they could hardly be blamed for them. In 1950, Britain's urban planners knew no better. By 1970 they certainly did, yet somehow it didn't stop them.

The fog began to lift as I drove away from Coventry, replaced by drizzle that in the light of ongoing technical issues restricted my view of Rugby to a pair of small arcs at the base of Craig's windscreen. Just past the BRITAIN IN BLOOM signs, there it was, at least a 15-degree wedge of its lower quarters: the Rugby Cement Works, a dust-shrouded collation of silos and vertiginous sheds, taller than Coventry cathedral. The plant had made number five on the *Demolition* list by virtue of its arrestingly residential situation, emerging from a nest of trim little terraced homes like some monstrous, grimy cuckoo. I pulled over and got out, waiting for a surge of outraged empathy that never came. Instead I saw Middlesbrough in its brass-from-muck heyday, Hartlepool getting filthy rich, Methil striking pay dirt. After passing through so many post-industrial downtown wastelands, it was a genuine, chest-swelling thrill to stand dwarfed beneath an old-time industrial behemoth that wasn't just alive but noisily, belchingly thriving. Sorry, residents of Lawford Road.

And sorry Northampton, for the bland curiosity that was all I could muster an hour or so later, confronted by the monolithic twin arses of hell its citizens know as Greyfriars bus station. Surveying this withering structure from the roundabout laid out before it, I was obliged to conclude that with Gateshead's Trinity Square now laboriously smashed off the map, here stood a genuine contender for the title of Britain's Most Loathsome Urban Edifice Outside Cumbernauld. Crowning the whole city centre with its dismal bulk, it looked less like an integrated transport hub than something hastily thrown up to cap a nuclear reactor in meltdown, or imprison Godzilla. I saw all this, yet all I could think was: Yeah, well, at least it's not a sodding car park. Though I've just discovered that large bits of it actually are.

Under a dimming, pink sky I steered Craig south into a gathering rush hour and a town that took shape in the now-traditional manner: an outlying belt of Harvesters and Premier Inns, then the Lidls and Tile Depots, the Polish grocers and the pound shops, all strung together between roundabouts of generous diameter. Culminating at the Brunel, cover star of the anti-celebration of rotary traffic-management that is *Roundabouts of Great Britain*, the tarmac jewel in the concrete crown of our nation's most famously insipid town-centre development. A sunken gyratory plaza girdled with cereal boxes the colour of Shredded Wheat and All Bran, viewed through the dun splatter of Craig's windscreen. It was my first circuit of the Brunel, but not his. Craig was back to where he once belonged. How now, brown Slough.

I did a couple of laps, inching across the log-jam to the inside lane. Down in the Brunel's sunken hub, that damp-slabbed plaza, a steady stream of heads-down, homebound David Brents scurried into the mouth of a wind-tunnel underpass. Here it was, the epicentre of England's grey unpleasant land, a what-not-to-do agglomeration of everything that made post-war British towns so very rubbish. The pathological deference to the motor car, and the parallel casting down of the pedestrian into a forlorn and sinister netherworld. That insatiable passion for pre-stressed concrete, showcased most overbearingly in the Brunel bus station, a cubist Connect 4 set whose grubby lozenges filled much of the world before me. And the default tendency to offset these massive wrongs with ever more massive superstores: the Pentagon-sized Tesco rearing up behind the bus station once ranked as the biggest in Europe, but now, just five years later, it wasn't even the biggest in Berkshire.

All the same, I felt a twinge of melancholy as I flicked the indicators on and exited the Brunel through the exhaust-fog and brake lights. Not for the first time, I knew I was surveying a townscape that would soon be swept away. Many of the public buildings around were already being prepared for demolition, and most are now no more. When you read this, the sunken plaza will have been filled in, and the monolithic bus station replaced with a metal-roofed wave of a structure, a rather silly and unconvincing affair that in the architects' sketches recalls a pair of Bacofoil flares hanging out to dry on a windy day. I think we can be certain that this will become a dated embarrassment even more quickly than its predecessor, but at least when that time comes it will be a lot less bother to knock down. 'Change and decay in all around I see,' I sang, sending off Slough with a snatch of the Cup Final hymn. 'O something, something else, abide with me.' Then it was away down the M4, east towards London, reeling in an increasingly familiar environment.

In my career as an accidental adventurer I have conquered Mount Kilimanjaro, traversed the ferociously bleak Icelandic interior on a bicycle, and pushed an inert donkey all the way across Spain. All these hard-won triumphs were eclipsed when I piloted Craig down the flyover ramp to Chiswick roundabout, and at Ozzy's behest took the first f-f-fookin exit, knowing that the third would have swiftly delivered me into the warm and welcoming bosom of my family home. I could almost smell the love, taste the goosedown, feel the steak Béarnaise and salad. Instead, just four minutes and one postal district later, I wanly cranked up the handbrake in the deserted car park of a hotel that had a strong statistical claim to be the very worst in Britain.

I'd chanced upon the Gresham Hotel on Hanger Lane many months before, while bottom-trawling TripAdvisor's reviews of its benighted namesake in Nottingham (the two establishments are in no way connected, beyond their shared homage to the esteemed and venerable Gresham Hotel in Dublin). This other Gresham's ratings were something else. Of the eighteen previous guests who had provided an opinion, no fewer than sixteen awarded it a single star (the one labelled 'terrible'). I spent an entire afternoon trying to find a hotel, any hotel, that bettered this ratio. When I failed, the final flag on my map almost planted itself. After all, my tour proper had begun down the other end of Hanger Lane, at Britain's worst road junction. This symmetry had seemed most satisfying right up to the point, just outside Slough, when I'd punched the Gresham Hotel's postcode into Ozzy's flat little face.

I stepped out into the fierce and frozen wind, issued a shuddering sigh and glanced around. The Gresham looked as sorry for itself as I felt. Hard up beside it, sharing a view of the ceaseless, roaring traffic, stood a rival hotel, another extended Edwardian building that was almost identical in every respect but one: not a single free space remained in its own forecourt parking area. Across a side street towered a sleek Ramada Inn, its softly lit reception area thronged with smart executives. The Gresham skulked in the streetlight shadows, forsaken and unloved, the runt of the litter.

I poked the bell and after a moment the huge front door was heaved slowly ajar by a young Asian man, startled to the point of abject terror. I explained that I wanted no more than a room for the night and to feast upon his flesh, then trailed him through the lofty, pungent hallway, and up to a little reception shelf fixed to the side of the breakfast bar. 'Is £45 please,' he whispered cravenly. 'You must pay now.'

I did so and followed him up a huge, bleak staircase, then across loud carpet and even louder floorboards to the door of room 5. The receptionist creaked it open and we were hit by a face-crumpling waft of stale fags. 'Good God,' I exclaimed, physically recoiling. 'Sorry, but can I have a no-smoking room?'

'All rooms no-smoke.'

'Well, can I have another room?'

'Is no other room.'

We had just walked past several numbered doors and everything suggested I was the Gresham's sole guest. The receptionist tried to smile, then switched the light on and turned to leave. 'Hang on – the key?'

'If you want, is £10.'

'For the key to my own room?' He appraised my slack-jawed silence and departed as discreetly as the shrieking floorboards allowed.

'Checked in, ten minutes later checked out.'

'I wouldn't let my dog stay there.'

'We found a cigarette butt under our bed, and we do not smoke.' (What rotten luck!)

The Gresham's TripAdvisor lowlights spooled through my mind as I patrolled my foinal fookin dustinoition. Room 5 was huge, but in the wrong direction: the ceiling a distant shadowy suggestion, the floorspace so meagre that the ends of my single bed touched both walls. Every small step around the modest bedless areas triggered an underfoot cacophony of squeaks and squeals, like a fat man sitting on an accordion. The en-suite shower had been grouted in with old toothpaste and clumps of pastry, and a shelf above the sink was home to many tubs of half-empty skin- and haircare products kindly donated by previous residents. Skeins of hairy fluff clung to the skirting boards and the hem of the bedspread: this would be a socks-on night.

By far the most compelling TripAdvisor review had been compiled by a guest striving to express profound dissatisfaction in a tongue that was not his own. 'I start to hearing weird sounds coming from the wall,' he began. 'It was of course a mouse. One staff came for look and we find two holes. After two mins he return with wood to cover the holes. I didn't like that.' The manager arrives with an explanation that fails to appease. 'He said I was hearing squirols in the garden . . . hahaha . . . how is that a squirol if I hear it running from my toilet to my window!!!' And so his story arrived at its predictable conclusion. 'I paid fifty pounds and I didn't spend the night there. It was not fair as I paid for a b. & b. and I didn't use the Bed or either the Breakfast.'

I sat down on the bed and it made that *Family Fortunes* noise. Room 5 was self-evidently a dump, but I waited in vain for trepidation and disgust to well up within me. Instead I found myself dwelling upon its attributes. There was a little telly and a beverage station. The water was hot and my word so was the room: a radiator the size of an up-and-over garage door filled one entire wall. My house, my lovely house with its lovely wife and children, lay just up the road, no more than a tearful, frosted stumble away. But something had happened to me over the last few months: I felt at home here. I had taken a crash course in grubby discomfort, and relearnt the lost native skills of taking the rough with the smooth, looking on the bright side, making the best of a bad job. This creaking, dishevelled, tobacco-fired sauna was now my kind of place.

I certainly began to miss it the minute I stepped outside. The traffic swished and roared, the wind stung my earlobes. I jogged stiffly past the Ramada Inn and round the corner, to an interwar parade that accommodated Ealing Common tube station and a number of convenience stores. Over the road their nemesis was taking shape in the ground floor of an office building: COMING SOON – YOUR NEW SAINSBURY'S LOCAL. Another era was ending, and this time it was mine: my primary school lay just two streets back from here, and these shops had for years kept me in sweet cigarettes and cream soda. On a melancholic whim, I ducked into the first one and vowed to purchase my last supper therein. My deep-fried flirtation with deficiency disease asserted an alarming influence upon the menu: I came back out into the cold with a thin blue plastic bag containing eleven carrots.

I took up residence at a bus shelter that looked out at the Gresham across six lanes of traffic, propping myself on one of those slanted half-seats especially designed to stop tramps like me from getting too comfortable. Halfway through my third carrot I spotted a man in a padded rally jacket giving Craig a surreptitious and sheepish once-over, the way you might look at a passing face half-remembered from some profoundly regretted night of drunken passion. As a shaming reminder of the nation's very lowest ebb, I understood all too well why Craig was shunned, deprived of the nostalgic affection that aged machinery generally inspires; why in a journey of – let me see – 3,812 miles, I had not encountered a single fellow survivor of the 600,000 Austin Maestros who once sat by Britain's roads with the bonnet up. This, I can only imagine, is why he remains in my care to this day: part incontinent, doddering object of pity, part dire warning from history. Some months later, during a deluge on the M4's hard shoulder, an AA serviceman reconstructed Craig's wiper linkage with a gout of superglue and several lusty hammer blows. 'They don't make them like this any more,' he said, letting the bonnet down with a hollow twang. 'Thank bloody Christ.'

My plastic bag flapped and snapped in the wind; a young tracksuited man of East European appearance struggled by, toting three huge holdalls that most likely contained all his worldly goods. I looked up at the Ramada Inn, stood there lazily sucking up the Gresham's life-blood, then extracted another carrot and dispatched it in memory of all those doomed remnants of the good old, bad old days: Pontin's holiday camps, the high-street Chinese restaurant, the Trinity Square car parks and Brunel bus stations, public houses from Leysdown to Lochgelly, closing down at the rate of one a day in London alone. All the shabby, strange or beguilingly dreadful museums and hotels that had shut their doors for the last time just before I arrived, or would do just after I left. The whiff of processed cocoa mass that would never again hang in the air of Kingston upon Hull, the blast furnaces of Redcar dimmed for ever after centuries of blazing clamour. If you'd traced my route on a map it would have looked as if I was trying to scribble out our former industrial heartlands. At times it felt like I'd succeeded.

A police van muscled through the traffic, whooping and flashing. I watched it slalom away towards the Sainsbury's Local, and crunched down the final ruminative carrot. What of all the many places that hadn't quite made my final cut? Wolverhampton, declared the world's fifth worst city by Lonely Planet; Salford, with its table-topping embarrassment of potholes and ASBOs; Stoke-on-Trent, thirteenth on the *Location* list, the home of Britain's laziest postmen and most doughty TV licence evaders. The Kentish emporium of cringe that called itself Dickensworld, the monstrous inhumanity of the booking-office staff at King's Cross, the bow-fronted, mirrored tombstone that was the reviled IMAX cinema in Bournemouth. I suspected, in fact was suddenly and dramatically certain, that whenever I got around to darkening all those doors and pavements and counters, everything that defined their outlandish wrongnesses would be long gone. Knocked down, rounded off, re-educated and otherwise swept away in Britain's relentless drive towards the competent, blandly inoffensive, ruthlessly focus-grouped middle ground, just another globalised consumer nation that shopped in the same vast retail parks and drove the same metallic-grey people carriers and conversed in the same droning upspeak. How glad I was to have celebrated, and in the nick of time, an age when this country of mine wasn't afraid to do things its own way, even if that meant doing most of them really badly. Then I slid gracelessly off the bus shelter's plastic bum-rest, and set off towards an awkward black shape marooned on a gloomy forecourt.